Microsoft Windows™ 3.1

Programmer's Reference

Volume 4

Resources

PUBLISHED BY
Microsoft Press
A Division of Microsoft Corporation
One Microsoft Way
Redmond, Washington 98052-6399

Library of Congress Cataloging-in-Publication Data
Microsoft Windows programmer's reference.
        p. cm.
    Includes indexes.
    Contents: v. 1. Overview -- v. 2. Functions -- v. 3. Messages,
structures, macros -- v. 4. Resources.
    ISBN 1-55615-453-4 (v. 1). -- ISBN 1-55615-463-1 (v. 2). -- ISBN
1-55615-464-X (v. 3). -- ISBN 1-55615-494-1 (v. 4)
    1. Microsoft Windows (Computer program) I. Microsoft
Corporation.
QA76.76.W56M532 1992
005.4'3--dc20   91-34199
                                                                  CIP

Printed and bound in the United States of America.

1 2 3 4 5 6 7 8 9 MLML 7 6 5 4 3 2

Distributed to the book trade in Canada by Macmillan of Canada, a division of Canada Publishing Corporation.

Distributed to the book trade outside the United States and Canada by Penguin Books Ltd.

Penguin Books Ltd., Harmondsworth, Middlesex, England
Penguin Books Australia Ltd., Ringwood, Victoria, Australia
Penguin Books N.Z. Ltd., 182-190 Wairau Road, Auckland 10, New Zealand

British Cataloging-in-Publication Data available.

The Symbol fonts provided with Windows version 3.1 are based on the CG Times font, a product of AGFA Compugraphic Division of Agfa Corporation.

U.S. Patent No. 4974159

Document No. PC30211-0492

Contents

Part 1   File Formats

Part 2   Tools Reference

Introduction

The Microsoft® Windows™ operating system is a single-user personal-computer operating system that employs a graphical user interface. This graphical interface uses a variety of resources that must be constructed in specific formats. This manual, the *Microsoft Windows Programmer's Reference*, *Volume 4*, describes these resource formats and executable-file headers.

Part 1, "File Formats," describes the formats for the principal types of files used by Windows applications. The chapters in this part provide detailed information about the file formats, as well as about the MS-DOS® and Windows executable-file headers and resource formats within executable files. Topics include the formats for the following types of files: graphics, clipboard, font, group, calendar, object-module, library, symbol, and metafile.

Part 2, "Tools Reference," provides detailed reference information about the statements, commands, and macros for tools used to create and maintain Windows resources. Topics include resource-definition statements, assembly-language macros, and help statements and macros. Each entry in this section gives the purpose of the command or macro; its complete syntax, parameters, and return values; and cross-references to related commands or macros. Many entries also include expanded comments on the use of the command or macro.

How to Use This Manual

This manual describes the Windows resource-file formats in individual chapters. Each chapter describes the format that should be used for the type of file associated with a specific resource or activity. For example, the chapter on graphics file formats describes the formats used with bitmap, icon, and cursor resource files.

Each chapter has two parts: a general description of the file type and a detailed presentation of the format. Chapters in Part 2, "Tools Reference," describe only the file format and not the tool. For more information about the associated tools, see *Microsoft Windows Programming Tools*.

Document Conventions

The following conventions are used throughout this manual to define syntax:

Convention	Meaning
Bold text	Denotes a term or character to be typed literally, such as a resource-definition statement or function name (**MENU** or **CreateWindow**), an MS-DOS command, or a command-line option (**/nod**). You must type these terms exactly as shown.
Italic text	Denotes a placeholder or variable: You must provide the actual value. For example, the statement **SetCursorPos**(X, Y) requires you to substitute values for the X and Y parameters.
[ ]	Enclose optional parameters.
|	Separates an either/or choice.
...	Specifies that the preceding item may be repeated.
BEGIN . . . END	Represents an omitted portion of a sample application.

In addition, certain text conventions are used to help you understand this material:

Convention	Meaning
SMALL CAPITALS	Indicate the names of keys, key sequences, and key combinations—for example, ALT+SPACEBAR.
FULL CAPITALS	Indicate filenames and paths, most type and structure names (which are also bold), and constants.
monospace	Sets off code examples and shows syntax spacing.

File Formats

Part 1

Graphics File Formats

This chapter describes the graphics-file formats used by the Microsoft Windows operating system. Graphics files include bitmap files, icon-resource files, and cursor-resource files.

1.1 Bitmap-File Formats

Windows bitmap files are stored in a device-independent bitmap (DIB) format that allows Windows to display the bitmap on any type of display device. The term "device independent" means that the bitmap specifies pixel color in a form independent of the method used by a display to represent color. The default filename extension of a Windows DIB file is .BMP.

1.1.1 Bitmap-File Structures

Each bitmap file contains a bitmap-file header, a bitmap-information header, a color table, and an array of bytes that defines the bitmap bits. The file has the following form:

```
BITMAPFILEHEADER  bmfh;
BITMAPINFOHEADER  bmih;
RGBQUAD           aColors[];
BYTE              aBitmapBits[];
```

The bitmap-file header contains information about the type, size, and layout of a device-independent bitmap file. The header is defined as a **BITMAPFILE-HEADER** structure.

The bitmap-information header, defined as a **BITMAPINFOHEADER** structure, specifies the dimensions, compression type, and color format for the bitmap.

The color table, defined as an array of **RGBQUAD** structures, contains as many elements as there are colors in the bitmap. The color table is not present for bitmaps with 24 color bits because each pixel is represented by 24-bit red-green-blue (RGB) values in the actual bitmap data area. The colors in the table should appear in order of importance. This helps a display driver render a bitmap on a device that cannot display as many colors as there are in the bitmap. If the DIB is in Windows version 3.0 or later format, the driver can use the **biClrImportant** member of the **BITMAPINFOHEADER** structure to determine which colors are important.

The **BITMAPINFO** structure can be used to represent a combined bitmap-information header and color table.

The bitmap bits, immediately following the color table, consist of an array of **BYTE** values representing consecutive rows, or "scan lines," of the bitmap. Each scan line consists of consecutive bytes representing the pixels in the scan line, in left-to-right order. The number of bytes representing a scan line depends on the color format and the width, in pixels, of the bitmap. If necessary, a scan line must be zero-padded to end on a 32-bit boundary. However, segment boundaries can appear anywhere in the bitmap. The scan lines in the bitmap are stored from bottom up. This means that the first byte in the array represents the pixels in the lower-left corner of the bitmap and the last byte represents the pixels in the upper-right corner.

The **biBitCount** member of the **BITMAPINFOHEADER** structure determines the number of bits that define each pixel and the maximum number of colors in the bitmap. These members can have any of the following values:

Value	Meaning
1	Bitmap is monochrome and the color table contains two entries. Each bit in the bitmap array represents a pixel. If the bit is clear, the pixel is displayed with the color of the first entry in the color table. If the bit is set, the pixel has the color of the second entry in the table.
4	Bitmap has a maximum of 16 colors. Each pixel in the bitmap is represented by a 4-bit index into the color table. For example, if the first byte in the bitmap is 0x1F, the byte represents two pixels. The first pixel contains the color in the second table entry, and the second pixel contains the color in the sixteenth table entry.
8	Bitmap has a maximum of 256 colors. Each pixel in the bitmap is represented by a 1-byte index into the color table. For example, if the first byte in the bitmap is 0x1F, the first pixel has the color of the thirty-second table entry.
24	Bitmap has a maximum of 2^{24} colors. The **bmiColors** (or **bmciColors**) member is NULL, and each 3-byte sequence in the bitmap array represents the relative intensities of red, green, and blue, respectively, for a pixel.

The **biClrUsed** member of the **BITMAPINFOHEADER** structure specifies the number of color indexes in the color table actually used by the bitmap. If the **biClrUsed** member is set to zero, the bitmap uses the maximum number of colors corresponding to the value of the **biBitCount** member.

An alternative form of bitmap file uses the **BITMAPCOREINFO**, **BITMAPCOREHEADER**, and **RGBTRIPLE** structures.

For a full description of the bitmap structures, see the *Microsoft Windows Programmer's Reference*, *Volume 3*.

1.1.2 Bitmap Compression

Windows versions 3.0 and later support run-length encoded (RLE) formats for compressing bitmaps that use 4 bits per pixel and 8 bits per pixel. Compression reduces the disk and memory storage required for a bitmap.

1.1.2.1 Compression of 8-Bits-per-Pixel Bitmaps

When the **biCompression** member of the **BITMAPINFOHEADER** structure is set to BI_RLE8, the DIB is compressed using a run-length encoded format for a 256-color bitmap. This format uses two modes: encoded mode and absolute mode. Both modes can occur anywhere throughout a single bitmap.

Encoded Mode   A unit of information in encoded mode consists of two bytes. The first byte specifies the number of consecutive pixels to be drawn using the color index contained in the second byte.

The first byte of the pair can be set to zero to indicate an escape that denotes the end of a line, the end of the bitmap, or a delta. The interpretation of the escape depends on the value of the second byte of the pair, which must be in the range 0x00 through 0x02. Following are the meanings of the escape values that can be used in the second byte:

Second byte	Meaning
0	End of line.
1	End of bitmap.
2	Delta. The two bytes following the escape contain unsigned values indicating the horizontal and vertical offsets of the next pixel from the current position.

Absolute Mode   Absolute mode is signaled by the first byte in the pair being set to zero and the second byte to a value between 0x03 and 0xFF. The second byte represents the number of bytes that follow, each of which contains the color index of a single pixel. Each run must be aligned on a word boundary.

Following is an example of an 8-bit RLE bitmap (the two-digit hexadecimal values in the second column represent a color index for a single pixel):

Compressed data	Expanded data
03 04	04 04 04
05 06	06 06 06 06 06
00 03 45 56 67 00	45 56 67
02 78	78 78
00 02 05 01	Move 5 right and 1 down
02 78	78 78
00 00	End of line
09 1E	1E 1E 1E 1E 1E 1E 1E 1E 1E
00 01	End of RLE bitmap

1.1.2.2 Compression of 4-Bits-per-Pixel Bitmaps

When the **biCompression** member of the **BITMAPINFOHEADER** structure is set to BI_RLE4, the DIB is compressed using a run-length encoded format for a 16-color bitmap. This format uses two modes: encoded mode and absolute mode.

Encoded Mode   A unit of information in encoded mode consists of two bytes. The first byte of the pair contains the number of pixels to be drawn using the color indexes in the second byte.

The second byte contains two color indexes, one in its high-order nibble (that is, its low-order 4 bits) and one in its low-order nibble. The first pixel is drawn using the color specified by the high-order nibble, the second is drawn using the color in the low-order nibble, the third is drawn with the color in the high-order nibble, and so on, until all the pixels specified by the first byte have been drawn.

The first byte of the pair can be set to zero to indicate an escape that denotes the end of a line, the end of the bitmap, or a delta. The interpretation of the escape depends on the value of the second byte of the pair. In encoded mode, the second byte has a value in the range 0x00 through 0x02. The meaning of these values is the same as for a DIB with 8 bits per pixel.

Absolute Mode   In absolute mode, the first byte contains zero, the second byte contains the number of color indexes that follow, and subsequent bytes contain color indexes in their high- and low-order nibbles, one color index for each pixel. Each run must be aligned on a word boundary.

Following is an example of a 4-bit RLE bitmap (the one-digit hexadecimal values in the second column represent a color index for a single pixel):

Compressed data	Expanded data
03 04	0 4 0
05 06	0 6 0 6 0
00 06 45 56 67 00	4 5 5 6 6 7
04 78	7 8 7 8
00 02 05 01	Move 5 right and 1 down
04 78	7 8 7 8
00 00	End of line
09 1E	1 E 1 E 1 E 1 E 1
00 01	End of RLE bitmap

1.1.3 Bitmap Example

The following example is a text dump of a 16-color bitmap (4 bits per pixel):

```
Win3DIBFile
                BitmapFileHeader
                     Type         19778
                     Size         3118
                     Reserved1  0
                     Reserved2  0
                     OffsetBits 118
                BitmapInfoHeader
                     Size               40
                     Width              80
                     Height             75
                     Planes             1
                     BitCount           4
                     Compression        0
                     SizeImage          3000
                     XPelsPerMeter      0
                     YPelsPerMeter      0
                     ColorsUsed         16
                     ColorsImportant 16
                Win3ColorTable
                          Blue   Green   Red   Unused
     [00000000]           84     252     84     0
     [00000001]          252     252     84     0
     [00000002]           84      84    252     0
     [00000003]          252      84    252     0
     [00000004]           84     252    252     0
     [00000005]          252     252    252     0
     [00000006]            0       0      0     0
     [00000007]          168       0      0     0
     [00000008]            0     168      0     0
     [00000009]          168     168      0     0
     [0000000A]            0       0    168     0
     [0000000B]          168       0    168     0
     [0000000C]            0     168    168     0
     [0000000D]          168     168    168     0
     [0000000E]           84      84     84     0
     [0000000F]          252      84     84     0
                Image
          .
          .                                        Bitmap data
          .
```

1.2 Icon-Resource File Format

An icon-resource file contains image data for icons used by Windows applications. The file consists of an icon directory identifying the number and types of icon images in the file, plus one or more icon images. The default filename extension for an icon-resource file is .ICO.

1.2.1 Icon Directory

Each icon-resource file starts with an icon directory. The icon directory, defined as an **ICONDIR** structure, specifies the number of icons in the resource and the dimensions and color format of each icon image. The **ICONDIR** structure has the following form:

```
typedef struct ICONDIR {
    WORD         idReserved;
    WORD         idType;
    WORD         idCount;
    ICONDIRENTRY idEntries[1];
} ICONHEADER;
```

Following are the members in the **ICONDIR** structure:

idReserved
Reserved; must be zero.

idType
Specifies the resource type. This member is set to 1.

idCount
Specifies the number of entries in the directory.

idEntries
Specifies an array of **ICONDIRENTRY** structures containing information about individual icons. The **idCount** member specifies the number of structures in the array.

The **ICONDIRENTRY** structure specifies the dimensions and color format for an icon. The structure has the following form:

```
struct IconDirectoryEntry {
    BYTE  bWidth;
    BYTE  bHeight;
    BYTE  bColorCount;
    BYTE  bReserved;
    WORD  wPlanes;
    WORD  wBitCount;
    DWORD dwBytesInRes;
    DWORD dwImageOffset;
};
```

Following are the members in the **ICONDIRENTRY** structure:

bWidth
Specifies the width of the icon, in pixels. Acceptable values are 16, 32, and 64.

bHeight
Specifies the height of the icon, in pixels. Acceptable values are 16, 32, and 64.

bColorCount
Specifies the number of colors in the icon. Acceptable values are 2, 8, and 16.

bReserved
Reserved; must be zero.

wPlanes
Specifies the number of color planes in the icon bitmap.

wBitCount
Specifies the number of bits in the icon bitmap.

dwBytesInRes
Specifies the size of the resource, in bytes.

dwImageOffset
Specifies the offset, in bytes, from the beginning of the file to the icon image.

1.2.2 Icon Image

Each icon-resource file contains one icon image for each image identified in the icon directory. An icon image consists of an icon-image header, a color table, an XOR mask, and an AND mask. The icon image has the following form:

```
BITMAPINFOHEADER     icHeader;
RGBQUAD              icColors[];
BYTE                 icXOR[];
BYTE                 icAND[];
```

The icon-image header, defined as a **BITMAPINFOHEADER** structure, specifies the dimensions and color format of the icon bitmap. Only the **biSize** through **biBitCount** members and the **biSizeImage** member are used. All other members (such as **biCompression** and **biClrImportant**) must be set to zero.

The color table, defined as an array of **RGBQUAD** structures, specifies the colors used in the XOR mask. As with the color table in a bitmap file, the **biBitCount** member in the icon-image header determines the number of elements in the array. For more information about the color table, see Section 1.1, "Bitmap-File Formats."

For a full description of the icon-resource structures, see the *Microsoft Windows Programmer's Reference, Volume 3*.

The XOR mask, immediately following the color table, is an array of **BYTE** values representing consecutive rows of a bitmap. The bitmap defines the basic shape and color of the icon image. As with the bitmap bits in a bitmap file, the bitmap data in an icon-resource file is organized in scan lines, with each byte representing one or more pixels, as defined by the color format. For more information about these bitmap bits, see Section 1.1, "Bitmap-File Formats."

The AND mask, immediately following the XOR mask, is an array of **BYTE** values, representing a monochrome bitmap with the same width and height as the XOR mask. The array is organized in scan lines, with each byte representing 8 pixels.

When Windows draws an icon, it uses the AND and XOR masks to combine the icon image with the pixels already on the display surface. Windows first applies the AND mask by using a bitwise AND operation; this preserves or removes existing pixel color. Windows then applies the XOR mask by using a bitwise XOR operation. This sets the final color for each pixel.

The following illustration shows the XOR and AND masks that create a monochrome icon (measuring 8 pixels by 8 pixels) in the form of an uppercase K:

AND mask

0	0	1	1	1	0	0	1
0	0	1	1	0	0	1	1
0	0	1	0	0	1	1	1
0	0	0	0	1	1	1	1
0	0	0	0	1	1	1	1
0	0	1	0	0	1	1	1
0	0	1	1	0	0	1	1
0	0	1	1	1	0	0	1

XOR mask

1	1	0	0	0	1	1	0
1	1	0	0	1	1	0	0
1	1	0	1	1	0	0	0
1	1	1	1	0	0	0	0
1	1	1	1	0	0	0	0
1	1	0	1	1	0	0	0
1	1	0	0	1	1	0	0
1	1	0	0	0	1	1	0

Resulting icon

K	K				K	K	
K	K			K	K		
K	K		K	K			
K	K	K	K				
K	K	K	K				
K	K		K	K			
K	K			K	K		
K	K				K	K	

1.2.3 Windows Icon Selection

Windows detects the resolution of the current display and matches it against the width and height specified for each version of the icon image. If Windows determines that there is an exact match between an icon image and the current device, it uses the matching image. Otherwise, it selects the closest match and stretches the image to the proper size.

If an icon-resource file contains more than one image for a particular resolution, Windows uses the icon image that most closely matches the color capabilities of the current display. If no image matches the device capabilities exactly, Windows selects the image that has the greatest number of colors without exceeding the number of display colors. If all images exceed the color capabilities of the current display, Windows uses the icon image with the least number of colors.

1.3 Cursor-Resource File Format

A cursor-resource file contains image data for cursors used by Windows applications. The file consists of a cursor directory identifying the number and types of cursor images in the file, plus one or more cursor images. The default filename extension for a cursor-resource file is .CUR.

1.3.1 Cursor Directory

Each cursor-resource file starts with a cursor directory. The cursor directory, defined as a **CURSORDIR** structure, specifies the number of cursors in the file and the dimensions and color format of each cursor image. The **CURSORDIR** structure has the following form:

```
typedef struct _CURSORDIR {
    WORD            cdReserved;
    WORD            cdType;
    WORD            cdCount;
    CURSORDIRENTRY  cdEntries[];
} CURSORDIR;
```

Following are the members in the **CURSORDIR** structure:

cdReserved
Reserved; must be zero.

cdType
Specifies the resource type. This member must be set to 2.

cdCount
Specifies the number of cursors in the file.

cdEntries
Specifies an array of **CURSORDIRENTRY** structures containing information about individual cursors. The **cdCount** member specifies the number of structures in the array.

A **CURSORDIRENTRY** structure specifies the dimensions and color format of a cursor image. The structure has the following form:

```
typedef struct _CURSORDIRENTRY {
    BYTE  bWidth;
    BYTE  bHeight;
    BYTE  bColorCount;
    BYTE  bReserved;
    WORD  wXHotspot;
    WORD  wYHotspot;
    DWORD lBytesInRes;
    DWORD dwImageOffset;
} CURSORDIRENTRY;
```

Following are the members in the **CURSORDIRENTRY** structure:

bWidth
Specifies the width of the cursor, in pixels.

bHeight
Specifies the height of the cursor, in pixels.

bColorCount
Reserved; must be zero.

bReserved
Reserved; must be zero.

wXHotspot
Specifies the x-coordinate, in pixels, of the hot spot.

wYHotspot
Specifies the y-coordinate, in pixels, of the hot spot.

lBytesInRes
Specifies the size of the resource, in bytes.

dwImageOffset
Specifies the offset, in bytes, from the start of the file to the cursor image.

1.3.2 Cursor Image

Each cursor-resource file contains one cursor image for each image identified in
the cursor directory. A cursor image consists of a cursor-image header, a color
table, an XOR mask, and an AND mask. The cursor image has the following
form:

```
BITMAPINFOHEADER    crHeader;
RGBQUAD             crColors[];
BYTE                crXOR[];
BYTE                crAND[];
```

The cursor hot spot is a single pixel in the cursor bitmap that Windows uses to
track the cursor. The **crXHotspot** and **crYHotspot** members specify the x- and
y-coordinates of the cursor hot spot. These coordinates are 16-bit integers.

The cursor-image header, defined as a **BITMAPINFOHEADER** structure, specifies the dimensions and color format of the cursor bitmap. Only the **biSize** through
biBitCount members and the **biSizeImage** member are used. The **biHeight** member specifies the combined height of the XOR and AND masks for the cursor. This
value is twice the height of the XOR mask. The **biPlanes** and **biBitCount** members must be 1. All other members (such as **biCompression** and **biClrImportant**)
must be set to zero.

The color table, defined as an array of **RGBQUAD** structures, specifies the colors used in the XOR mask. For a cursor image, the table contains exactly two structures, since the **biBitCount** member in the cursor-image header is always 1.

The XOR mask, immediately following the color table, is an array of **BYTE** values representing consecutive rows of a bitmap. The bitmap defines the basic shape and color of the cursor image. As with the bitmap bits in a bitmap file, the bitmap data in a cursor-resource file is organized in scan lines, with each byte representing one or more pixels, as defined by the color format. For more information about these bitmap bits, see Section 1.1, "Bitmap-File Formats."

The AND mask, immediately following the XOR mask, is an array of **BYTE** values representing a monochrome bitmap with the same width and height as the XOR mask. The array is organized in scan lines, with each byte representing 8 pixels.

When Windows draws a cursor, it uses the AND and XOR masks to combine the cursor image with the pixels already on the display surface. Windows first applies the AND mask by using a bitwise AND operation; this preserves or removes existing pixel color. Window then applies the XOR mask by using a bitwise XOR operation. This sets the final color for each pixel.

The following illustration shows the XOR and the AND masks that create a cursor (measuring 8 pixels by 8 pixels) in the form of an arrow:

Following are the bit-mask values necessary to produce black, white, inverted, and transparent results:

Pixel result	AND mask	XOR mask
Black	0	0
White	0	1
Transparent	1	0
Inverted	1	1

1.3.3 Windows Cursor Selection

If a cursor-resource file contains more than one cursor image, Windows determines the best match for a particular display by examining the width and height of the cursor images.

Clipboard File Format

Microsoft Windows Clipboard (CLIPBRD.EXE) saves and reads its data in files with the .CLP extension. A .CLP file contains a value identifying it as a Clipboard data file; one or more structures defining the format, size, and location of the data; and one or more blocks of actual data.

2.1 Clipboard-File Header

The Clipboard data file begins with a header consisting of two members. Following are the members in this header:

FileIdentifier
Identifies the file as a Clipboard data file. This member must be set to CLP_ID. This is a 2-byte value.

FormatCount
Specifies the number of clipboard formats contained in the file. This is a 2-byte value.

2.2 Clipboard-File Structure

The header is followed by one or more structures, each of which identifies the format, size, and offset of a block containing clipboard data. Following are the members in this structure:

FormatID
Specifies the clipboard-format identifier of the clipboard data. For information on clipboard formats, see the description of the **SetClipboardData** function in the *Microsoft Windows Programmer's Reference*, *Volume 2*. This is a 2-byte value.

LenData
Specifies the length, in bytes, of the clipboard data. This is a 4-byte value.

OffData
Specifies the offset, in bytes, of the clipboard-data block. The offset is from the beginning of the file. This is a 4-byte value.

Name
Identifies a 79-character array specifying the format name of a private clipboard format.

The first block of clipboard data follows the last of these structures. For bitmaps and metafiles, the bits follow immediately after the bitmap header and the **META-FILEPICT** structures. For a description of the **METAFILEPICT** structure, see the *Microsoft Windows Programmer's Reference*, *Volume 3*.

Metafile Format

A metafile for the Microsoft Windows operating system consists of a collection of graphics device interface (GDI) functions that describe an image. Because metafiles take up less space and are more device-independent than bitmaps, they provide convenient storage for images that appear repeatedly in an application or need to be moved from one application to another.

To generate a metafile, a Windows application creates a special device context that sends GDI commands to a file or memory for storage. The application can later play back the metafile and display the image.

During playback, Windows breaks the metafile down into records and identifies each object with an index to a handle table. When a META_DELETEOBJECT record is encountered during playback, the associated object is deleted from the handle table. The entry is then reused by the next object that the metafile creates. To ensure compatibility, an application that explicitly manipulates records or builds its own metafile should manage the handle table in the same way. For more information on the format of the handle table, see the **HANDLETABLE** structure in the *Microsoft Windows Programmer's Reference, Volume 3*.

In some cases, there are two variants of a metafile record, one representing the record created by Windows versions before 3.0 and the second representing the record created by Windows versions 3.0 and later. Windows versions 3.0 and later play all metafile versions but store only 3.0 and later versions. Windows versions earlier than 3.0 do not play metafiles recorded by Windows versions 3.0 and later.

A metafile consists of two parts: a header and a list of records. The header and records (both typical and function-specific records) are described in the next three sections of this chapter.

3.1 Metafile Header

The metafile header contains a description of the size of the metafile and the number of drawing objects it uses. The drawing objects can be pens, brushes, bitmaps, or fonts.

The metafile header has the following form:

```
typedef struct tagMETAHEADER {
    WORD   mtType;
    WORD   mtHeaderSize;
    WORD   mtVersion;
    DWORD  mtSize;
    WORD   mtNoObjects;
    DWORD  mtMaxRecord;
    WORD   mtNoParameters;
} METAHEADER;
```

Following are the members in the metafile header:

mtType

Specifies whether the metafile is stored in memory or recorded in a file. This member has one of the following values:

Value	Meaning
0	Metafile is in memory.
1	Metafile is in a file.

mtHeaderSize

Specifies the size, in words, of the metafile header.

mtVersion

Specifies the Windows version number. The version number for Windows version 3.0 and later is 0x300.

mtSize

Specifies the size, in words, of the file.

mtNoObjects

Specifies the maximum number of objects that can exist in the metafile at the same time.

mtMaxRecord

Specifies the size, in words, of the largest record in the metafile.

mtNoParameters

Not used.

3.2 Typical Metafile Record

The graphics device interface stores most of the GDI functions that an application can use to create metafiles in typical records.

A typical metafile record has the following form:

```
struct {
    DWORD rdSize;
    WORD  rdFunction;
    WORD  rdParm[];
}
```

Following are the members in a typical metafile record:

rdSize

Specifies the size, in words, of the record.

rdFunction
Specifies the function number. This value may be the number of any function in the table at the end of this section.

rdParm
Identifies an array of words containing the function parameters (listed in the reverse order in which they are passed to the function).

Following are the GDI functions found in typical records, along with their hexadecimal values:

GDI function	Value
Arc	0x0817
Chord	0x0830
Ellipse	0x0418
ExcludeClipRect	0x0415
FloodFill	0x0419
IntersectClipRect	0x0416
LineTo	0x0213
MoveTo	0x0214
OffsetClipRgn	0x0220
OffsetViewportOrg	0x0211
OffsetWindowOrg	0x020F
PatBlt	0x061D
Pie	0x081A
RealizePalette (3.0 and later)	0x0035
Rectangle	0x041B
ResizePalette (3.0 and later)	0x0139
RestoreDC	0x0127
RoundRect	0x061C
SaveDC	0x001E
ScaleViewportExt	0x0412
ScaleWindowExt	0x0400
SetBkColor	0x0201
SetBkMode	0x0102
SetMapMode	0x0103
SetMapperFlags	0x0231
SetPixel	0x041F
SetPolyFillMode	0x0106
SetROP2	0x0104
SetStretchBltMode	0x0107

GDI function	Value
SetTextAlign	0x012E
SetTextCharExtra	0x0108
SetTextColor	0x0209
SetTextJustification	0x020A
SetViewportExt	0x020E
SetViewportOrg	0x020D
SetWindowExt	0x020C
SetWindowOrg	0x020B

For more information on GDI functions, see the *Microsoft Windows Programmer's Reference, Volume 2*. For more information on the function-specific metafile records, see Section 3.6, "Function-Specific Metafile Records."

3.3 Placeable Windows Metafiles

A placeable Windows metafile is a standard Windows metafile that has an additional 22-byte header. The header contains information about the aspect ratio and original size of the metafile, permitting applications to display the metafile in its intended form.

The header for a placeable Windows metafile has the following form:

```
typedef struct {
    DWORD   key;
    HANDLE  hmf;
    RECT    bbox;
    WORD    inch;
    DWORD   reserved;
    WORD    checksum;
} METAFILEHEADER;
```

Following are the members of a placeable metafile header:

key
Specifies the binary key that uniquely identifies this file type. This member must be set to 0x9AC6CDD7L.

hmf
Unused; must be zero.

bbox
Specifies the coordinates of the smallest rectangle that encloses the picture. The coordinates are in metafile units as defined by the **inch** member.

inch

Specifies the number of metafile units to the inch. To avoid numeric overflow, this value should be less than 1440. Most applications use 576 or 1000.

reserved

Unused; must be zero.

checksum

Specifies the checksum. It is the sum (using the XOR operator) of the first 10 words of the header.

The actual content of the Windows metafile immediately follows the header. The format for this content is identical to that for standard Windows metafiles. For some applications, a placeable Windows metafile must not exceed 64K.

Note   Placeable Windows metafiles are not compatible with the **GetMetaFile** function. Applications that intend to use the metafile functions to read and play placeable Windows metafiles must read the file by using an input function (such as **_lread**), strip the 22-byte header, and create a standard Windows metafile by using the remaining bytes and the **SetMetaFileBits** function.

3.4 Guidelines for Windows Metafiles

To ensure that metafiles can be transported between different computers and applications, any application that creates a metafile should make sure the metafile is device-independent and sizable.

The following guidelines ensure that every metafile can be accepted and manipulated by other applications:

1. Set a mapping mode as one of the first records. Many applications, including OLE applications, only accept metafiles that are in MM_ANISOTROPIC mode.

2. Call the **SetWindowOrg** and **SetWindowExt** functions. Do not call the **SetViewportExt** or **SetViewportOrg** functions if the user will be able to resize or change the dimensions of the object.

3. Use the **MFCOMMENT** printer escape to add comments to the metafile.

4. Rely primarily on the functions listed in Section 3.2, "Typical Metafile Record." Observe the following limitations on the functions you use:

   - Do not use functions that retrieve data (for example, **GetActiveWindow** or **EnumFontFamilies**).

   - Do not use any of the region functions (because they are device dependent).

   - Use **StretchBlt** or **StretchDIB** instead of **BitBlt**.

3.5 Sample of Metafile Program Output

This section describes a sample program and the metafile that it creates. The sample program creates a small metafile that draws a purple rectangle with a green border and writes the words "Hello People" in the rectangle.

```
MakeAMetaFile(hDC)
HDC hDC;
{
    HPEN      hMetaGreenPen;
    HBRUSH    hMetaVioletBrush;
    HDC       hDCMeta;
    HANDLE    hMeta;

    /* Create the metafile with output going to the disk. */

    hDCMeta = CreateMetaFile( (LPSTR) "sample.met");

    hMetaGreenPen = CreatePen(0, 0, (DWORD) 0x0000FF00);
    SelectObject(hDCMeta, hMetaGreenPen);

    hMetaVioletBrush = CreateSolidBrush((DWORD) 0x00FF00FF);
    SelectObject(hDCMeta, hMetaVioletBrush);

    Rectangle(hDCMeta, 0, 0, 150, 70);

    TextOut(hDCMeta, 10, 10, (LPSTR) "Hello People", 12);

    /* We are done with the metafile. */

    hMeta = CloseMetaFile(hDCMeta);

    /* Play the metafile that we just created. */

    PlayMetaFile(hDC, hMeta);
}
```

The resulting metafile, SAMPLE.MET, consists of a metafile header and six records. It has the following binary form:

```
0001          mtType... disk metafile
0009          mtSize...
0300          mtVersion
0000 0036     mtSize
0002          mtNoObjects
0000 000C     mtMaxRecord
0000          mtNoParameters
```

```
0000 0008    rdSize
02FA         rdFunction (CreatePenIndirect function)
0000 0000 0000 0000 FF00  rdParm (LOGPEN structure defining pen)

0000 0004    rdSize
012D         rdFunction (SelectObject)
0000         rdParm (index to object #0... the above pen)

0000 0007    rdSize
02FC         rdFunction (CreateBrushIndirect)
0000 00FF 00FF 0000 rdParm (LOGBRUSH structure defining the brush)

0000 0004    rdSize
012D         rdFunction (SelectObject)
0001         rdParm (index to object #1... the brush)

0000 0007    rdSize
041B         rdFunction (Rectangle)
0046 0096 0000 0000 rdParm (parameters sent to Rectangle...
                    in reverse order)

0000 000C    rdSize
0521         rdFunction (TextOut)
rdParm
000C         count
string
48 65 6C 6C 6F 20 50 65 6F 70 6C 65    "Hello People"
000A              y-value
000A              x-value
```

3.6 Function-Specific Metafile Records

The graphics-device interface stores most of the GDI functions for creating meta-files in typical records. The remainder are stored in function-specific records that contain structures in the **rdParm** member. This section contains definitions for these records.

AnimatePalette

```
struct {
    DWORD rdSize;
    WORD  rdFunction;
    WORD  rdParm[];
}
```

Members

rdSize
Specifies the record size, in words.

rdFunction
Specifies the GDI function number 0x0436.

rdParm
Contains the following elements:

Element	Description
start	First entry to be animated
numentries	Number of entries to be animated
entries	**PALETTEENTRY** blocks (for a description of the **PALETTEENTRY** structure, see the *Microsoft Windows Programmer's Reference*, *Volume 3*)

BitBlt

```
struct {
    DWORD rdSize;
    WORD  rdFunction;
    WORD  rdParm[];
}
```

The **BitBlt** record stored by Windows versions earlier than 3.0 contains a device-dependent bitmap that may not be suitable for playback on all devices.

Members

rdSize
Specifies the record size, in words.

rdFunction
Specifies the GDI function number 0x0922.

rdParm
Contains the following elements:

Element	Description
raster op	High-order word of the raster operation
SY	Y-coordinate of the source origin
SX	X-coordinate of the source origin
DYE	Destination y-extent
DXE	Destination x-extent
DY	Y-coordinate of the destination origin
DX	X-coordinate of the destination origin
bmWidth	Width of bitmap, in pixels
bmHeight	Height of bitmap, in raster lines
bmWidthBytes	Number of bytes in each raster line
bmPlanes	Number of color planes in the bitmap
bmBitsPixel	Number of adjacent color bits
bits	Actual device-dependent bitmap bits

BitBlt

3.0

```
struct {
    DWORD rdSize;
    WORD  rdFunction;
    WORD  rdParm[];
}
```

The **BitBlt** record contains a device-independent bitmap suitable for playback on any device.

Members

rdSize
Specifies the record size, in words.

rdFunction
Specifies the GDI function number 0x0940.

rdParm
Contains the following elements:

Element	Description
raster op	High-order word of the raster operation
SY	Y-coordinate of the source origin
SX	X-coordinate of the source origin
DYE	Destination y-extent

Element	Description
DXE	Destination x-extent
DY	Y-coordinate of the destination origin
DX	X-coordinate of the destination origin
BitmapInfo	**BITMAPINFO** structure (for a description of the **BIT-MAPINFO** structure, see the *Microsoft Windows Programmer's Reference*, *Volume 3*)
bits	Actual device-independent bitmap bits

CreateBrushIndirect

```
struct {
    DWORD    rdSize;
    WORD     rdFunction;
    LOGBRUSH rdParm;
}
```

Members   **rdSize**
Specifies the record size, in words.

rdFunction
Specifies the GDI function number 0x02FC.

rdParm
Specifies the logical brush.

CreateFontIndirect

```
struct {
    DWORD    rdSize;
    WORD     rdFunction;
    LOGFONT  rdParm;
}
```

Members

rdSize
: Specifies the record size, in words.

rdFunction
: Specifies the GDI function number 0x02FB.

rdParm
: Specifies the logical font.

CreatePalette

```
struct {
    DWORD     rdSize;
    WORD      rdFunction;
    LOGPALETTE rdParm;
}
```

Members

rdSize
: Specifies the record size, in words.

rdFunction
: Specifies the GDI function number 0x00F7.

rdParm
: Specifies the logical palette.

CreatePatternBrush

```
struct {
    DWORD rdSize;
    WORD  rdFunction;
    WORD  rdParm[];
}
```

The **CreatePatternBrush** record contains a device-dependent bitmap that may not be suitable for playback on all devices.

Members

rdSize
: Specifies the record size, in words.

rdFunction
: Specifies the GDI function number 0x01F9.

rdParm

Contains the following elements:

Element	Description
bmWidth	Bitmap width
bmHeight	Bitmap height
bmWidthBytes	Bytes per raster line
bmPlanes	Number of color planes
bmBitsPixel	Number of adjacent color bits that define a pixel
bmBits	Pointer to bit values
bits	Actual bits of pattern

CreatePatternBrush

3.0

```
struct {
    DWORD rdSize;
    WORD  rdFunction;
    WORD  rdParm[];
}
```

The **CreatePatternBrush** record contains a device-independent bitmap suitable for playback on all devices.

Members

rdSize

Specifies the record size, in words.

rdFunction

Specifies the GDI function number 0x0142.

rdParm

Contains the following elements:

Element	Description
type	Bitmap type. This element may be either of these two values:
	BS_PATTERN—Brush is defined by a device-dependent bitmap through a call to the **CreatePatternBrush** function.
	BS_DIBPATTERN—Brush is defined by a device-independent bitmap through a call to the **CreateDIB-PatternBrush** function.

Element	Description
wUsage	Color-table type. This element specifies whether the **bmi-Colors** member of the **BITMAPINFO** structure contains explicit RGB values or indexes to the currently realized logical palette. This element must be one of the following values:
	DIB_RGB_COLORS—The color table contains literal RGB values.
	DIB_PAL_COLORS—The color table consists of an array of indexes to the currently realized logical palette.
bmi	**BITMAPINFO** structure (for a description of the **BITMAPINFO** structure, see the *Microsoft Windows Programmer's Reference*, *Volume 3*).
bits	Actual device-independent bitmap bits.

CreatePenIndirect

```
struct {
    DWORD  rdSize;
    WORD   rdFunction;
    LOGPEN rdParm;
}
```

Members

rdSize
Specifies the record size, in words.

rdFunction
Specifies the GDI function number 0x02FA.

rdParm
Specifies the logical pen.

CreateRegion

```
struct {
    DWORD rdSize;
    WORD  rdFunction;
    WORD  rdParm[];
}
```

Members

rdSize
Specifies the record size, in words.

rdFunction
Specifies the GDI function number 0x06FF.

rdParm
Specifies the region to be created.

DeleteObject

```
struct {
    DWORD rdSize;
    WORD  rdFunction;
    WORD  rdParm;
}
```

Members

rdSize
Specifies the record size, in words.

rdFunction
Specifies the GDI function number 0x01F0.

rdParm
Specifies the index to the handle table for the object to be deleted.

Escape

```
struct {
    DWORD rdSize;
    WORD  rdFunction;
    WORD  rdParm[];
}
```

Members

rdSize
Specifies the record size, in words.

rdFunction
Specifies the GDI function number 0x0626.

rdParm
Contains the following elements:

Element	Description
escape number	Number identifying individual escape.
count	Number of bytes of information.
input data	Variable-length field. The member is ((count+1) >> 1) words long.

ExtTextOut

```
struct{
    DWORD rdSize;
    WORD  rdFunction;
    WORD  rdParm[];
}
```

Members

rdSize
Specifies the record size, in words.

rdFunction
Specifies the GDI function number 0x0A32.

rdParm
Contains the following elements:

Element	Description
y	Logical y-value of the starting point for the string.
x	Logical x-value of the starting point for the string.
count	Length of the string.
options	Rectangle type. An application should use the AND (&) operator to determine if this element has either the ETO_CLIPPED or ETO_OPAQUE bits set. Using the equality operator (==) is discouraged in this case, because some applications set additional bits in the *wOptions* parameter of the rectangular region in which the **ExtTextOut** function writes text.
rectangle	**RECT** structure defining the rectangular region in which the **ExtTextOut** function writes text. This element does not exist if the options element is zero. (For a description of the **RECT** structure, see the *Microsoft Windows Programmer's Reference*, *Volume 3*.)
string	Byte array containing the string. The array is ((count + 1) >> 1) words long.

Element	Description
dxarray	Optional word array of intercharacter distances.

Polygon

```
struct {
    DWORD rdSize;
    WORD  rdFunction;
    WORD  rdParm[];
}
```

Members

rdSize
Specifies the record size, in words.

rdFunction
Specifies the GDI function number 0x0324.

rdParm
Contains the following elements:

Element	Description
count	Number of points
list of points	List of individual points

PolyPolygon

```
struct {
    DWORD rdSize;
    WORD  rdFunction;
    WORD  rdParm[];
}
```

Members

rdSize
Specifies the record size, in words.

rdFunction
Specifies the GDI function number 0x0538.

rdParm
Contains the following elements:

Element	Description
count	Total number of polygons
list of polygon counts	List of number of points for each polygon
list of points	List of individual points

Polyline

```
struct {
    DWORD rdSize;
    WORD  rdFunction;
    WORD  rdParm[];
}
```

Members

rdSize
Specifies the record size, in words.

rdFunction
Specifies the GDI function number 0x0325.

rdParm
Contains the following elements:

Element	Description
count	Number of points
list of points	List of individual points

SelectClipRgn

```
struct{
    DWORD rdSize;
    WORD  rdFunction;
    WORD  rdParm;
}
```

Members   **rdSize**
Specifies the record size, in words.

rdFunction
Specifies the GDI function number 0x012C.

rdParm
Specifies the index to the handle table for the region being selected.

SelectObject

```
struct{
    DWORD rdSize;
    WORD  rdFunction;
    WORD  rdParm;
}
```

Members   **rdSize**
Specifies the record size, in words.

rdFunction
Specifies the GDI function number 0x012D.

rdParm
Specifies the index to the handle table for the object being selected.

SelectPalette

```
struct {
    DWORD rdSize;
    WORD  rdFunction;
    WORD  rdParm;
}
```

Members   **rdSize**
Specifies the record size, in words.

rdFunction
Specifies the GDI function number 0x0234.

rdParm
Specifies the index to the handle table for the logical palette being selected.

SetDIBitsToDevice

```
struct {
    DWORD rdSize;
    WORD  rdFunction;
    WORD  rdParm[];
}
```

Members

rdSize

Specifies the record size, in words.

rdFunction

Specifies the GDI function number 0x0D33.

rdParm

Contains the following elements:

Element	Description
wUsage	Flag indicating whether the bitmap color table contains RGB values or indexes to the currently realized logical palette
numscans	Number of scan lines in the bitmap
startscan	First scan line in the bitmap
srcY	Y-coordinate for the origin of the source rectangle in the bitmap
srcX	X-coordinate for the origin of the source rectangle in the bitmap
extY	Height of the source rectangle in the bitmap
extX	Width of the source rectangle in the bitmap
destY	Y-coordinate of the origin of the destination rectangle
destX	X-coordinate of the origin of the destination rectangle
BitmapInfo	**BITMAPINFO** structure (For a description of the **BIT-MAPINFO** structure, see the *Microsoft Windows Programmer's Reference, Volume 3*.)
bits	Actual device-independent bitmap bits

SetPaletteEntries

```
struct {
    DWORD rdSize;
    WORD  rdFunction;
    WORD  rdParm[];
}
```

Members

rdSize
Specifies the record size, in words.

rdFunction
Specifies the GDI function number 0x0037.

rdParm
Contains the following elements:

Element	Description
start	First entry to be set in the palette
numentries	Number of entries to be set in the palette
entries	**PALETTEENTRY** blocks (For a description of the **PALETTEENTRY** structure, see the *Microsoft Windows Programmer's Reference*, *Volume 3*.)

StretchBlt

```
struct {
    DWORD rdSize;
    WORD  rdFunction;
    WORD  rdParm[];
}
```

The **StretchBlt** record contains a device-dependent bitmap that may not be suitable for playback on all devices.

Members

rdSize
Specifies the record size, in words.

rdFunction
Specifies the GDI function number 0x0B23.

rdParm
Contains the following elements:

Element	Description
raster op	Low-order word of the raster operation
raster op	High-order word of the raster operation
SYE	Source y-extent
SXE	Source x-extent
SY	Y-coordinate of the source origin
SX	X-coordinate of the source origin
DYE	Destination y-extent
DXE	Destination x-extent
DY	Y-coordinate of the destination origin
DX	X-coordinate of the destination origin
bmWidth	Width of the bitmap, in pixels
bmHeight	Height of the bitmap, in raster lines
bmWidthBytes	Number of bytes in each raster line
bmPlanes	Number of color planes in the bitmap
bmBitsPixel	Number of adjacent color bits
bits	Actual bitmap bits

StretchBlt

3.0

```
struct {
    DWORD rdSize;
    WORD  rdFunction;
    WORD  rdParm[];
}
```

The **StretchBlt** record contains a device-independent bitmap suitable for playback on all devices.

Members

rdSize
Specifies the record size, in words.

rdFunction
Specifies the GDI function number 0x0B41.

rdParm
Contains the following elements:

Element	Description
raster op	Low-order word of the raster operation
raster op	High-order word of the raster operation
SYE	Source y-extent
SXE	Source x-extent
SY	Y-coordinate of the source origin
SX	X-coordinate of the source origin
DYE	Destination y-extent
DXE	Destination x-extent
DY	Y-coordinate of the destination origin
DX	X-coordinate of the destination origin
BitmapInfo	**BITMAPINFO** structure (For a description of the **BITMAPINFO** structure, see the *Microsoft Windows Programmer's Reference, Volume 3*.)
bits	Actual device-independent bitmap bits

StretchDIBits

```
struct {
    DWORD rdSize;
    WORD  rdFunction;
    WORD  rdParm[];
}
```

Members

rdSize
Specifies the record size, in words.

rdFunction
Specifies the GDI function number 0x0F43.

rdParm
Contains the following elements:

Element	Description
dwRop	Raster operation to be performed
Usag	Flag indicating whether the bitmap color table contains RGB values or indexes to the currently realized logical palette
srcYExt	Height of the source in the bitmap
srcXExt	Width of the source in the bitmap
srcY	Y-coordinate of the origin of the source in the bitmap

Element	Description
srcX	X-coordinate of the origin of the source in the bitmap
dstYExt	Height of the destination rectangle
dstXExt	Width of the destination rectangle
dstY	Y-coordinate of the origin of the destination rectangle
dstX	X-coordinate of the origin of the destination rectangle
BitmapInfo	**BITMAPINFO** structure (For a description of the **BIT-MAPINFO** structure, see the *Microsoft Windows Programmer's Reference, Volume 3*.)
bits	Actual device-independent bitmap bits

TextOut

```
struct {
    DWORD rdSize;
    WORD  rdFunction;
    WORD  rdParm[];
}
```

Members

rdSize
Specifies the record size, in words.

rdFunction
Specifies the GDI function number 0x0521.

rdParm
Contains the following elements:

Element	Description
count	Length of the string
string	Actual string
y-value	Logical y-coordinate of the starting point for the string
x-value	Logical x-coordinate of the starting point for the string

Font File Format

Chapter **4**

This chapter describes the file formats for raster and vector fonts used by the Microsoft Windows operating system. These file formats may be used by smart text generators in some support modules for the graphics device interface (GDI). Vector formats, however, are more frequently used by GDI than by the support modules. TrueType font files are described in *TrueType Font Files*, available from Microsoft Corporation.

4.1 Organization of a Font File

Raster and vector font files begin with information that is common to both types of file and then continue with information that differs for each type. These font files are stored with an .FNT extension.

In Windows version 3.0 and later, the font-file header for raster and vector fonts includes six new members: **dFlags**, **dfAspace**, **dfBspace**, **dfCspace**, **dfColorPointer**, and **dfReserved1**. All device drivers support the fonts in Windows 2.*x*. However, not all drivers support those in versions 3.0 and later.

In Windows, font files for raster and vector fonts include the glyph table in the **dfCharTable** member, which consists of structures describing the bits for characters in the font file.The use of 32-bit offsets to the character glyphs in the **dfCharTable** member enables fonts to exceed 64K, the size limit of Windows 2.*x* fonts.

Because of their 32-bit offsets and potentially large size, the newer fonts are designed for use on systems that are running Windows versions 3.0 and later in protected (standard or 386-enhanced) mode and are using an 80386 (or higher) processor whose 32-bit registers can access the character glyphs. Typically, newer drivers use the newer version of a font only when both of these conditions are true.

4.2 Font-File Structure

Font information is found at the beginning of both raster and vector font files. The **FONTINFO** structure has the following form:

```
struct FONTINFO {
        WORD  dfVersion;
        DWORD dfSize;
        char  dfCopyright[60];
        WORD  dfType;
        WORD  dfPoints;
        WORD  dfVertRes;
        WORD  dfHorizRes;
        WORD  dfAscent;
        WORD  dfInternalLeading;
        WORD  dfExternalLeading;
        BYTE  dfItalic;
        BYTE  dfUnderline;
        BYTE  dfStrikeOut;
        WORD  dfWeight;
        BYTE  dfCharSet;
        WORD  dfPixWidth;
        WORD  dfPixHeight;
        BYTE  dfPitchAndFamily;
        WORD  dfAvgWidth;
        WORD  dfMaxWidth;
        BYTE  dfFirstChar;
        BYTE  dfLastChar;
        BYTE  dfDefaultChar;
        BYTE  dfBreakChar;
        WORD  dfWidthBytes;
        DWORD dfDevice;
        DWORD dfFace;
        DWORD dfBitsPointer;
        DWORD dfBitsOffset;
        BYTE  dfReserved;
        DWORD dfFlags;
        WORD  dfAspace;
        WORD  dfBspace;
        WORD  dfCspace;
        WORD  dfColorPointer;
        DWORD dfReserved1;
        WORD  dfCharTable[];
};
```

Following are the members of the **FONTINFO** structure:

dfVersion
Specifies the version (0x0200 or 0x0300) of the file.

dfSize
Specifies the total size of the file, in bytes.

dfCopyright
Specifies copyright information.

dfType

Specifies the type of font file. This information is organized as follows:

Byte	Description
Low-order	Exclusively for GDI use. If the low-order bit of the word is zero, it is a bitmap (raster) font file. If the low-order bit is 1, it is a vector font file. The second bit is reserved and must be zero. If no bits follow in the file and the bits are located in memory at a fixed address specified by the **dfBitsOffset** member, the third bit is set to 1. Otherwise, the bit is set to zero. If the font is realized by a device, the high-order bit of the low-order byte is set. The remaining bits in the low-order byte are then reserved and set to zero.
High-order	Reserved for device use and is always set to zero for standard fonts realized by GDI. Physical fonts that set the high-order bit of the low-order byte may use this byte to describe themselves. GDI never inspects the high-order byte.

dfPoints

Specifies the nominal point size (that is, the number identifying the point size) at which this character set looks best.

dfVertRes

Specifies the nominal vertical resolution (that is, the number identifying the vertical resolution), in dots per inch, at which this character set was digitized.

dfHorizRes

Specifies the nominal horizontal resolution (that is, the number identifying the horizontal resolution), in dots per inch, at which this character set was digitized.

dfAscent

Specifies the distance from the top of a character-definition cell to the base line of the typographical font. The **dfAscent** member is useful for aligning the base lines of fonts with different heights.

dfInternalLeading

Specifies the amount of leading inside the bounds set by the **dfPixHeight** member. Accent marks can occur in this area. The designer can set the value to zero.

dfExternalLeading

Specifies the amount of extra leading that the designer requests the application to add between rows. Since this area is outside the font proper, it contains no marks and is not altered by text-output calls in either opaque or transparent mode. The designer can set the value to zero.

dfItalic

Specifies whether the character-definition data represents an italic font. If the flag is set, the low-order bit is 1. All other bits are zero.

dfUnderline

Specifies whether the character-definition data represents an underlined font. If the flag is set, the low-order bit is 1. All other bits are zero.

dfStrikeOut

Specifies whether the character-definition data represents a strikeout font. If the flag is set, the low-order bit is 1. All other bits are zero.

dfWeight

Specifies the weight of the characters in the character-definition data, on a scale of 1 through 1000. A **dfWeight** value of 400 specifies a regular weight.

dfCharSet

Specifies the character set defined by this font.

dfPixWidth

Specifies the width of the grid on which a vector font was digitized. For raster fonts, if the **dfPixWidth** member is nonzero, it represents the width for all the characters in the bitmap. If the member is zero, the font has variable-width characters whose widths are specified in the array for the **dfCharTable** member.

dfPixHeight

Specifies the height of the character bitmap for raster fonts or the height of the grid on which a vector font was digitized.

dfPitchAndFamily

Specifies the pitch and font family. If the font is variable pitch, the low bit is set. The four high bits give the family name of the font. Font families describe the general look of a font. They identify fonts when the exact name is not available. The font families are described as follows:

Family	Description
FF_DONTCARE	Unknown.
FF_ROMAN	Proportionally spaced fonts with serifs.
FF_SWISS	Proportionally spaced fonts without serifs.
FF_MODERN	Fixed-pitch fonts.
FF_SCRIPT	Cursive or script fonts. (Both are designed to look similar to handwriting. Script fonts have joined letters; cursive fonts do not.)
FF_DECORATIVE	Novelty fonts.

dfAvgWidth

Specifies the width of characters in the font. For fixed-pitch fonts, this value is the same as the value for the **dfPixWidth** member. For variable-pitch fonts, it is the width of the character "X".

dfMaxWidth

Specifies the maximum pixel width of any character in the font. For fixed-pitch fonts, this value is the same as the value of the **dfPixWidth** member.

dfFirstChar

Specifies the first character code defined by the font. Character definitions are stored only for the characters actually present in the font. Use this member, therefore, when calculating indexes for either the **dfBits** or **dfCharOffset** member.

dfLastChar

Specifies the last character code defined by the font. All characters with codes between the values for the **dfFirstChar** and **dfLastChar** members must be present in the character definitions for the font.

dfDefaultChar

Specifies the character to substitute whenever a string contains a character that is out of range. The character is given relative to the **dfFirstChar** member so that the **dfDefaultChar** member is the actual value of the character less the value of the **dfFirstChar** member. The **dfDefaultChar** member indicates a special character that is not a space.

dfBreakChar

Specifies the character that defines word breaks for word wrapping and word-spacing justification. The character is given relative to the **dfFirstChar** member so that the **dfBreakChar** member is the actual value of the character less that of the **dfFirstChar** member. The **dfBreakChar** member is normally 32 minus the value of the **dfFirstChar** member (the ASCII space character).

dfWidthBytes

Specifies the number of bytes in each row of the bitmap. This value is always even so that the rows start on word boundaries. For vector fonts, this member has no meaning.

dfDevice

Specifies the offset in the file to the string giving the device name. For a generic font, this value is zero.

dfFace

Specifies the offset in the file to the null-terminated string that names the face.

dfBitsPointer

Specifies the absolute machine address of the bitmap. This is set by GDI at load time. The value of the **dfBitsPointer** member is guaranteed to be even.

dfBitsOffset

Specifies the offset in the file to the beginning of the bitmap information. If the third bit in the **dfType** member is set, the **dfBitsOffset** member is an absolute address of the bitmap (probably in read-only memory).

For raster fonts, the **dfBitsOffset** member points to a sequence of bytes that make up the bitmap of the font. The height of the bitmap is the height of the font, and its width is the sum of the widths of the characters in the font, rounded up to the next word boundary.

For vector fonts, the **dfBitsOffset** member points to a string of bytes or words (depending on the size of the grid on which the font was digitized) that specify the strokes for each character of the font. The value of the **dfBitsOffset** member must be even.

dfReserved

Not used.

dfFlags

Specifies the bit flags that define the format of the glyph bitmap, as follows:

Pitch value	Address
DFF_FIXED	0x0001
DFF_PROPORTIONAL	0x0002
DFF_ABCFIXED	0x0004
DFF_ABCPROPORTIONAL	0x0008
DFF_1COLOR	0x0010
DFF_16COLOR	0x0020
DFF_256COLOR	0x0040
DFF_RGBCOLOR	0x0080

dfAspace

Specifies the global A space, if any. The value of the **dfAspace** member is the distance from the current position to the left edge of the bitmap.

dfBspace

Specifies the global B space, if any. The value of the **dfBspace** member is the width of the character.

dfCspace

Specifies the global C space, if any. The value of the **dfCspace** member is the distance from the right edge of the bitmap to the new current position. The increment of a character is the sum of the A, B, and C spaces. These spaces apply to all glyphs, including DFF_ABCFIXED.

dfColorPointer

Specifies the offset to the color table for color fonts, if any. The format of the bits is like a device-independent bitmap (DIB), but without the header. (That is, the characters are not split into disjoint bytes; instead, they are left intact.) If no color table is needed, this entry is NULL.

dfReserved1

Not used.

dfCharTable

Specifies an array of entries for raster, fixed-pitch vector, and proportionally spaced vector fonts, as follows:

Font type	Description
Raster	Each entry in the array consists of two 2-byte words for Windows 2.x and three 2-byte words for Windows 3.0 and later. The first word of each entry is the character width. The second word of each entry is the byte offset from the beginning of the **FONTINFO** structure to the character bitmap. For Windows 3.0 and later, the second and third words are used for the offset.
Fixed-pitch vector	Each 2-byte entry in the array specifies the offset from the start of the bitmap to the beginning of the string of stroke specification units for the character. The number of bytes or words to be used for a particular character is calculated by subtracting its entry from the next one, so that there is a sentinel at the end of the array of values.
Proportionally-spaced vector	Each 4-byte entry in the array is divided into two 2-byte fields. The first field gives the starting offset from the start of the bitmap of the character strokes. The second field gives the pixel width of the character.

One extra entry at the end of the character table describes an absolute-space character, which is guaranteed to be blank. This character is not part of the normal character set.

The number of entries in the table is calculated as follows: (**dfLastChar** – **dfFirstChar**) + 2. This number includes a "spare," the sentinel offset.

For more information on the **dfCharTable** member, see Section 4.3, "Version-Specific Glyph Tables."

facename
Specifies an ASCII character string that constitutes the name of the font face. The size of this member is the length of the string plus a null terminating character.

devicename
Specifies an ASCII character string that constitutes the name of the device if this font file is for a specific one. The size of this member is the length of the string plus a null terminating character.

bitmaps
Specifies character bitmap definitions. Unlike the old font format, each character is stored as a contiguous set of bytes.

The first byte contains the first 8 bits of the first scan line (that is, the top line of the character). The second byte contains the first 8 bits of the second scan line.

This continues until the first "column" is completely defined. The subsequent byte contains the next 8 bits of the first scan line, padded with zeros on the right if necessary (and so on, down through the second "column"). If the glyph is quite narrow, each scan line is covered by one byte, with bits set to zero as necessary for padding. If the glyph is very wide, a third or even fourth set of bytes can be present.

Character bitmaps must be stored contiguously and arranged in ascending order. The bytes for a 12-pixel by 14-pixel "A" character, for example, are given in two sets, because the character is less than 17 pixels wide:

```
00 06 09 10 20 20 20 3F 20 20 20 00 00 00
00 00 00 80 40 40 40 C0 40 40 40 00 00 00
```

Note that in the second set of bytes, the second digit of the byte is always zero. The zeros correspond to the thirteenth through sixteenth pixels on the right side of the character, which are not used by this character bitmap.

4.3 Version-Specific Glyph Tables

The **dfCharTable** member for Windows 2.x has a **GlyphEntry** structure with the following format:

```
GlyphEntry      struc
geWidth                 dw      ? ; width of char bitmap, pixels
geOffset                dw      ? ; pointer to the bits
GlyphEntry      ends
```

The **dfCharTable** member in Windows 3.0 and later is dependent on the format of the glyph bitmap. The only formats supported are DFF_FIXED and DFF_PROPORTIONAL.

```
DFF_FIXED
DFF_PROPORTIONAL
```

```
GlyphEntry      struc
geWidth                 dw      ? ; width of char bitmap, pixels
geOffset                dd      ? ; pointer to the bits
GlyphEntry      ends
```

```
DFF_ABCFIXED
DFF_ABCPROPORTIONAL
```

```
GlyphEntry      struc
geWidth                 dw      ?  ; width of char bitmap, pixels
geOffset                dd      ?  ; pointer to the bits
geAspace                dd      ?  ; A space, fract pixels (16.16)
geBspace                dd      ?  ; B space, fract pixels (16.16)
geCspace                dw      ?  ; C space, fract pixels (16.16)
GlyphEntry      ends
```

Fractional pixels are expressed as 32-bit signed numbers with an implicit binary point between bits 15 and 16. This is referred to as a 16.16 ("sixteen dot sixteen") fixed-point number.

The ABC spacing in the following example is the same as defined previously. However, specific sets are defined for each character:

```
DFF_1COLOR                              ; 8 pixels per byte
DFF_16COLOR                             ; 2 pixels per byte
DFF_256COLOR                            ; 1 pixel per byte
DFF_RGBCOLOR                            ; RGB quads

GlyphEntry      struc
geWidth                 dw      ?  ; width of char bitmap, pixels
geOffset                dd      ?  ; pointer to the bits
geHeight                dw      ?  ; height of char bitmap, pixels
geAspace                dd      ?  ; A space, fract pixels (16.16)
geBspace                dd      ?  ; B space, fract pixels (16.16)
geCspace                dd      ?  ; C space, fract pixels (16.16)
GlyphEntry      ends
```

Group File Format

This chapter describes the format of group files used by the Microsoft Windows operating system. A group file contains data that Microsoft Windows Program Manager (PROGMAN.EXE) uses to display the icons of the applications in a group, start the applications in a group, and open related documents.

5.1 Organization of a Group File

The first element in a group file is the group-file header. The data in the group-file header includes an identifier, a count of bytes, a count of items in the file, and information that the system uses to display group icons.

The group-file header is followed by one or more entries that contain item data describing the icon of an application. These entries include the coordinates that the system uses to display the icon; the count of bytes in the header, AND mask, and XOR mask for the icon; and the offset to the header, AND mask, and XOR mask for the icon.

The item data entries are followed by entries that contain the color data for the application icons. For more information about these entries, see Chapter 1, "Graphics File Formats."

For Windows version 3.1, the icon data is followed by tag data. The tag data contains information that Program Manager uses when it displays the Program Item Properties dialog box. This data identifies the directory in which the application is stored and the shortcut key (if one exists). It also specifies the state of the Run Minimized box.

5.2 Group-File Structures

This chapter uses C structures to depict the organization of data within a group file. These structures were created solely to show the organization of data in a resource; they do not appear in any of the include files shipped with the Microsoft Windows 3.1 Software Development Kit (SDK).

5.2.1 Group-File Header

The group-file header contains general information about the group file. The **GROUPHEADER** structure has the following form:

```
struct tagGROUPHEADER {
    char  cIdentifier[4];
    WORD  wCheckSum;
    WORD  cbGroup;
    WORD  nCmdShow;
    RECT  rcNormal;
    POINT ptMin;
    WORD  pName;
    WORD  wLogPixelsX;
    WORD  wLogPixelsY;
    WORD  wBitsPerPixel;
    WORD  wPlanes;
    WORD  cItems;
    WORD  rgiItems[cItems];
};
```

Following are the members in the **GROUPHEADER** structure:

cIdentifier
Identifies an array of 4 characters. If the file is a valid group file, this array must contain the string "PMCC".

wCheckSum
Specifies the negative sum of all words in the file (including the value specified by the **wCheckSum** member).

cbGroup
Specifies the size of the group file, in bytes.

nCmdShow
Specifies whether Program Manager should display the group in minimized, normal, or maximized form. This member can be one of the following values:

Value	Flag
0x00	SW_HIDE
0x01	SW_SHOWNORMAL
0x02	SW_SHOWMINIMIZED
0x03	SW_SHOWMAXIMIZED
0x04	SW_SHOWNOACTIVATE
0x05	SW_SHOW
0x06	SW_MINIMIZE
0x07	SW_SHOWMINNOACTIVATE
0x08	SW_SHOWNA
0x09	SW_RESTORE

rcNormal
Specifies the coordinates of the group window (the window in which the group icons appear). It is a rectangular structure.

ptMin

Specifies the coordinate of the lower-left corner of the group window with respect to the parent window. It is a point structure.

pName

Specifies an offset from the beginning of the file to a null-terminated string that specifies the group name.

wLogPixelsX

Specifies the horizontal display resolution for which the group icons were created.

wLogPixelsY

Specifies the vertical display resolution for which the group icons were created.

wBitsPerPixel

Specifies the format of the icon bitmaps, in bits per pixel.

wPlanes

Specifies the count of planes in the icon bitmaps.

cItems

Specifies the number of **ITEMDATA** structures in the **rgiItems** array. (There may also be NULL entries in the **rgiItems** array.)

rgiItems[cItems]

Specifies an array of **ITEMDATA** structures.

5.2.2 Item Data

The item data contains information about a particular application and its icon. The **ITEMDATA** structure has the following form:

```
struct tagITEMDATA {
    POINT pt;
    WORD  iIcon;
    WORD  cbResource;
    WORD  cbANDPlane;
    WORD  cbXORPlane;
    WORD  pHeader;
    WORD  pANDPlane;
    WORD  pXORPlane;
    WORD  pName;
    WORD  pCommand;
    WORD  pIconPath;
};
```

Following are the members in the **ITEMDATA** structure:

pt

Specifies the coordinates for the lower-left corner of an icon in the group window. It is a point structure.

iIcon

Specifies the index value for an icon. This value indicates the position of the icon in an executable file.

cbResource

Specifies the count of bytes in the icon resource, which appears in the executable file for the application.

cbANDPlane

Specifies the count of bytes in the AND mask for the icon.

cbXORPlane

Specifies the count of bytes in the XOR mask for the icon.

pHeader

Specifies an offset from the beginning of the group file to the resource header for the icon.

pANDPlane

Specifies an offset from the beginning of the group file to the AND mask for the icon.

pXORPlane

Specifies an offset from the beginning of the group file to the XOR mask for the icon.

pName

Specifies an offset from the beginning of the group file to a string that specifies the item name.

pCommand

Specifies an offset from the beginning of the group file to a string that specifies the name of the executable file containing the application and the icon resource(s).

pIconPath

Specifies an offset from the beginning of the group file to a string that specifies the path where the executable file is located. This path can be used to extract icon data from an executable file.

5.2.3 Tag Data

The tag data contains general information used to display the Program Item Properties dialog box. The **TAGDATA** structure has the following form:

```
struct tagTAGDATA{
    WORD wID;
    WORD wItem;
    WORD cb;
    BYTE rgb[1];
};
```

Following are the members in the **TAGDATA** structure:

wID

Specifies the type of tag data. This member can have one of the following values:

Value	Meaning
0x8101	Array at which the **rgb** member points is a null-terminated string that identifies the path for the application.
0x8102	Array at which the **rgb** member points is a 16-bit word value that identifies the shortcut key specified by the user.
0x8103	Minimized version of the item is displayed. If this value is specified, the array to which the **rgb** member points is not present in the structure and the value of the **cb** member is 0x06.

wItem

Specifies the index to the item the tag data refers to. If the data is not specific to a particular item, this value is 0xFFFF.

cb

Specifies the size of the **TAGDATA** structure, in bytes.

rgb

Specifies an array of byte values. The length of this array can be found by subtracting 6 from the value of the **cb** member.

Executable-File Header Format

An executable (.EXE) file for the Microsoft Windows operating system contains a combination of code and data or a combination of code, data, and resources. The executable file also contains two headers: an MS-DOS header and a Windows header. The next two sections describe these headers; the third section describes the code and data contained in a Windows executable file.

6.1 MS-DOS Header

The MS-DOS (old-style) executable-file header contains four distinct parts: a collection of header information (such as the signature word, the file size, and so on), a reserved section, a pointer to a Windows header (if one exists), and a stub program. The following illustration shows the MS-DOS executable-file header:

Beginning of file

MS-DOS header info	*00h (offset)*
Reserved	*20h (offset)*
Windows offset	*3Ch (offset)*
MS-DOS stub program	*40h (offset)*
	Beginning of Windows header
⋮	

If the word value at offset 18h is 40h or greater, the word value at 3Ch is an offset to a Windows header.

MS-DOS uses the stub program to display a message if Windows has not been loaded when the user attempts to run a program.

For more information about the MS-DOS executable-file header, see the *Microsoft MS-DOS Programmer's Reference* (Redmond, Washington: Microsoft Press, 1991).

6.2 Windows Header

The Windows (new-style) executable-file header contains information that the loader requires for segmented executable files. This information includes the linker version number, data specified by the linker, data specified by the resource compiler, tables of segment data, tables of resource data, and so on. The following illustration shows the Windows executable-file header:

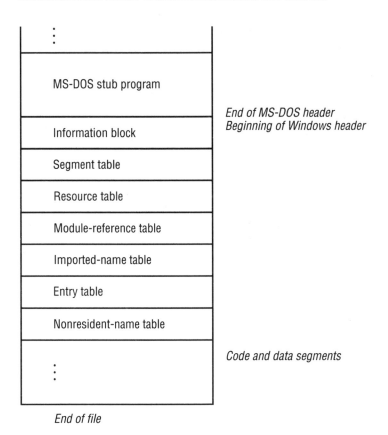

The following sections describe the entries in the Windows executable-file header.

6.2.1 Information Block

The information block in the Windows header contains the linker version number, the lengths of various tables that further describe the executable file, the offsets from the beginning of the header to the beginning of these tables, the heap and stack sizes, and so on. The following list summarizes the contents of the header information block (the locations are relative to the beginning of the block):

Location	Description
00h	Specifies the signature word. The low byte contains "N" (4Eh) and the high byte contains "E" (45h).
02h	Specifies the linker version number.
03h	Specifies the linker revision number.
04h	Specifies the offset to the entry table (relative to the beginning of the header).
06h	Specifies the length of the entry table, in bytes.
08h	Reserved.
0Ch	Specifies flags that describe the contents of the executable file. This value can be one or more of the following bits:

Bit	Meaning
0	The linker sets this bit if the executable-file format is **SINGLEDATA**. An executable file with this format contains one data segment. This bit is set if the file is a dynamic-link library (DLL).
1	The linker sets this bit if the executable-file format is **MULTIPLEDATA**. An executable file with this format contains multiple data segments. This bit is set if the file is a Windows application.
	If neither bit 0 nor bit 1 is set, the executable-file format is **NOAUTODATA**. An executable file with this format does not contain an automatic data segment.
2	Reserved.
3	Reserved.
8	Reserved.
9	Reserved.
11	If this bit is set, the first segment in the executable file contains code that loads the application.
13	If this bit is set, the linker detects errors at link time but still creates an executable file.
14	Reserved.

Location	Description

	Bit	**Meaning**
	15	If this bit is set, the executable file is a library module.

If bit 15 is set, the CS:IP registers point to an initialization procedure called with the value in the AX register equal to the module handle. The initialization procedure must execute a far return to the caller. If the procedure is successful, the value in AX is nonzero. Otherwise, the value in AX is zero.

The value in the DS register is set to the library's data segment if **SINGLEDATA** is set. Otherwise, DS is set to the data segment of the application that loads the library.

Location	Description
0Eh	Specifies the automatic data segment number. (0Eh is zero if the **SINGLEDATA** and **MULTIPLEDATA** bits are cleared.)
10h	Specifies the initial size, in bytes, of the local heap. This value is zero if there is no local allocation.
12h	Specifies the initial size, in bytes, of the stack. This value is zero if the SS register value does not equal the DS register value.
14h	Specifies the segment:offset value of CS:IP.
18h	Specifies the segment:offset value of SS:SP.

The value specified in SS is an index to the module's segment table. The first entry in the segment table corresponds to segment number 1.

If SS addresses the automatic data segment and SP is zero, SP is set to the address obtained by adding the size of the automatic data segment to the size of the stack.

Location	Description
1Ch	Specifies the number of entries in the segment table.
1Eh	Specifies the number of entries in the module-reference table.
20h	Specifies the number of bytes in the nonresident-name table.
22h	Specifies a relative offset from the beginning of the Windows header to the beginning of the segment table.
24h	Specifies a relative offset from the beginning of the Windows header to the beginning of the resource table.
26h	Specifies a relative offset from the beginning of the Windows header to the beginning of the resident-name table.
28h	Specifies a relative offset from the beginning of the Windows header to the beginning of the module-reference table.
2Ah	Specifies a relative offset from the beginning of the Windows header to the beginning of the imported-name table.

Location	Description
2Ch	Specifies a relative offset from the beginning of the file to the beginning of the nonresident-name table.
30h	Specifies the number of movable entry points.
32h	Specifies a shift count that is used to align the logical sector. This count is $\log_2$ of the segment sector size. It is typically 4, although the default count is 9. (This value corresponds to the **/alignment** [**/a**] linker switch. When the linker command line contains **/a:16**, the shift count is 4. When the linker command line contains **/a:512**, the shift count is 9.)
34h	Specifies the number of resource segments.
36h	Specifies the target operating system, depending on which bits are set:

Bit	Meaning
0	Operating system format is unknown.
1	Reserved.
2	Operating system is Microsoft Windows.
3	Reserved.
4	Reserved.

Location	Description
37h	Specifies additional information about the executable file. It can be one or more of the following values:

Bit	Meaning
1	If this bit is set, the executable file contains a Windows 2.x application that runs in version 3.x protected mode.
2	If this bit is set, the executable file contains a Windows 2.x application that supports proportional fonts.
3	If this bit is set, the executable file contains a fast-load area.

Location	Description
38h	Specifies the offset, in sectors, to the beginning of the fast-load area. (Only Windows uses this value.)
3Ah	Specifies the length, in sectors, of the fast-load area. (Only Windows uses this value.)
3Ch	Reserved.
3Eh	Specifies the expected version number for Windows. (Only Windows uses this value.)

6.2.2 Segment Table

The segment table contains information that describes each segment in an executable file. This information includes the segment length, segment type, and segment-relocation data. The following list summarizes the values found in the segment table (the locations are relative to the beginning of each entry):

Location	Description
00h	Specifies the offset, in sectors, to the segment data (relative to the beginning of the file). A value of zero means no data exists.
02h	Specifies the length, in bytes, of the segment, in the file. A value of zero indicates that the segment length is 64K, unless the selector offset is also zero.
04h	Specifies flags that describe the contents of the executable file. This value can be one or more of the following:

Bit	Meaning
0	If this bit is set, the segment is a data segment. Otherwise, the segment is a code segment.
1	If this bit is set, the loader has allocated memory for the segment.
2	If this bit is set, the segment is loaded.
3	Reserved.
4	If this bit is set, the segment type is **MOVEABLE**. Otherwise, the segment type is **FIXED**.
5	If this bit is set, the segment type is **PURE** or **SHAREABLE**. Otherwise, the segment type is **IMPURE** or **NONSHAREABLE**.
6	If this bit is set, the segment type is **PRELOAD**. Otherwise, the segment type is **LOADONCALL**.
7	If this bit is set and the segment is a code segment, the segment type is **EXECUTEONLY**. If this bit is set and the segment is a data segment, the segment type is **READONLY**.
8	If this bit is set, the segment contains relocation data.
9	Reserved.
10	Reserved.
11	Reserved.
12	If this bit is set, the segment is discardable.
13	Reserved.

Location	Description

	Bit	Meaning
	14	Reserved.
	15	Reserved.

06h	Specifies the minimum allocation size of the segment, in bytes. A value of zero indicates that the minimum allocation size is 64K.

6.2.3 Resource Table

The resource table describes and identifies the location of each resource in the executable file. The table has the following form:

```
WORD      rscAlignShift;
TYPEINFO  rscTypes[];
WORD      rscEndTypes;
BYTE      rscResourceNames[];
BYTE      rscEndNames;
```

Following are the members in the resource table:

rscAlignShift
Specifies the alignment shift count for resource data. When the shift count is used as an exponent of 2, the resulting value specifies the factor, in bytes, for computing the location of a resource in the executable file.

rscTypes
Specifies an array of **TYPEINFO** structures containing information about resource types. There must be one **TYPEINFO** structure for each type of resource in the executable file.

rscEndTypes
Specifies the end of the resource type definitions. This member must be zero.

rscResourceNames
Specifies the names (if any) associated with the resources in this table. Each name is stored as consecutive bytes; the first byte specifies the number of characters in the name.

rscEndNames
Specifies the end of the resource names and the end of the resource table. This member must be zero.

6.2.3.1 Type Information

The **TYPEINFO** structure has the following form:

```
typedef struct _TYPEINFO {
    WORD        rtTypeID;
    WORD        rtResourceCount;
    DWORD       rtReserved;
    NAMEINFO    rtNameInfo[];
} TYPEINFO;
```

Following are the members in the **TYPEINFO** structure:

rtTypeID
Specifies the type identifier of the resource. This integer value is either a resource-type value or an offset to a resource-type name. If the high bit in this member is set (0x8000), the value is one of the following resource-type values:

Value	Resource type
RT_ACCELERATOR	Accelerator table
RT_BITMAP	Bitmap
RT_CURSOR	Cursor
RT_DIALOG	Dialog box
RT_FONT	Font component
RT_FONTDIR	Font directory
RT_GROUP_CURSOR	Cursor directory
RT_GROUP_ICON	Icon directory
RT_ICON	Icon
RT_MENU	Menu
RT_RCDATA	Resource data
RT_STRING	String table

If the high bit of the value in this member is not set, the value represents an offset, in bytes relative to the beginning of the resource table, to a name in the **rscResourceNames** member.

rtResourceCount
Specifies the number of resources of this type in the executable file.

rtReserved
Reserved.

rtNameInfo
Specifies an array of **NAMEINFO** structures containing information about individual resources. The **rtResourceCount** member specifies the number of structures in the array.

6.2.3.2 Name Information

The **NAMEINFO** structure has the following form:

```
typedef struct _NAMEINFO {
    WORD rnOffset;
    WORD rnLength;
    WORD rnFlags;
    WORD rnID;
    WORD rnHandle;
    WORD rnUsage;
} NAMEINFO;
```

Following are the members in the **NAMEINFO** structure:

rnOffset
Specifies an offset to the contents of the resource data (relative to the beginning of the file). The offset is in terms of alignment units specified by the **rscAlign-Shift** member at the beginning of the resource table.

rnLength
Specifies the resource length, in bytes.

rnFlags
Specifies whether the resource is fixed, preloaded, or shareable. This member can be one or more of the following values:

Value	Meaning
0x0010	Resource is movable (**MOVEABLE**). Otherwise, it is fixed.
0x0020	Resource can be shared (**PURE**).
0x0040	Resource is preloaded (**PRELOAD**). Otherwise, it is loaded on demand.

rnID
Specifies or points to the resource identifier. If the identifier is an integer, the high bit is set (8000h). Otherwise, it is an offset to a resource string, relative to the beginning of the resource table.

rnHandle
Reserved.

rnUsage
Reserved.

6.2.4 Resident-Name Table

The resident-name table contains strings that identify exported functions in the executable file. As the name implies, these strings are resident in system memory and are never discarded. The resident-name strings are case-sensitive and are not null-terminated. The following list summarizes the values found in the resident-name table (the locations are relative to the beginning of each entry):

Location	Description
00h	Specifies the length of a string. If there are no more strings in the table, this value is zero.
01h – xxh	Specifies the resident-name text. This string is case-sensitive and is not null-terminated.
xxh + 01h	Specifies an ordinal number that identifies the string. This number is an index into the entry table.

The first string in the resident-name table is the module name.

6.2.5 Module-Reference Table

The module-reference table contains offsets for module names stored in the imported-name table. Each entry in this table is 2 bytes long.

6.2.6 Imported-Name Table

The imported-name table contains the names of modules that the executable file imports. Each entry contains two parts: a single byte that specifies the length of the string and the string itself. The strings in this table are not null-terminated.

6.2.7 Entry Table

The entry table contains bundles of entry points from the executable file (the linker generates each bundle). The numbering system for these ordinal values is 1-based—that is, the ordinal value corresponding to the first entry point is 1.

The linker generates the densest possible bundles under the restriction that it cannot reorder the entry points. This restriction is necessary because other executable files may refer to entry points within a given bundle by their ordinal values.

The entry-table data is organized by bundle, each of which begins with a 2-byte header. The first byte of the header specifies the number of entries in the bundle (a value of 00h designates the end of the table). The second byte specifies whether the corresponding segment is movable or fixed. If the value in this byte is 0FFh, the segment is movable. If the value in this byte is 0FEh, the entry does not refer to a segment but refers, instead, to a constant defined within the module. If the value in this byte is neither 0FFh nor 0FEh, it is a segment index.

For movable segments, each entry consists of 6 bytes and has the following form:

Location	Description
00h	Specifies a byte value. This value can be a combination of the following bits:

Bit(s)	Meaning
0	If this bit is set, the entry is exported.
1	If this bit is set, the segment uses a global (shared) data segment.
3–7	If the executable file contains code that performs ring transitions, these bits specify the number of words that compose the stack. At the time of the ring transition, these words must be copied from one ring to the other.

Location	Description
01h	Specifies an **int 3fh** instruction.
03h	Specifies the segment number.
04h	Specifies the segment offset.

For fixed segments, each entry consists of 3 bytes and has the following form:

Location	Description
00h	Specifies a byte value. This value can be a combination of the following bits:

Bit(s)	Meaning
0	If this bit is set, the entry is exported.
1	If this bit is set, the entry uses a global (shared) data segment. (This may be set only for **SINGLEDATA** library modules.)
3–7	If the executable file contains code that performs ring transitions, these bits specify the number of words that compose the stack. At the time of the ring transition, these words must be copied from one ring to the other.

Location	Description
01h	Specifies an offset.

6.2.8 Nonresident-Name Table

The nonresident-name table contains strings that identify exported functions in the executable file. As the name implies, these strings are not always resident in system memory and are discardable. The nonresident-name strings are case-sensitive; they are not null-terminated. The following list summarizes the values found in the nonresident-name table (the specified locations are relative to the beginning of each entry):

Location	Description
00h	Specifies the length, in bytes, of a string. If this byte is 00h, there are no more strings in the table.
01h – xxh	Specifies the nonresident-name text. This string is case-sensitive and is not null-terminated.
xx + 01h	Specifies an ordinal number that is an index to the entry table.

The first name that appears in the nonresident-name table is the module description string (which was specified in the module-definition file).

6.3 Code Segments and Relocation Data

Code and data segments follow the Windows header. Some of the code segments may contain calls to functions in other segments and may, therefore, require relocation data to resolve those references. This relocation data is stored in a relocation table that appears immediately after the code or data in the segment. The first 2 bytes in this table specify the number of relocation items the table contains. A relocation item is a collection of bytes specifying the following information:

- Address type (segment only, offset only, segment and offset)
- Relocation type (internal reference, imported ordinal, imported name)
- Segment number or ordinal identifier (for internal references)
- Reference-table index or function ordinal number (for imported ordinals)
- Reference-table index or name-table offset (for imported names)

Each relocation item contains 8 bytes of data, the first byte of which specifies one of the following relocation-address types:

Value	Meaning
0	Low byte at the specified offset
2	16-bit selector
3	32-bit pointer
5	16-bit offset

Value	Meaning
11	48-bit pointer
13	32-bit offset

The second byte specifies one of the following relocation types:

Value	Meaning
0	Internal reference
1	Imported ordinal
2	Imported name
3	**OSFIXUP**

The third and fourth bytes specify the offset of the relocation item within the segment.

If the relocation type is imported ordinal, the fifth and sixth bytes specify an index to a module's reference table and the seventh and eighth bytes specify a function ordinal value.

If the relocation type is imported name, the fifth and sixth bytes specify an index to a module's reference table and the seventh and eighth bytes specify an offset to an imported-name table.

If the relocation type is internal reference and the segment is fixed, the fifth byte specifies the segment number, the sixth byte is zero, and the seventh and eighth bytes specify an offset to the segment. If the relocation type is internal reference and the segment is movable, the fifth byte specifies 0FFh, the sixth byte is zero; and the seventh and eighth bytes specify an ordinal value found in the segment's entry table.

Resource Formats Within Executable Files

This chapter describes the format of executable-file resources used by the Microsoft Windows operating system. A resource, or collection of binary data, can be one of two types: standard or user-defined. The data in a standard resource describes an icon, cursor, menu, dialog box, bitmap, font, string table, or accelerator. The data in a user-defined resource describes an application-specific object. This chapter describes standard resources.

A Windows executable file contains a resource table that describes each of the resources in the file. The data in this table includes an offset from the beginning of the file to each resource. It also includes values that specify the resource type, the resource length, and so on. For more information about the organization of the resource table, see Chapter 6, "Executable-File Header Format."

This chapter uses C structures to depict the organization of data in resources. In some cases, these structures are not true C structures, because they contain members that can be variable-length strings. These structures were created only to depict the organization of data within a resource; they do not appear in any of the include files shipped with the Microsoft Windows 3.1 Software Development Kit (SDK).

7.1 Icon Resource

An icon resource is identical in format to an icon image in an icon-resource file. The resource contains the icon-image header, color table, and XOR and AND masks. For more information about the icon-image format, see Chapter 1, "Graphics File Formats."

Each icon resource must have a corresponding entry in the resource table of the executable file. This means the resource table must contain a **TYPEINFO** structure in which the **rscTypeID** member is set to the RT_ICON value.

7.2 Icon-Directory Resource

An icon-directory resource is nearly identical in format to an icon directory in an icon-resource file. The resource specifies the number of icon images associated with this resource, as well as the dimensions and color formats for each icon. However, the last member of the **ICONDIRENTRY** structure (**dwImageOffset**) is replaced with a 16-bit value that specifies the resource-table index of the corresponding icon-image resource. The index is 1-based. If an executable file contains multiple icon resources, the index must be unique across all directories. For more information about the icon-directory format, see Chapter 1, "Graphics File Formats."

Each icon-directory resource must have a corresponding entry in the resource table of the executable file. This means the resource table must contain a **TYPEINFO** structure in which the **rscTypeID** member is set to the RT_GROUP_ICON value.

7.3 Cursor Resource

A cursor resource is nearly identical in format to a cursor image in a cursor-resource file. The resource contains the cursor hot spot as well as the cursor-image header, color table, and XOR and AND masks. The x- and y-coordinates for the cursor hot spot (both 16-bit values) appear first in the resource, immediately followed by the cursor-image header. For more information about the cursor-image format, see Chapter 1, "Graphics File Formats."

Each cursor resource must have a corresponding entry in the resource table of the executable file. This means the resource table must contain a **TYPEINFO** structure in which the **rscTypeID** member is set to the RT_CURSOR value.

7.4 Cursor-Directory Resource

A cursor-directory resource is nearly identical in format to a cursor directory in a cursor-resource file. The resource specifies the number of cursor images associated with this resource, as well as the dimensions of the images, but it does not include the hot-spot data. Furthermore, the last member of the **ICONDIRENTRY** structure (**dwImageOffset**) is replaced with a 16-bit value that specifies the resource-table index of the corresponding cursor-image resource.

In an executable file, the **CURSORDIRENTRY** structure has the following form:

```
typedef struct _CURSORDIRENTRY {
    WORD   wWidth;
    WORD   wHeight;
    WORD   wPlanes;
    WORD   wBitCount;
    DWORD  lBytesInRes;
    WORD   wImageIndex;
} CURSORDIRENTRY;
```

Following are the members in the **CURSORDIRENTRY** structure:

wWidth
    Specifies the width of the cursor, in pixels.

wHeight
    Specifies the height of the cursor, in pixels.

wPlanes

Specifies the number of color planes in the bitmap. This member must be set to 1.

wBitCount

Specifies the number of color bits per pixel in the bitmap. This member must be set to 1.

lBytesInRes

Specifies the size of the resource, in bytes.

wImageIndex

Specifies the 1-based index identifying the cursor image associated with this cursor-directory resource. If an executable file contains multiple icon resources, the index must be unique across all directories.

Each cursor-directory resource must have a corresponding entry in the resource table of the executable file. This means the resource table must contain a **TYPE-INFO** structure in which the **rscTypeID** member is set to the RT_GROUP_CURSOR value.

7.5 Menu Resource

A menu resource contains a header followed by a list of normal and pop-up menu items.

Each entry in the executable file's resource table contains a member that identifies the resource type. The RT_MENU constant identifies a menu resource.

7.5.1 Menu Header

The menu header contains version information for the menu resource. The header consists of two 16-bit values (which must be zero for Windows version 3.0 and later). A **MenuHeader** structure has the following form:

```
struct MenuHeader {
    WORD wVersion;
    WORD wReserved;
};
```

Following are the members in the **MenuHeader** structure:

wVersion

Specifies the version number. (For Windows 3.0 and later, this value is zero.)

wReserved

Reserved; must be zero.

7.5.2 Pop-up Menu Item

A menu resource contains data for each pop-up item in a menu. The first 16 bits indicate whether the item is grayed, inactive, checked, and so on. This data also includes a string that appears in the rectangle corresponding to that item. A **PopupMenuItem** structure has the following form:

```
struct PopupMenuItem {
    WORD fItemFlags;
    char szItemText[];
};
```

Following are the members in the **PopupMenuItem** structure:

fItemFlags
Specifies menu-item information. This member can have one or more of the following values:

Value	Meaning
MF_GRAYED	Item is grayed.
MF_DISABLED	Item is inactive.
MF_CHECKED	Item can be checked.
MF_POPUP	Item is a popup (must be specified for pop-up items).
MF_MENUBARBREAK	Item is a menu-bar break.
MF_MENUBREAK	Item is a menu break.
MF_END	Item ends the menu.

szItemText
Specifies a null-terminated string that appears in the menu and identifies the menu item. There is no fixed limit on the size of this string.

7.5.3 Normal Menu Item

A normal menu item is very similar to a pop-up menu item, except that it has an additional menu identifier. A **NormalMenuItem** structure has the following form:

```
struct NormalMenuItem {
    WORD fItemFlags;
    WORD wMenuID;
    char szItemText[];
};
```

Following are the members in the **NormalMenuItem** structure:

fItemFlags
Specifies menu-item information. This member can have one or more of the following values:

Value	Meaning
MF_GRAYED	Item is grayed.
MF_DISABLED	Item is inactive.
MF_CHECKED	Item can be checked.
MF_MENUBARBREAK	Item is a menu-bar break.
MF_MENUBREAK	Item is a menu break.
MF_END	Item ends the menu.

wMenuID
Identifies the menu item.

szItemText
Specifies a null-terminated string that appears in the menu and identifies the menu item. There is no fixed limit on the size of this string.

A menu separator is a normal menu item for which **fItemFlags** is zero, **wMenuID** is zero, and the **szItemText** array is empty.

7.5.4 Combined Menu Items

Pop-up and normal menu items are often combined in menus. A mixture of the two is shown in the following example:

```
POPUP ITEM
    NORMAL ITEM
    NORMAL ITEM
    .
    .
    .
    NORMAL ITEM
    NORMAL ITEM (fItemFlags contains the MF_END constant)
```

Note that the terminating item is a normal menu item, not a pop-up item, and that the **fItemFlags** member in the last item contains the MF_END constant.

Pop-up and normal menu items can also be nested to create hierarchical blocks, as shown in the following example:

```
POPUP ITEM
    NORMAL ITEM
    NORMAL ITEM
    .
    .
    .
    NORMAL ITEM
    POPUP ITEM
        NORMAL ITEM
        NORMAL ITEM
        NORMAL ITEM
        POPUP ITEM (fItemFlags contains the MF_END constant)
            NORMAL ITEM
            NORMAL ITEM (fItemFlags contains the MF_END constant)
    NORMAL ITEM (fItemFlags contains the MF_END constant)
```

Note that, although the pop-up menu item has its own terminating item, the terminating item for the entire menu is again a normal menu item.

7.6 Dialog Box Resource

A dialog box resource contains a dialog box header and data for each control within the dialog box.

Each entry in the executable file's resource table contains a member that identifies the resource type. The RT_DIALOG constant identifies a dialog box resource.

7.6.1 Dialog Box Header

The dialog box header contains general dialog box data, such as the dialog box window style, the number of controls in the dialog box, the coordinates of the upper-left corner of the box, the width and height of the box, the name of the menu to be displayed, and so on. The **DialogBoxHeader** structure has the following form:

```
struct DialogBoxHeader {
    DWORD  lStyle;
    BYTE   bNumberOfItems;
    WORD   x;
    WORD   y;
    WORD   cx;
    WORD   cy;
    char   szMenuName[];
    char   szClassName[];
    char   szCaption[];
    WORD   wPointSize;    /* only if DS_SETFONT */
    char   szFaceName[];  /* only if DS_SETFONT */
};
```

Following are the members in the **DialogBoxHeader** structure:

lStyle
Specifies the dialog-window style. This member is a combination of the window-style and dialog-style flags that are found in the WINDOWS.H include file.

bNumberOfItems
Specifies the number of controls in the dialog box.

x
Specifies the x-coordinate of the upper-left corner of the dialog box. This coordinate is a horizontal distance from the left edge of the parent window. This distance is specified by using a special horizontal dialog box unit equivalent to the average character width of the font divided by 4. If the DS_SETFONT flag is set, the average character width of the font specified in the dialog box header is used. Otherwise, the average character width of the system font is used.

y
Specifies the y-coordinate of the lower-left corner of the dialog box. This coordinate is a vertical distance from the top of the parent window. This distance is specified by using a special vertical dialog box unit equivalent to the character height of the current font divided by 8. If the DS_SETFONT flag is set, the height of the font specified in the dialog box header is used. Otherwise, the height of the system font is used.

cx
Specifies the width of the dialog box, in horizontal dialog units. (See the description of the **x** member for a definition of horizontal dialog units.)

cy
Specifies the height of the dialog box, in vertical dialog units. (See the description of the **y** member for a definition of vertical dialog units.)

szMenuName
Identifies a menu resource associated with the dialog box. If no menu is associated with the dialog box, this array contains a single-byte value of zero. If the menu has an ordinal identifier, the first byte of this member contains 0xFF and the subsequent two bytes contain the ordinal value. If the menu has a name identifier, the member contains a null-terminated string that specifies the menu name.

szClassName
Specifies the class name for the dialog box. If the dialog box uses the default class, this member contains a single-byte value of zero. Otherwise, this member contains a null-terminated string that specifies the name of the dialog class.

szCaption
Specifies a dialog box caption. This array must contain a null-terminated string.

wPointSize
Specifies the point size of a font that is unique to the dialog box. (This member is present only if the DS_SETFONT flag is set by the **lStyle** member.)

szFaceName
Specifies the typeface name of a dialog box font. This array must contain a null-terminated string. (This member is present only if the DS_SETFONT flag is set by the **lStyle** member.)

7.6.2 Control Data

A dialog box resource contains data for each control in a given dialog box. This data contains the coordinates of the upper-left corner of the control, the dimensions of the control, a control identifier, and so on. A **ControlData** structure has the following form:

```
struct ControlData {
    WORD  x;
    WORD  y;
    WORD  cx;
    WORD  cy;
    WORD  wID;
    DWORD lStyle;
    union
    {
        BYTE class;     /* if (class & 0x80) */
        char szClass[]; /* otherwise         */
    } ClassID;
    szText;
};
```

Following are the members in the **ControlData** structure:

x
Specifies the x-coordinate of the upper-left corner of the control.

y
Specifies the y-coordinate of the upper-left corner of the control.

cx
Specifies the width of the control, in horizontal dialog box units. For a definition of these units, see the **DialogBoxHeader** structure in the preceding section.

cy
Specifies the height of the control, in vertical dialog box units. For a definition of these units, see the **DialogBoxHeader** structure in the preceding section.

wID
Identifies the control.

lStyle

Specifies the control style. This member is a combination of the window-style flags that appear in the WINDOWS.H file.

ClassID

Specifies the class type. This member is either a single-byte value or a null-terminated string.

If this member is a byte value, it can be one of the following:

Value	Class type
0x80	Button
0x81	Edit
0x82	Static
0x83	List box
0x84	Scroll bar
0x85	Combo box

If this number is not a byte value, it takes the form described in the **szClass** member.

szClass

Identifies the class type. This member is a null-terminated string.

szText

Specifies the control text. This member is a null-terminated string.

7.7 Bitmap Resource

A bitmap resource is identical in format to a Windows bitmap file with its **BITMAPFILEHEADER** structure removed. In other words, the bitmap resource contains only the bitmap header, color table, and bitmap bits. For more information about the bitmap format, see Chapter 1, "Graphics File Formats."

Each bitmap resource must have a corresponding entry in the resource table of the executable file. This means the resource table must contain a **TYPEINFO** structure in which the **rscTypeID** member is set to the RT_BITMAP value.

7.8 Font Resource

A font resource consists of two parts: a directory and its components. The font-directory data describes all the fonts in a resource. This data includes a value specifying the number of fonts in the resource and a table of metrics for each of these fonts. The font-component data describes a single font in the resource. There is one component for each of the fonts in the resource. The component data is identical to the data found in a Windows font file (.FNT).

Each entry in the executable file's resource table contains a member that identifies the resource type. The RT_FONTDIR and RT_FONT constants identify a font directory and a font component, respectively.

7.8.1 Font-Directory Data

Font-directory data consists of a font count and one or more font directory entries.

7.8.1.1 Font Count

The font count is an integer that specifies the number of fonts in the resource. This value also corresponds to the number of font directories and font components.

7.8.1.2 Font Directory

The font directory is a collection of font metrics for a particular font. These metrics specify the point size for the font, aspect ratio, stroke width, and so on. The **FontDirEntry** structure has the following form:

```
struct FontDirEntry {
        WORD   fontOrdinal;
        WORD   dfVersion;
        DWORD  dfSize;
        char   dfCopyright[60];
        WORD   dfType;
        WORD   dfPoints;
        WORD   dfVertRes;
        WORD   dfHorizRes;
        WORD   dfAscent;
        WORD   dfInternalLeading;
        WORD   dfExternalLeading;
        BYTE   dfItalic;
        BYTE   dfUnderline;
        BYTE   dfStrikeOut;
        WORD   dfWeight;
        BYTE   dfCharSet;
        WORD   dfPixWidth;
        WORD   dfPixHeight;
```

```
            BYTE  dfPitchAndFamily;
            WORD  dfAvgWidth;
            WORD  dfMaxWidth;
            BYTE  dfFirstChar;
            BYTE  dfLastChar;
            BYTE  dfDefaultChar;
            BYTE  dfBreakChar;
            WORD  dfWidthBytes;
            DWORD dfDevice;
            DWORD dfFace;
            DWORD dfReserved;
            char  szDeviceName[];
            char  szFaceName[];
};
```

For a full description of these members, see the **TEXTMETRIC** and **LOGFONT**
structures in the *Microsoft Windows Programmer's Reference, Volume 3*.

7.8.2 Font-Component Data

Font-component data consists of one or more font-component entries.

7.8.2.1 Font Component

Each font-component entry consists of a header, extension data, extended text
metrics, kerning-pair data, and track-kerning data.

Following are the five parts of the font component entries:

Data structure	Contents
Header	Font metrics, such as the aspect ratio for which the font was created; leading values; italic, underline, strikeout, and bold descriptions; width information; first and last character identifiers; default and break character identifiers; and a pointer to the actual character data
Extension data	Offset to the extended font metrics, offset to the extent table, offset to the origin table, and offset to the table of kerning data
Extended text metrics	Additional font metrics, such as the point size of the font, the minimum point size to which it can be scaled, the maximum point size to which it can be scaled, the "X" height, the lowercase ascent and descent values, superscript metrics and offsets, subscript metrics and offsets, underline offset and width, strikeout offset and width, and the number of kerning pairs associated with the font

Data structure	Contents
Kerning-pair data	An identifier for each character in the pair of kerned characters, and a kerning value
Track-kerning data	Additional kerning data

For a complete description of Windows font files, see the Microsoft Windows Device Development Kit documentation.

7.9 String-Table Resources

A string table consists of one or more separate resources, each containing exactly 16 strings. The maximum length of each string is 255 bytes. One or more strings in a block can be null or empty. The first byte in the string specifies the number of characters in the string. (For null or empty strings, the first byte contains the value zero.)

Windows uses a 16-bit identifier to locate a string in a string-table resource. Bits 4 through 15 specify the block in which the string appears; bits 0 through 3 specify the location of that string relative to the beginning of the block.

Each entry in an executable file's resource table contains a member that identifies the resource type. The RT_STRING constant identifies a string table.

7.10 Accelerator Resource

An accelerator resource contains one or more accelerator entries.

Each entry in an executable file's resource table contains a member that identifies the resource type. The RT_ACCELERATOR constant identifies an accelerator resource.

The accelerator entry is a 5-byte entry with the following form:

```
struct AccelTableEntry {
        BYTE fFlags;
        WORD wEvent;
        WORD wId;
};
```

Following are the members in the **AccelTableEntry** structure:

fFlags
Specifies accelerator characteristics. It can be one or more of the following values:

Value	Meaning
0x02	Top-level menu item is not highlighted when accelerator is used.
0x04	Accelerator is activated only if user presses the SHIFT key. This flag applies only to virtual keys.
0x08	Accelerator is activated only if user presses the CONTROL key. This flag applies only to virtual keys.
0x10	Accelerator is activated only if user presses the ALT key. This flag applies only to virtual keys.
0x80	Entry is last entry in accelerator table.

wEvent
Specifies an ASCII character value or a virtual-key code that identifies the accelerator key.

wID
Identifies the accelerator. This is the value passed to the window procedure when the user presses the key.

7.11 Name-Table Resource

Name-table entries are not used in Windows 3.1. They are supported in Windows 3.0, but they can adversely affect system performance.

The header in a Windows executable file contains a resource table. This table contains data that describes many of the resources in the file. In Windows 3.0, the resource table does not describe named resources or resources that use a type name as a unique identifier. Instead, a name-table structure in the resource table maps a unique integer value to each resource name or type.

Each entry in an executable file's resource table contains a member that identifies the resource type. The decimal value 15 identifies a name-table resource.

7.11.1 Name-Table Entry

There is one name-table entry for each resource that uses either a named resource or a named-resource identifier. The **NameTable** structure depicts the form of these entries:

```
struct NameTable {
        WORD wBytesInEntry;
        WORD wTypeOrdinal;
        WORD wIDOrdinal;
        char szType[];
        char szID[];
};
```

Following are the members in the **NameTable** structure:

wBytesInEntry
Specifies the number of bytes in the name-table entry.

wTypeOrdinal
Specifies the ordinal value of the resource type for this name-table entry. If the high-order bit of this member is set, the named type of the resource was replaced with an ordinal value by the resource compiler. If this bit is not set, the resource type was not a named-type member and the **szType** member contains a single null byte.

wIDOrdinal
Specifies the ordinal value of the resource identifier for this name-table entry. If the high-order bit of this member is set, the named identifier of the resource was replaced with an ordinal value by the resource compiler and the named-identifier string appears in the **szID** array. If this bit is not set, a named-resource identifier does not exist and the **szID** array contains a single null byte.

szType
Specifies the resource type. This array must contain a null-terminated string. If the high bit of the **wTypeOrdinal** member is not set, this array contains a single-byte value of zero.

szID
Specifies a resource name. This array must be a null-terminated string. If the high bit of the **wIDOrdinal** member is not set, this array contains a single-byte value of zero.

Note Name-table entries are supported in Windows 3.0, but they are not required. Name-table entries do not appear in Windows 3.1.

7.12 Version-Information Resource

A version-information resource contains data that identifies the version, language, and distribution of the application, dynamic-link library, driver, or device containing the resource. Installation programs use the functions in the File Installation library (VER.DLL) to retrieve the version-information resource from a file and to extract the version-information blocks from the resource. (For more information about the File Installation library, see the *Microsoft Windows Programmer's Reference, Volume 1*.)

A version-information resource consists of one or more information blocks, each with the following form:

```
WORD    cbBlock;
WORD    cbValue;
char    szKey[];
BYTE    abValue[];
```

Following are the members in a version-information block:

cbBlock
> Specifies the size, in bytes, of the complete block. This value includes the size of nested blocks, if any.

cbValue
> Specifies the size, in bytes, of the **abValue** member.

szKey
> Specifies the name of the block. This value is a null-terminated string. Additional zero bytes are appended to the string to align the last byte on a 32-bit boundary.

abValue
> Specifies either an array of word values or a null-terminated string. The format of this member depends on the **szKey** value. Additional zero bytes are appended to align the last byte on a 32-bit boundary.

A block can contain nested blocks. In such cases, the nested block immediately follows the **abValue** member and the size specified by the **cbBlock** member in the first block is the sum of the two sizes. If a block contains more than one nested block, the nested blocks are stored sequentially and the **cbBlock** member in the first block specifies the total size of all blocks.

A version-information resource usually contains the following predefined blocks:

- Root
- Variable information
- String information
- Language-specific

In addition, the string and variable information blocks usually contain nested blocks that define the details about the file. This section describes the predefined information blocks.

7.12.1 Root Block

A root block is always the first block in the version resource. It contains such information as the file version, product version, release status, operating system, file type, and date the file was created.

The name of the root block, as specified by the **szKey** member, is VS_VERSION_INFO. The value (in **abValue**) is a **VS_FIXEDFILEINFO** structure. For a description of the **VS_FIXEDFILEINFO** structure, see the *Microsoft Windows Programmer's Reference*, *Volume 3*.

The variable and string information blocks in the resource are nested within the root block.

7.12.2 Variable Information Block

A variable information block typically contains a single nested block that defines the languages and character sets supported by the file.

The variable information block has the name **VarFileInfo** but has no corresponding value. Instead, the block is immediately followed by a nested block that has the name **Translation** and has a value consisting of an array of language and character-set identifiers. Each element in the array consists of two 16-bit values. The first value is a language identifier, the second a character-set identifier.

The language identifier can be one of the following values:

Value	Language
0x0401	Arabic
0x0402	Bulgarian
0x0403	Catalan
0x0404	Traditional Chinese
0x0405	Czech
0x0406	Danish
0x0407	German
0x0408	Greek
0x0409	U.S. English
0x040A	Castilian Spanish
0x040B	Finnish
0x040C	French
0x040D	Hebrew
0x040E	Hungarian
0x040F	Icelandic
0x0410	Italian
0x0411	Japanese
0x0412	Korean
0x0413	Dutch
0x0414	Norwegian – Bokmål

Value	Language
0x0415	Polish
0x0416	Brazilian Portuguese
0x0417	Rhaeto-Romanic
0x0418	Romanian
0x0419	Russian
0x041A	Croato-Serbian (Latin)
0x041B	Slovak
0x041C	Albanian
0x041D	Swedish
0x041E	Thai
0x041F	Turkish
0x0420	Urdu
0x0421	Bahasa
0x0804	Simplified Chinese
0x0807	Swiss German
0x0809	U.K. English
0x080A	Mexican Spanish
0x080C	Belgian French
0x0810	Swiss Italian
0x0813	Belgian Dutch
0x0814	Norwegian – Nynorsk
0x0816	Portuguese
0x081A	Serbo-Croatian (Cyrillic)
0x0C0C	Canadian French
0x100C	Swiss French

The character-set identifier can be one of the following values:

Value	Character set
0	7-bit ASCII
932	Windows, Japan (Shift – JIS X-0208)
949	Windows, Korea (Shift – KSC 5601)
950	Windows, Taiwan (GB5)
1200	Unicode
1250	Windows, Latin-2 (Eastern European)
1251	Windows, Cyrillic
1252	Windows, Multilingual
1253	Windows, Greek

Value	Character set
1254	Windows, Turkish
1255	Windows, Hebrew
1256	Windows, Arabic

Character set 1252 is typically given for files designed for the U.S. English version of Windows.

7.12.3 String Information Block

A string information block contains version information in the form of null-terminated strings.

The string information block has the name **StringFileInfo** but has no corresponding value. Instead, the block contains one or more nested blocks. Each nested block corresponds to one pair of language and character-set identifiers given in the variable information block.

7.12.4 Language-Specific Blocks

A language-specific block contains nested blocks that specify such information as the product name, company name, copyrights, trademarks, operating system, and so on.

A language-specific block can contain any number of nested blocks. Each block corresponds to one of the language and character-set identifier pairs given in the resource's variable information block. The name of the language-specific block is a null-terminated string consisting of a concatenation of the language and character-set identifiers. The block has no corresponding value.

Each nested block contains a name that identifies version-specific information and a string that represents the value associated with the name. A nested block can have one of the following predefined names and associated values:

Name	Value
Comments	Specifies additional information that should be displayed for diagnostic purposes.
CompanyName	Specifies the company that produced the file—for example, "Microsoft Corporation" or "Standard Microsystems Corporation, Inc.". This string is required.

Name	Value
FileDescription	Specifies a file description to be presented to users. This string may be displayed in a list box when the user is choosing files to install—for example, "Keyboard Driver for AT-Style Keyboards" or "Microsoft Word for Windows". This string is required.
FileVersion	Specifies the version number of the file—for example, "3.10" or "5.00.RC2". This string is required.
InternalName	Specifies the internal name of the file, if one exists—for example, a module name if the file is a dynamic-link library. If the file has no internal name, this string should be the original filename, without extension. This string is required.
LegalCopyright	Specifies all copyright notices that apply to the file. This should include the full text of all notices, legal symbols, copyright dates, and so on—for example, "Copyright Microsoft Corp. 1990,1991". This string is optional.
LegalTrademarks	Specifies all trademarks and registered trademarks that apply to the file. This should include the full text of all notices, legal symbols, trademark numbers, and so on—for example, "Windows(TM) is a trademark of Microsoft Corporation". This string is optional.
OriginalFilename	Specifies the original name of the file, not including a path. This information enables an application to determine whether a file has been renamed by a user. The format of the name depends on the file system for which the file was created. This string is required.
PrivateBuild	Specifies information about a private version of the file—for example, "Built by TESTER1 on \TESTBED". This string should be present only if the VS_FF_PRIVATEBUILD flag is set in the **dwFileFlags** member of the **VS_FIXEDFILEINFO** structure of the root block.
ProductName	Specifies the name of the product with which the file is distributed—for example, "Microsoft Windows". This string is required.
ProductVersion	Specifies the version of the product with which the file is distributed—for example, "3.10" or "5.00.RC2". This string is required.
SpecialBuild	Specifies how this version of the file differs from the standard version—for example, "Private build for TESTER1 solving mouse problems on M250 and M250E computers". This string should be present only if the VS_FF_SPECIALBUILD flag is set in the **dwFileFlags** member of the **VS_FIXEDFILEINFO** structure in the root block.

Write File Format

This chapter describes the binary file format used by Microsoft Write. A Write binary file contains information about file content, text and pictures (including object-linking-and-embedding, or OLE, objects), and formatting.

8.1 Write-File Header

The Write-file header describes the content of the file. It contains data, pointers to subdivisions of the formatting section, and information about the length of the file. The file header has the following form:

Word	Name	Description
0	wIdent	Must be 0137061 octal (or 0137062 octal if the file contains OLE objects)
1	dty	Must be zero
2	wTool	Must be 0125400 octal
3		Reserved; must be zero
4		Reserved; must be zero
5		Reserved; must be zero
6		Reserved; must be zero
7–8	fcMac	Number of bytes of actual text plus 128, the bytes in one sector (low-order word first)
9	pnPara	Page number for start of paragraph information
10	pnFntb	Page number of footnote table (FNTB) or pnSep, if none
11	pnSep	Page number of section property (SEP) or pnSetb, if none
12	pnSetb	Page number of section table (SETB) or pnPgtb, if none
13	pnPgtb	Page number of page table (PGTB) or pnFfntb, if none
14	pnFfntb	Page number of font face-name table (FFNTB) or pnMac, if none
15–47	szSsht	Reserved for Microsoft Word compatibility
48	pnMac	Count of pages in whole file (last page number plus 1)

In the preceding list, a "page number" means an offset in 128-byte blocks from the start of the file. For example, if pnPara equals 10, the paragraph information is at offset 10*128 = 1280 in the file.

The starting page number of character information (pnChar) is not stored but is computable, as follows:

pnChar = (fcMac + 127) / 128

Examining the value of word 48 of the header is a good way to distinguish Write files from Microsoft Word files. If **pnMac** equals zero, the file originated in Word. Any other value identifies a Write file.

8.2 Text and Pictures

After the header comes information about text and pictures. This information constitutes a separate section of the file.

8.2.1 Text

The text of the Write file starts at word 64 (page 1). Write uses the Windows character set (except for the pictures in the file) as well as the following special characters:

- ASCII character codes 13, 10 (carriage return, linefeed) for paragraph ends. No other occurrences of these two characters are allowed.
- ASCII character code 12 for explicit page breaks.
- ASCII character code 9 (normal) for tab characters.

Other line-break or wordwrap information is not stored.

8.2.2 Pictures

Pictures (including OLE objects) are stored as a sequence of bytes in the text stream. These bytes can be identified as picture information by examining their paragraph formatting. One picture is exactly one paragraph. Paragraphs that are pictures have a special bit set in their paragraph property (PAP) structure. For more information on the PAP structure, see Section 8.3, "Formatting."

Each picture consists of a descriptive header followed by the data that makes up the picture. The header for OLE objects is different from the one used for pictures. The picture header has the following form:

Byte	Name	Description
0–7	**mfp**	Windows **METAFILEPICT** structure (**hMF** member undefined)
8–9	**dxaOffset**	Offset of picture from left margin, in twips (1/1440 inch)
10–11	**dxaSize**	Horizontal size, in twips
12–13	**dyaSize**	Vertical size, in twips
14–15	**cbOldSize**	Number of following bytes (actual metafile or bitmap bits); set to zero

Byte	Name	Description
16–29	**bm**	Additional information for bitmaps only
30–31	**cbHeader**	Number of bytes in this header
32–35	**cbSize**	Number of following bytes (actual metafile or bitmap bits), replacing **cbOldSize** for new files
36–37	**mx**	Scaling factor (*x*)
38–39	**my**	Scaling factor (*y*)
40–?	**cbHeader**	Picture contents, through **cbHeader+cbSize–1**

The **mm** member (bytes 0–1) of the **METAFILEPICT** structure specifies the mapping mode used to draw the picture. The last set of bytes will be bitmap bits if the value of the **mm** member is 0xE3. This is a special value used only in Write. Otherwise, the bytes will be metafile contents.

If the picture has never been rescaled with the Size Picture command in Write, the scaling factors in each direction will be 1000 (decimal). If the picture has been re-sized, the scaling factor will be the percentage of the original size that the picture is now, relative to 1000 (100 per cent).

For information about the **METAFILEPICT** structure and bitmaps, see the *Microsoft Windows Guide to Programming* and the *Microsoft Windows Programmer's Reference*, *Volumes 1* and *3*.

The descriptive header for OLE objects is similar to the one used for pictures. The OLE object header has the following form:

Byte	Name	Description
0–1	**mm**	Must be 0xE4
2–5		Not used
6–7	**objectType**	Type: 1=static, 2=embedded, 3=link
8–9	**dxaOffset**	Offset of picture from left margin, in twips (1/1440 inch)
10–11	**dxaSize**	Horizontal size, in twips
12–13	**dyaSize**	Vertical size, in twips
14–15		Not used
16–19	**dwDataSize**	Number of bytes in the object data that follows the header
20–23		Not used
24–27	**dwObjNum**	Hexadccimal number that, when converted to an 8-digit string, represents the object's unique name
28–29		Not used
30–31	**cbHeader**	Number of bytes in this header
32–35		Not used

Byte	Name	Description
36–37	**mx**	Scaling factor (x)
38–39	**my**	Scaling factor (y)
40–?	**cbHeader**	Object contents, through **cbHeader+dwDataSize–1**

The scaling factors for OLE objects work the same way as they do with pictures.

8.3 Formatting

Write files contain both character and paragraph formatting information. There can be no gaps in either; each must begin with the first text character (byte 128) and continue through the last. The format descriptors (FODs) for the first and last paragraph must, therefore, have the value of **fcLim** equal to the value of **fcMac**, as defined in the header section.

There is a difference between paragraph and character FODs. A character FOD may describe any number of consecutive characters with the same formatting. However, there must be exactly one paragraph FOD for each text paragraph. In either case, it is advisable to have multiple FODs point to the same formatting properties (FPROPs) on a given page because it saves space in the file. No FOD may point off its page.

8.3.1 Characters and Paragraphs

Both the character and paragraph sections are structured as a set of pages. Each page contains an array of FODs and a group of FPROPs, both of which are described later in this section. Following is the format of a page:

Byte	Name	Description
0–3	**fcFirst**	Byte number of first character covered by this page of formatting information; equals 128 for first character in the text (low-order byte first)
4–**n**	**rgfod**	Array of FODs
n+1–126	**grpfprop**	Group of FPROPs
127	**cfod**	Number of FODs on this page

An FOD is fixed in size. It contains the byte offset to the corresponding FPROP. Following is the structure of an FOD:

Word	Name	Description
0–1	**fcLim**	Byte number after last character covered by this FOD
2	**bfprop**	Byte offset from beginning of FOD array to corresponding FPROP for these characters or this paragraph

An FPROP is variable in size. It contains the prefix for a character property (CHP) or paragraph property (PAP), both of which are described later in this section. Following is the structure of an FPROP:

Byte	Name	Description
0	**cch**	Number of bytes in this FPROP
1–n	**rgchProp**	Prefix for a CHP (for characters) or a PAP (for paragraphs) sufficient to include all bits that differ from the default CHP or PAP

Following is the format of a CHP:

Byte	Bit	Name	Description
0			Reserved; ignored by Write
1	0	**fBold**	Bold characters
	1	**fItalic**	Italic characters
	2–7	**ftc**	Font code (low bits); index into the FFNTB
2		**hps**	Size of font, in half points (standard is 24)
3	0	**fUline**	Underlined characters
	1	**fStrike**	Reserved; ignored by Write
	2	**fDline**	Reserved; ignored by Write
	3	**fOverset**	Reserved; ignored by Write
	4–5	**csm**	Reserved; ignored by Write
	6	**fSpecial**	Set for "(page)" only
	7		Reserved; ignored by Write
4	0–2	**ftcXtra**	Font code (high-order bits, concatenated with **ftc**)
	3	**fOutline**	Reserved; ignored by Write
	4	**fShadow**	Reserved; ignored by Write
	5–7		Reserved; ignored by Write
5		**hpsPos**	Position: 0=normal, 1–127=superscript, 128–255=subscript

If the user doesn't select any special character properties, the CHP is filled with the following default values:

Byte	Value
0	1
2	24
3–5	0

Each character FPROP must, therefore, have a count of characters (**cch**) greater than or equal to 1.

Each PAP can contain up to 14 tab descriptors (TBDs), which are described later in this section. Following is the structure of a PAP:

Byte	Bit	Name	Description
0			Reserved; must be zero
1	0–1	**jc**	Justification: 0=left, 1=center, 2=right, 3=both
	2–7		Reserved; must be zero
2			Reserved; must be zero
3			Reserved; must be zero
4–5		**dxaRight**	Right indent, in 20ths of a point
6–7		**dxaLeft**	Left indent, in 20ths of a point
8–9		**dxaLeft1**	First-line left indent (relative to **dxaLeft**)
10–11		**dyaLine**	Interline spacing (standard is 240)
12–13		**dyaBefore**	Reserved; ignored by Write (standard is zero)
14–15		**dyaAfter**	Reserved; ignored by Write (standard is zero)
16	0	**rhcPage**	0=header, 1=footer
	1–2		Reserved; 0=normal paragraph, non-zero=header or footer paragraph
	3	**rhcFirst**	Start of printing: 1=print on first page, 0=do not print on first page
	4	**fGraphics**	Paragraph type: 1=picture, 0=text
	5–7		Reserved; must be zero
17–21			Reserved; must be zero
22–78			Tab descriptors (up to 14)

Following is the format of a TBD:

Byte	Bit	Name	Description
0–1		**dxa**	Indent from left margin of tab stop, in 20ths of a point
2	0–2	**jcTab**	Tab type: 0=normal tabs, 3=decimal tabs
	3–5	**tlc**	Reserved; ignored by Write
	6–7		Reserved; must be zero

Byte	Bit	Name	Description
3		**chAlign**	Reserved; ignored by Write

If the user doesn't select any special paragraph properties, the PAP is filled with the following default values:

Byte	Value
0	61
2	30
10–11	240 (word)
12–78	0

Each paragraph FPROP must have a count of characters (**cch**) greater than or equal to 1.

8.3.2 Footnotes

Write documents do not have footnote tables (FNTBs), so **pnFntb** is always equal to **pnSep**. In fact, all their header and footer paragraphs appear at the beginning of the document before any normal paragraphs. When reading files created by Word, Write recognizes only those headers and footers that appear at the beginning of the document; it treats all others as normal text.

8.3.3 Sections

A Write document has only one section. If the section properties of a Write document differ from the defaults, the document contains a section property (SEP) section and a section table (SETB) section. If not, then neither section is present and **pnSep** and **pnSetb** are both equal to **pnPgtb**.

Following is the format of an SEP:

Byte	Name	Description
0	**cch**	Count of bytes used, excluding this byte (all properties at byte positions greater than **cch** are set to their default values)
1–2		Reserved; must be zero
3–4	**yaMac**	Page length, in 20ths of a point (default is 11*1440=15840)
5–6	**xaMac**	Page width, in 20ths of a point (default is 8.5*1440=12240)
7–8		Reserved; must be 0xFFFF

Byte	Name	Description
9–10	**yaTop**	Top margin, in 20ths of a point (default is 1440)
11–12	**dyaText**	Height of text, in 20ths of a point (default is 9*1440=12960)
13–14	**xaLeft**	Left margin, in 20ths of a point (default is 1.25*1440=1800)
15–16	**dxaText**	Width of text area, in 20ths of a point (default is 6*1440=8640)

The page length (**yaMac**) is equal to **yaTop+dyaText**. The page width (**xaMac**) is equal to **xaLeft+dxaText+**(right margin, not stored).

If all the above properties are set to their defaults, no SEP or SETB is needed. Otherwise, the count of characters (**cch**) is greater than or equal to 1 and less than or equal to 16.

The SETB section contains an array of section descriptors (SEDs), described later in this section. Following is the structure of an SETB:

Word	Name	Description
0	**csed**	Number of sections (always 2 for Write documents)
1	**csedMax**	Undefined
2–n	**rgsed**	Array of SEDs plus zero-padding to fill the sector

Following is the structure of an SED:

Word	Name	Description
0–1	**cp**	Byte address of first character following section
2	**fn**	Undefined
3–4	**fcSep**	Byte address of associated SEP

A Write document always has exactly two SED entries. The **cp** value of the first entry indicates that it affects all the characters in the document. The **fcSep** value of the first entry points to the one SEP in the file. The second SED entry is a dummy with **fcSep** set to 0xFFFFFFFF.

The PGTB section (optional) is on the page immediately after the SEP section.

Note The term "page" used in the rest of this section refers to printed pages of a Write document, not 128-byte "pages" of a disk file.

The page table (PGTB) contains an array of page descriptors (PGDs), which are described later in this section. Following is the structure of a PGTB:

Word	Name	Description
0	**cpgd**	Number of PGDs (1 or more)
1	**cpgdMac**	Undefined
2–**n**	**rgpgd**	Array of PGDs plus zero padding to fill the sector

Following is the structure of a PGD:

Word	Name	Description
0	**pgn**	Page number in printed Word documents
1–2	**cpMin**	Byte address of first character on printed page

8.3.4 Font Table

The font face-name table (FFNTB) contains the number of font face names (FFNs) and a list of FFNs. Following is the structure of an FFNTB:

Byte	Name	Description
0–1	**cffn**	Number of FFNs
2–**n**	**grpffn**	List of FFNs

Following is the structure of an FFN:

Byte	Name	Description
0–1	**cbFfn**	Number of bytes following in this FFN (not including these 2 bytes)
2	**ffid**	Font family identifier
3–(**cbffn**+2)	**szFfn**	Font name (variable length; null-terminated)

A **cbFfn** value of 0xFFFF means that the next FFN entry will be found at the start of the next 128-byte page. A **cbFfn** value of zero means that there are no more FFN entries in the table.

Possible values for **ffid** are FF_DONTCARE, FF_ROMAN, FF_SWISS, FF_MODERN, FF_SCRIPT, and FF_DECORATIVE. These constants are defined in WINDOWS.H. Additional values may be added to the list in future versions of Windows.

Calendar File Format

This chapter describes the binary file format used by Microsoft Windows Calendar (CALENDAR.EXE). A Calendar binary file contains information about file content, dates, days, and appointments.

9.1 Calendar-File Header

The first 8 bytes of a Calendar file are a character array identifying the file as a Calendar file. Following are the contents of the array:

```
'C' + 'r' = b5
'A' + 'a' = a2
'L' + 'd' = b0
'E' + 'n' = b3
'N' + 'e' = b3
'D' + 'l' = b0
'A' + 'a' = a2
'R' + 'c' = b5
```

The next 2 bytes (**cDateDescriptors**) contain the integer count of dates described in the file.

The next 12 bytes contain six 2-byte fields of information that is global to the entire file. These variables are normally set by the user through the Alarm Controls and Options Day dialog boxes. The header information has the following form:

```
WORD    MinEarlyRing
BOOL    fSound
int     interval
int     mininterval
BOOL    f24HourFormat
int     StartTime
```

Following are the members in the header structure:

MinEarlyRing
Specifies an early ring, in minutes.

fSound
Specifies whether alarms should be audible.

interval
Specifies the interval between appointments: 0 = 15 minutes, 1 = 30 minutes, 2 = 60 minutes.

mininterval
Specifies the interval, in minutes.

f24HourFormat
Specifies the time format: nonzero=24-hour format.

StartTime
Specifies the starting time in day mode—that is, the time that normally appears first in the display, in minutes past midnight.

The rest of the first 64 bytes are reserved.

9.2 Date Descriptors

A date-descriptor array appears next. Each entry in the array describes one day. The number of entries in the array is **cDateDescriptors** (described in the preceding section). Each element in the array consists of 12 bytes, in six 2-byte fields. The date-descriptor array has the following form:

```
unsigned    Date
int         fMarked
int         cAlarms
unsigned    FileBlockOffset
int         reserved
unsigned    reserved
```

Following are the members in the date-descriptor array:

Date
Specifies the date, in days past 1/1/1980.

fMarked
Specifies which mark(s) are set for the date: box = 128, parentheses = 256, circle = 512, cross = 1024, underscore = 2048.

cAlarms
Specifies the number of alarms set for the day.

FileBlockOffset
Specifies the file offset, in 64-byte blocks, to the day's information. Only the low 15 bits are used (the high bit will be zero). Thus, if this offset is 6, the day's information is stored at byte 6*64 in the file.

reserved
Reserved; must be 0xFFF.

reserved
Reserved; must be 0xFFF.

9.3 Day-Specific Information

All day information is stored after the date-descriptor array, on even 64-byte boundaries. The day-information structure has the following form:

```
unsigned    reserved
unsigned    Date
unsigned    reserved
unsigned    cbNotes
unsigned    cbAppointment
char        Notes[cbNotes]
BYTE        ApptInfo[]
```

Following are the members in the day-information structure:

reserved
Reserved; must be zero.

Date
Specifies the date, in days past 1/1/1980.

reserved
Reserved; must be 1.

cbNotes
Specifies the number of bytes of note information, including null bytes. This information appears in the note array below the appointment list.

cbAppointment
Specifies the count of bytes of appointment information.

Notes
Contains the text of the note.

ApptInfo
Contains the block of appointments.

9.4 Appointment-Specific Information

The information in the appointment block is stored as a list of single appointments. Each appointment consists of a structure similar to the following:

```
struct {
    char cb;
    char flags;
    int  time;
    char szApptDesc[];
};
```

Following are the members in each appointment structure:

cb
Specifies the size, in bytes, of the structure containing the appointment. The structure address of the next appointment is the current appointment plus the value of the **cb** member.

flags
Contains various flags. This member can have one or more of the following values:

Value	Meaning
1	Alarm will go off at the specified time of the appointment.
2	Appointment is a special time.

time
Specifies the number of minutes past midnight.

szApptDesc
Contains a null-terminated string consisting of text associated with an appointment.

Windows Object-Module Format

This chapter describes the object module format (OMF) for the Microsoft Windows operating system. Although this chapter lists all OMF records, it does not provide complete information for all of them. For an explanation of the Microsoft object-module format and details about the records not defined in this chapter, see *The MS-DOS Encyclopedia* (Redmond, Washington: Microsoft Press, 1988).

10.1 Object-Module Format Records

The object files and object modules in the libraries and import libraries provided with the SDK contain the following OMF records:

Record type	Identifier
THEADR	80h
COMENT	88h
DOSSEG	88h, 9Eh
IMPDEF	88h, A0h, 01h
EXPDEF	88h, A0h, 02h
LIBMOD	88h, A3h
MODEND	8Ah
EXTDEF	8Ch
PUBDEF	90h
LINNUM	94h
LNAMES	96h
SEGDEF	98h
GRPDEF	9Ah
FIXUPP	9Ch
LEDATA	A0h
LIDATA	A2h
COMDEF	B0h
LEXTDEF	B4h
LPUBDEF	B6h

This chapter describes the **EXPDEF**, **IMPDEF**, **LEXTDEF**, **LIBMOD**, and **LPUBDEF** records. The rest of the records listed are documented in *The MS-DOS Encyclopedia.*

10.2 Record Reference

This section contains detailed descriptions for OMF records not defined in *The MS-DOS Encyclopedia*.

EXPDEF

```
EXPDEF  STRUC
    edRecordType   db 88h              ; COMENT record
    edLength       dw ?                ; length of record
    edAttribute    db ?                ; attributes
    edClass        db 0A0h             ; comment class
    edSubType      db 02h              ; EXPDEF subtype
    edExpFlag      db ?                ; export flags
    edExportedName db ? dup(?)         ; exported name (var-length)
    edInternalName db ? dup(?)         ; internal name (var-length)
    edExportOrdinal dw ?               ; export ordinal (conditional)
EXPDEF  ENDS
```

The **EXPDEF** record defines one exported symbol.

Members

edRecordType
Specifies the record type. This member must be 88h.

edLength
Specifies the length of the record.

edAttribute
Specifies the record attributes. These are as defined for the **COMENT** record.

edClass
Specifies the comment class. This member must be 0A0h.

edSubType
Specifies the **EXPDEF** subtype. This member must be 02h.

edExpFlag
Specifies the export flags. The bits in this 8-bit member have the following meanings:

Bit	Meaning
OrdBit (80h)	If set, the item is exported by using the ordinal value of a function. In this case, the **edExportOrdinal** member is present.

Bit	Meaning
ResName (40h)	If set, the exported name is to be kept resident by the system loader. Keeping the exported name resident is an optimization for frequently used items imported by name.
NoData (20h)	If set, the entry point does not use initialized data.
ParmCount (1Fh)	Set to zero for all but call gates to 16-bit segments. This bit specifies the number of parameter words.

edExportedName
Contains a character string defining the exported symbol. This name is used when the symbol is imported by name. The first byte in this member specifies the number of characters in the string.

edInternalName
Contains a character string defining the internal name. This name is used within the module that defines the symbol. The first byte in this member specifies the number of characters in the string. If the first byte is zero, the internal name is the same as the exported name given in the **edExportedName** member.

edExportOrdinal
Specifies the ordinal value representing the exported symbol. This member is present only if the OrdBit bit (80h) is set in the **edExpFlag** member.

Comments   Microsoft compilers generate the **EXPDEF** record when the keyword _export is used in a source file. Microsoft Segmented Executable Linker (LINK) limits the **edExportOrdinal** value to 16,384 (16K) or less.

IMPDEF

```
IMPDEF   STRUC
    idRecordType    db 88h          ; COMENT record
    idLength        dw ?            ; length of record
    idAttribute     db ?            ; attributes
    idClass         db 0A0h         ; comment class
    idSubType       db 01h          ; IMPDEF subtype
    idOrdFlag       db ?            ; ordinal flag
    idInternalName  db ? dup(?)     ; imported symbol (var-length)
    idModuleName    db ? dup(?)     ; module name (var-length)
    idEntryIdent    dw ?            ; ordinal or name (var-length)
IMPDEF   ENDS
```

The **IMPDEF** record defines one imported symbol.

Members

idRecordType
Specifies the record type. This member must be 88h.

idLength
Specifies the length of the record.

idAttribute
Specifies the record attributes. These are as defined for the **COMENT** record.

idClass
Specifies the comment class. This member must be 0A0h.

idSubType
Specifies the **IMPDEF** subtype. This member must be 01h.

idOrdFlag
Specifies the ordinal type. If this member is zero, the imported symbol is identified by name. If nonzero, it is identified by ordinal value.

idInternalName
Contains a character string defining the imported symbol. The first byte in this member specifies the number of bytes in the character string.

idModuleName
Contains a character string defining the name of the module with the definition for the imported symbol. The first byte in this member specifies the number of bytes in the character string.

idEntryIdent
Specifies an ordinal value or the name used by the exporting module for the symbol. The content of this member depends on the **idOrdFlag** member as follows:

idOrdFlag	idEntryIdent
Nonzero	16-bit value that specifies the ordinal value for the imported symbol.
Zero	Character string that defines the symbol corresponding to the imported symbol. The first byte in this member specifies the number of bytes in the character string. If the first byte is zero, the exported name is the same as the imported name (as given in the **idInternalName** member).

Comments

Microsoft Import Library Manager (IMPLIB) creates **IMPDEF** records and builds an import library from a module-definition file or dynamic-link library. For more information about import libraries, see Chapter 11, "Library and Import-Library Formats."

LEXTDEF

```
LEXTDEF STRUC
    ledRecordType    db 0B4h      ; LEXTDEF record
    ledLength        dw ?         ; length of record

                                  ; next 3 fields repeated
    ledNameLength    db ?         ; length of name
    ledExternalName  db ? dup(?)  ; external name (var-length)
    ledTypeIndex     db ?         ; type index
                     db ?         ; type index (conditional)

    ledCheckSum      db ?         ; checksum
LEXTDEF ENDS
```

The **LEXTDEF** record is identical in form to the **EXTDEF** record. However, the symbols named in this record are visible only inside the module in which they are defined.

For complete details about the members in this record, see the **EXTDEF** record in *The MS-DOS Encyclopedia*.

Comments **LEXTDEF** records are associated with corresponding **LPUBDEF** and **LCOMDEF** records. The name string, when stored by LINK in internal data structures, is encoded with spaces and digits at the beginning of the name.

Examples This record type is produced in C from static functions, as in the following example:

```
static int myfunc() { }
```

LIBMOD

```
LIBMOD  STRUC
    lmRecordType    db 88h        ; COMENT record
    lmLength        dw ?          ; length of record
    lmAttribute     db ?          ; attributes
    lmClass         db 0A3h       ; comment class
    lmModuleName    db ? dup(?)   ; module name (var-length)
LIBMOD  ENDS
```

The **LIBMOD** record specifies the name of an object module. Microsoft Library Manager (LIB) uses this record to preserve the module name of the object module while storing the filename of the module's original source file in the **THEADR** record.

Members

lmRecordType
Specifies the record type. This member must be 88h.

lmLength
Specifies the length of the record.

lmAttribute
Specifies the record attributes. These are as defined for the **COMENT** record.

lmClass
Specifies the comment class. This member must be 0A3h.

lmModuleName
Contains the character string defining the module name. The first byte of the member specifies the number of characters in the name. The module name does not include a path or extension.

Comments

The **LIBMOD** record is used only by LIB and not by LINK. LIB adds a **LIB-MOD** record when an .OBJ file is added to a library and strips the **LIBMOD** record when an .OBJ file is removed from a library. In general, a library file contains one **LIBMOD** record for each object module that was combined to build the library.

LPUBDEF

```
LPUBDEF STRUC
    lpdRecordType    db 0B6h      ; LPUBDEF record; 0B7h also allowed
    lpdLength        dw ?         ; length of record
    lpdBaseGrp       db ?         ; base group
                     db ?         ; base group (conditional)
    lpdBaseSeg       db ?         ; base segment
                     db ?         ; base segment (conditional)
    lpdBaseFrame     dw ?         ; base frame (conditional)

                                  ; next 4 fields repeated
    lpdNameLength    db ?         ; length of name
    lpdName          db ? dup(?)  ; local name (variable-length)
    lpdLocalOffset   dw ?         ; local offset
    lpdTypeIndex     db ?         ; type index
                     db ?         ; type index (conditional)

    lpdCheckSum      db ?         ; checksum
```

The **LPUBDEF** record is identical in form to the **PUBDEF** record. However, the symbols named in this record are visible only inside the module in which they are defined.

For complete details about the members in this record, see the **PUBDEF** record in *The MS-DOS Encyclopedia.*

Comments   In C, the **static** keyword on functions or initialized variables produces **LPUBDEF** records. Uninitialized static variables produce **LCOMDEF** records.

Library and Import-Library Formats

This chapter describes the file formats for the libraries and import libraries used by the Microsoft Windows operating system.

11.1 Organization of Libraries

Libraries and import libraries have identical formats but typically differ in content. Each library consists of one or more 512-byte blocks and has the following general form:

- A **LibraryHeader** record
- One or more object modules
- A **Marker** record
- A dictionary containing a prime number of **DictionaryBlock** structures

The first record in the library, the **LibraryHeader** record, marks the beginning of the library and contains information that specifies the page size of the library and the location of the dictionary.

Immediately following the **LibraryHeader** record are one or more object modules. Each module, in Microsoft object-module format (OMF), starts with a **THEADR** record containing the module name and ends with a **MODEND** record. Each module is also aligned on a page boundary. If an object module is not an exact multiple of the library's page size, it is padded with null bytes.

A **Marker** record follows the last object module in the library. This record marks the end of the object modules and the start of the dictionary.

The remaining blocks in the library make up the dictionary, which contains entries that specify the locations of public symbols defined in the object modules for the library. The number of blocks in the dictionary is given in the **LibraryHeader** record.

11.2 Dictionary

The dictionary consists of a prime number of 512-byte blocks, each having the following form:

```
DictionaryBlock STRUC
    dbBuckets    db 37 dup(0)
    dbFreeSpace  db ?
    dbEntries    db (512-37) dup(0)
DictionaryBlock ENDS
```

Following are the descriptions of the entries in a dictionary block:

dbBuckets

Specifies a 37-byte array in which each byte contains either zero, indicating a free bucket, or an offset to one of the dictionary entries in the block.

dbFreeSpace

Specifies the next free byte in the block or contains 0FFh to indicate a full block.

dbEntries

Contains the dictionary entries for the block. Each entry includes a character string defining the symbol and the page number for the start of the object module containing the symbol.

The dictionary is a hashed index of public symbols in the library. A symbol is hashed twice, generating both a block index and a bucket index. The block index specifies which block contains a given symbol, and the bucket index specifies which bucket contains the given symbol's block offset.

The bucket value, multiplied by 2, specifies the offset from the beginning of the block to the beginning of the dictionary entry containing the symbol. Since this offset is a multiple of 2, all dictionary entries start on word boundaries. Furthermore, since the **dbBuckets** member occupies bytes 0 through 36 (decimal) of each dictionary block and the **dbFreeSpace** member occupies another byte, the first dictionary entry starts at byte 38. For a complete description of the **DictionaryEntry** record, see Section 11.3, "Record Reference."

A dictionary block can be full even though one or more buckets in the block are free. This can happen, for example, if the character strings defining the symbols are longer on average than 9 characters each.

11.2.1 Collision Resolution

A collision occurs whenever two or more distinct public symbols in the library have the same block and bucket indexes. A technique known as linear open addressing is used to resolve collisions. It relies on two values, the block and bucket deltas, that are produced at the same time as the block and bucket indexes.

If a symbol collides with a symbol already in the dictionary, the library-management program (librarian) attempts to find an empty bucket for it by adding the bucket delta to the bucket index and using the result (modulo 37) as a new bucket index. If this new bucket index points to a bucket that is empty, the librarian installs the symbol in that bucket. If the bucket is not empty, the librarian applies the bucket delta repeatedly until an empty bucket is found or all buckets in the block have been tried.

If the block has no empty buckets, the librarian adds the block delta to the block index and uses the result (modulo the number of blocks in the dictionary) as a new block index. With the new block index and the original bucket index, the librarian repeats the procedure to find an empty bucket. Since the number of blocks and the number of buckets are both prime numbers, this procedure guarantees that all possible block-bucket combinations are tried no matter what block and bucket indexes and deltas are initially generated for the symbol.

11.3 Record Reference

This section contains detailed descriptions of the records mentioned in Section 11.1, "Organization of Libraries."

DictionaryEntry

```
DictionaryEntry STRUC
    deSymbolLength   db  SYMBOLLENGTH
    deSymbol         db  SYMBOLLENGTH dup(?)
    dePageNumber     dw  ?
    deAlignByte      db  ?
DictionaryEntry ENDS
```

The **DictionaryEntry** record specifies the name of a public symbol and the location of the object module that contains the definition of the public symbol.

Members

deSymbolLength

Specifies the number of bytes in the character string defining the symbol.

deSymbol

Contains the character string defining the symbol. The string contains exactly the number of bytes specified in the **deSymbolLength** member.

dePageNumber

Specifies the page number of the object module in which the symbol is defined. The **LibraryHeader** record is at page 0.

deAlignByte

Contains a trailing null byte used to align the next dictionary entry on a word boundary.

LibraryHeader

```
LibraryHeader STRUC
    lhRecordType        db 0F0h
    lhPageSize          dw ?
    lhDictionaryOffset  dd ?
    lhDictionarySize    dw ?
    lhFlags             db ?
    lhPad               db ? dup(0)
LibraryHeader ENDS
```

The **LibraryHeader** record marks the beginning of the library and contains information about the library's page size and dictionary.

Members

lhRecordType
Specifies the record type. This member must be 0F0h.

lhPageSize
Specifies the number of bytes remaining in the record and defines the page size for the library. Modules in a library always start at the beginning of a page. Page size is determined by adding 3 to the value of this member—the library header record always occupies exactly one page. The page size must be a power of 2 in the range 16 through 32,768.

lhDictionaryOffset
Specifies the offset to the first byte of the 512-byte block in the dictionary. The offset is relative to the start of the **LibraryHeader** record.

lhDictionarySize
Specifies the number of 512-byte blocks in the dictionary. Although this member can have any value, the dictionary itself must not exceed 251 blocks. Microsoft Library Manager (LIB) cannot create a library with more blocks than this.

lhFlags
Contains the library flags. This member can contain the following value:

Value	Meaning
01h	Case-sensitive

All other values are reserved for future use.

lhPad
Contains any remaining bytes needed to pad the **LibraryHeader** record to the length specified by the **lhPageSize** member. These bytes are not used.

Comments   The **LibraryHeader** record does not include a checksum at the end of the record.

Marker

```
Marker STRUC
    mkRecordType     db 0F1h
    mkLength         dw ?
    mkPad            db ? dup(0)
Marker ENDS
```

The **Marker** record marks the end of the object modules and the beginning of the dictionary.

Members

mkRecordType
Specifies the record type. This member must be 0F1h.

mkLength
Specifies the number of bytes remaining in the record. This member must be set so that the dictionary begins on a 512-byte boundary.

mkPad
Contains any remaining bytes needed to pad the marker record to the length specified by the **mkLength** member. These bytes are not used.

Comments

As with the **LibraryHeader** record, the last byte in this record is not a checksum.

Symbol File Format

This chapter describes the format of symbol files created by Microsoft Symbol File Generator (MAPSYM). Symbol files contain information that the Microsoft Windows 80386 Debugger (WDEB386.EXE) can use to locate program modules and global data in an executable module.

12.1 Map Definitions

Every symbol file contains a list that links two or more map definitions. Each map definition describes a module in the executable file.

The first map definition in the chain starts at the beginning of the file, as follows:

```
/* File is loaded at pFileBuffer. */

pMapDef = (MAPDEF *)pFileBuffer;
```

Each map definition (except the last) contains a pointer to the next map definition in the chain. This pointer is a 16-bit number that, when multiplied by 16, gives the byte offset of the next map definition in the file, as follows:

```
pNextMapDef = (MAPDEF *)(pFileBuffer + (pMapDef->ppNextMap * 16));
```

The pointer in the last map definition is zero.

The **MAPDEF** structure for each map definition (except the last) has the following form:

```
typedef struct {
    WORD ppNextMap;      /* paragraph pointer to next map          */
    BYTE bFlags;         /* symbol types                           */
    BYTE bReserved1;     /* reserved                               */
    WORD pSegEntry;      /* segment entry-point value              */
    WORD cConsts;        /* count of constants in map              */
    WORD pConstDef;      /* pointer to constant chain              */
    WORD cSegs;          /* count of segments in map               */
    WORD ppSegDef;       /* paragraph pointer to first segment     */
    BYTE cbMaxSym;       /* maximum symbol-name length             */
    BYTE cbModName;      /* length of module name                  */
    char achModName[1];  /* n bytes of module-name member          */
} MAPDEF;
```

The last **MAPDEF** structure contains the version and release number for the version of Symbol File Generator used to create the symbol file. It has the following form:

```
typedef struct {
    WORD ppNextMap; /* always zero                            */
    BYTE release;   /* release number (minor version number) */
    BYTE version;   /* major version number                   */
} LAST_MAPDEF;
```

Following are the members of the **MAPDEF** structure:

ppNextMap
Specifies the offset from the beginning of the file to the next **MAPDEF** structure in the chain. Multiply the value of the **ppNextMap** member by 16 to obtain the offset.

bFlags
Specifies the type of symbols in the file. The **bFlags** member can be one or more of the following values:

Value	Meaning
0	Contains 16-bit symbols.
1	Contains 32-bit symbols.
2	Includes alphabetic symbol table.

bReserved1
Reserved.

pSegEntry
Specifies the segment of the entry point for the application.

cConsts
Specifies the number of constants in this module.

pConstDef
Specifies a 16-bit offset from the beginning of the file to an array of pointers to constant definitions. This value is not multiplied by 16 to obtain the offset.

cSegs
Specifies the number of segments in this module.

ppSegDef
Specifies the offset from the beginning of the file to the first segment definition in this module. Multiply the value of the **ppSegDef** member by 16 to obtain the offset.

cbMaxSym
Specifies the length of the longest symbol name in this module.

cbModName
Specifies the length of the module name.

achModName
Specifies a variable-length array of characters containing the module name. The name is not null-terminated.

12.2 Segment Definitions

Each module in the symbol file contains a linked list of segment definitions. To obtain a pointer to the first segment definition, multiply the value of the **ppSegDef** member in the current **MAPDEF** structure by 16, as follows:

```
/* File is loaded at pFileBuffer. */

pSegDef = (SEGDEF *)(pFileBuffer + (md.ppSegDef * 16));
```

Each segment definition contains a pointer to the next segment definition in the chain. This pointer is a 16-bit number that, when multiplied by 16, gives the byte offset of the next segment definition in the file, as follows:

```
pNextSegDef = (SEGDEF *)(pFileBuffer + (pSegDef->ppNextSeg * 16));
```

The pointer in the last segment definition is not zero. The linked list of segment definitions is circular—the pointer in the last segment definition gives the offset of the first segment definition. You can use the **cSegs** member in the **MAPDEF** structure to determine the number of segments in the module.

The **SEGDEF** structure for these lists has the following form:

```
typedef struct {
    WORD ppNextSeg;       /* paragraph pointer to next segment    */
    WORD cSymbols;        /* count of symbols in list             */
    WORD pSymDef;         /* offset of symbol chain               */
    WORD wReserved1;      /* reserved                             */
    WORD wReserved2;      /* reserved                             */
    WORD wReserved3;      /* reserved                             */
    WORD wReserved4;      /* reserved                             */
    BYTE bFlags;          /* symbol types                         */
    BYTE bReserved1;      /* reserved                             */
    WORD ppLineDef;       /* offset of line-number record         */
    BYTE bReserved2;      /* reserved                             */
    BYTE bReserved3;      /* reserved                             */
    BYTE cbSegName;       /* length of segment name               */
    char achSegName[1];   /* n bytes of segment-name member       */
} SEGDEF;
```

Following are the members of the **SEGDEF** structure:

ppNextSeg
Specifies the offset from the beginning of the file to the next **SEGDEF** structure in the chain. Multiply the value of the **ppNextSeg** member by 16 to obtain the offset.

cSymbols
Specifies the number of symbols in this segment.

pSymDef

Specifies the offset from the beginning of the segment definition to an array of pointers to symbol definitions. This value is not multiplied by 16 to obtain the offset. For more details, see Section 12.3, "Symbol Definitions."

wReserved1

Reserved.

wReserved2

Reserved.

wReserved3

Reserved.

wReserved4

Reserved.

bFlags

Specifies the type of symbols in this segment. The **bFlags** member can be one or more of the following values:

Value	Meaning
0	Contains 16-bit symbols.
1	Contains 32-bit symbols.
2	Includes alphabetic symbol table.

bReserved1

Reserved.

ppLineDef

Specifies the offset from the beginning of the file to the first line-number definition. Multiply the value of the **ppLineDef** member by 16 to obtain the offset.

bReserved2

Reserved.

bReserved3

Reserved.

cbSegName

Specifies the length of the segment name.

achSegName

Specifies a variable-length array of characters containing the segment name. The name is not null-terminated.

12.3 Symbol Definitions

Each segment definition contains a pointer to an array of pointers to symbol definitions.

All symbol files contain an array of pointers to symbols, sorted by symbol value. The **bFlags** member in the **SEGDEF** structure indicates whether the segment has an alphabetic symbol table. To obtain a pointer to the numerically ordered array of symbol-definition pointers, add the **pSymDef** pointer in the current segment definition to the pointer to the current segment definition, as follows:

```
aSymPtr = (WORD *)((BYTE *)pSegDef + pSegDef->pSymDef);
```

In addition, symbol files created by MAPSYM versions 5.0 and later may contain an array of pointers sorted alphabetically by symbol name. This array begins immediately after the numeric array:

```
aSymPtrAlpha = (WORD *)((BYTE *)pSegDef +
        pSegDef->pSymDef + pSegDef->cSymbols * sizeof(WORD));
```

To obtain a pointer to each symbol definition, add the offset specified by each element in the array of symbol-definition pointers to the pointer to the current segment definition, as follows:

```
for (n = 0; n < pSegDef->cSymbols; n++) {
    pSymDef = (SYMDEF *)((BYTE *)pSegDef + aSymPtr[n]);
    .
    .
    /* Use the symbol information here. */
    .
    .
}
```

The **SYMDEF** structure for these symbol definitions has the following form:

```
typedef struct {
    WORD wSymVal;        /* symbol address or constant    */
    BYTE cbSymName;      /* length of symbol name         */
    char achSymName[1];  /* n bytes of symbol-name member */
} SYMDEF;
```

Following are the members of the **SYMDEF** structure:

wSymVal
  Specifies the address of the symbol or the value of a constant.

cbSymName
  Specifies the length of the symbol name.

achSymName
   Specifies a variable-length array of characters containing the segment name.
   The name is not null-terminated.

The **wSymVal** member in the **SYMDEF** structure is a doubleword value for 32-bit symbols.

12.4 Constant Definitions

Each **MAPDEF** structure contains a pointer to an array of pointers to constant definitions. The format of a constant definition is the same as that of a symbol definition (you can use the **SYMDEF** structure described in Section 12.3, "Symbol Definitions").

The **ppConstDef** member in the current **MAPDEF** structure specifies the file offset of the array of constant-definition pointers, and the offset to each constant definition can be calculated from each element in the array, as follows:

```
aConstPtr = (WORD *)(pFileBuffer + md.ppConstDef);

for (n = 0; n < md.cConsts; n++) {
    pConstDef = (SYMDEF *)(pFileBuffer + aConstPtr[n]);
    .
    .
    /* Use the symbol information here. */
    .
    .
}
```

12.5 Line Definitions

Symbol files created by linking with the **/LI** option also contain line-number information. Each segment definition contains a pointer to the first line definition in a circularly linked list. If the pointer in the **SEGDEF** structure is zero, the segment has no line-number information.

12.5.1 LINEDEF Structure

To obtain a pointer to the first **LINEDEF** structure in the linked list, multiply the value of the **ppLineDef** member in the current **SEGDEF** structure by 16, as follows:

```
pLineDef = (LINEDEF *)(pBuf + (pSegDef->ppLineDef * 16));
```

Each **LINEDEF** structure (except the last) contains a pointer to the next **LINEDEF** structure in the linked list. The pointer in the last **LINEDEF** structure is zero.

The **LINEDEF** structure for each line definition has the following form:

```
typedef struct {
    WORD ppNextLine;        /* ptr to next linedef (0 if last) */
    WORD wReserved1;        /* reserved                        */
    WORD pLines;            /* pointer to line numbers         */
    WORD wReserved2;        /* reserved                        */
    int  cLines;            /* count of line numbers           */
    BYTE cbFileName;        /* filename length                 */
    char achFileName[1];    /* filename (contains lines)       */
} LINEDEF;
```

Following are the members of the **LINEDEF** structure:

ppNextLine
Specifies the offset from the beginning of the file to the next **LINEDEF** structure in the chain. Multiply the value of the **ppNextLine** member by 16 to obtain the offset. If this member is zero, there is no line-number information for this segment.

wReserved1
Reserved.

pLines
Specifies the offset from the beginning of the current **LINEDEF** structure to the array of line-information structures.

wReserved2
Reserved.

cLines
Specifies the number of lines in the line-information array.

cbFileName
Specifies the number of characters in the name of the source file. This file was compiled and linked to produce the map file.

achFileName
Specifies a variable-length array of characters containing the name of the source file. The name is not null-terminated.

12.5.2 LINEINF Structure

To obtain a pointer to the first **LINEINF** structure in the array for the line-definition structure, add the **pLines** pointer in the current **LINEDEF** structure to the current **LINEDEF** pointer, as follows:

```
pLines = (LINEINF *)((BYTE *)pLineDef + pLineDef->pLines);
```

Each element in the line-information array contains the offset into the source file for a line and the offset into the executable file for the code resulting from the source line.

The **LINEINF** structure has the following form:

```
typedef struct {
    WORD wCodeOffset;    /* executable offset */
    WORD dwFileOffset;   /* source offset     */
} LINEINF;
```

Following are the members of the **LINEINF** structure:

wCodeOffset
Specifies the offset in this segment to the code resulting from compiling this line in the source file.

dwFileOffset
Specifies the offset to this line in the source file.

Tools Reference

Part 2

Resource-Definition Statements

This chapter describes statements defining the resources that the Microsoft Windows Resource Compiler (RC) adds to an application's executable file. Once a resource is added to the executable file, the application can load the resource as it is needed at run time.

All resource statements associate an identifying name or number with a given resource. Most statements can also include load and memory options for the resource, specifying whether the resource should be preloaded or loaded on demand and whether the memory allocated for the resource should be discardable.

13.1 Alphabetic Reference

This section describes in detail the resource-definition statements used by the Microsoft Windows Resource Compiler (RC). It lists the statements in alphabetic order.

ACCELERATORS

acctablename **ACCELERATORS**
BEGIN
   event, *idvalue*, [*type*] [*options*]
   .
   .
   .
END

The **ACCELERATORS** statement defines one or more accelerators for an application. An accelerator is a keystroke defined by the application to give the user a quick way to perform a task. The **TranslateAccelerator** function is used to translate accelerator messages from the application queue into WM_COMMAND or WM_SYSCOMMAND messages.

Parameters

acctablename
   Specifies either a unique name or an integer value that identifies the resource.

event
   Specifies the keystroke to be used as an accelerator. It can be any one of the following character types:

Type	Description
"char"	A single ASCII character enclosed in double quotation marks. The character can be preceded by a caret (^), meaning that the character is a control character.
ASCII character	An integer value representing an ASCII character. The *type* parameter must be **ASCII**.
Virtual-key character	An integer value representing a virtual key. The virtual key for alphanumeric keys can be specified by placing the uppercase letter or number in double quotation marks (for example, "9" or "C"). The *type* parameter must be **VIRTKEY**.

idvalue
Specifies an integer value that identifies the accelerator.

type
Required only when the *event* parameter is an ASCII character or a virtual-key character. The *type* parameter specifies either **ASCII** or **VIRTKEY**; the integer value of *event* is interpreted accordingly. When **VIRTKEY** is specified and *event* contains a string, *event* must be uppercase.

options
Specifies the options that define the accelerator. This parameter can be one or more of the following values:

Option	Description
NOINVERT	Specifies that no top-level menu item is highlighted when the accelerator is used. This is useful when defining accelerators for actions such as scrolling that do not correspond to a menu item. If **NOINVERT** is omitted, a top-level menu item will be highlighted (if possible) when the accelerator is used.
ALT	Causes the accelerator to be activated only if the ALT key is down.
SHIFT	Causes the accelerator to be activated only if the SHIFT key is down.
CONTROL	Defines the character as a control character (the accelerator is only activated if the CONTROL key is down). This has the same effect as using a caret (^) before the accelerator character in the *event* parameter.

The **ALT**, **SHIFT**, and **CONTROL** options apply only to virtual keys.

Examples

The following example demonstrates the usage of accelerator keys:

```
1 ACCELERATORS
BEGIN
  "^C",   IDDCLEAR        ; control C
  "K",    IDDCLEAR        ; shift K
  "k",    IDDELLIPSE, ALT ; alt K
  98,     IDDRECT, ASCII  ; b
  66,     IDDSTAR, ASCII  ; B (shift b)
  "g",    IDDRECT         ; g
  "G",    IDDSTAR         ; G (shift G)
  VK_F1, IDDCLEAR, VIRTKEY                ; F1
  VK_F1, IDDSTAR, CONTROL, VIRTKEY        ; control F1
  VK_F1, IDDELLIPSE, SHIFT, VIRTKEY       ; shift F1
  VK_F1, IDDRECT, ALT, VIRTKEY            ; alt F1
  VK_F2, IDDCLEAR, ALT, SHIFT, VIRTKEY    ; alt shift F2
  VK_F2, IDDSTAR, CONTROL, SHIFT, VIRTKEY ; ctrl shift F2
  VK_F2, IDDRECT, ALT, CONTROL, VIRTKEY   ; alt control F2
END
```

BITMAP

nameID **BITMAP** [*load-option*] [*mem-option*] *filename*

The **BITMAP** resource-definition statement specifies a custom bitmap that an application uses in its screen display or as an item in a menu.

Parameters

nameID
Specifies either a unique name or an integer value identifying the resource.

load-option
Specifies when the resource is to be loaded. The parameter must be one of the following:

Option	Description
PRELOAD	Resource is loaded immediately.
LOADONCALL	Resource is loaded when called. This is the default option.

mem-option
Specifies whether the resource is fixed or movable and whether it is discardable. The parameter must be one of the following:

Option	Description
FIXED	Resource remains at a fixed memory location.
MOVEABLE	Resource can be moved if necessary in order to compact memory.
DISCARDABLE	Resource can be discarded if no longer needed.

The default for bitmap resources is **MOVEABLE**.

filename
Specifies the name of the file that contains the resource. The name must be a valid MS-DOS filename; it must be a full path if the file is not in the current working directory. The path can either be a quoted or non-quoted string.

Examples

The following example specifies two bitmap resources:

```
disk1    BITMAP disk.bmp
12       BITMAP PRELOAD diskette.bmp
```

See Also

LoadBitmap

CAPTION

CAPTION *captiontext*

The **CAPTION** statement defines the title for the dialog box. The title appears in the box's caption bar (if it has one).

The default caption is empty.

Parameters

captiontext
Specifies an ASCII character string enclosed in double quotation marks.

Examples

The following example demonstrates the usage of the **CAPTION** statement:

```
CAPTION "Error!"
```

CHECKBOX

CHECKBOX *text*, *id*, *x*, *y*, *width*, *height*, [*style*]

The **CHECKBOX** statement creates a check box control. The control is a small rectangle (check box) that has the specified text displayed next to it (typically, to the right). When the user selects the control, the control highlights the rectangle and sends a message to its parent window. The **CHECKBOX** statement, which can only be used in a **DIALOG** statement, defines the text, identifier, dimensions, and attributes of the control.

Parameters

text

Specifies text that is displayed to the right of the control. This parameter must contain zero or more characters enclosed in double quotation marks. Character values must be in the range 1 through 255. If a double quotation mark is required in the text, you must include the double quotation mark twice. An ampersand (&) character in the text indicates that the following character is used as a mnemonic character for the control. When the control is displayed, the ampersand is not shown, but the mnemonic character is underlined. The user can choose the control by pressing the key corresponding to the underlined mnemonic character. To use the ampersand as a character in a string, insert two ampersands (&&).

id

Specifies the control identifier. This value must be an integer in the range 0 through 65,535 or a simple expression that evaluates to a value in that range.

x

Specifies the x-coordinate of the left side of the control relative to the left side of the dialog box. This value must be an integer in the range 0 through 65,535 or an expression consisting of integers and the addition (+) or subtraction (–) operator. The coordinate is assumed to be in dialog units and is relative to the origin of the dialog box, window, or control containing the specified control.

y

Specifies the y-coordinate of the top side of the control relative to the top of the dialog box. This value must be an integer in the range 0 through 65,535 or an expression consisting of integers and the addition (+) or subtraction (–) operator. The coordinate is assumed to be in dialog units and is relative to the origin of the dialog box, window, or control containing the specified control.

width

Specifies the width of the control. This value must be an integer in the range 1 through 65,535 or an expression consisting of integers and the addition (+) or subtraction (–) operator. The width is in 1/4-character units.

height
Specifies the height of the control. This value must be an integer in the range 1 through 65,535 or an expression consisting of integers and the addition (+) or subtraction (–) operator. The height is in 1/8-character units.

style
Specifies the control styles. This value can be a combination of the button class style BS_CHECKBOX and the WS_TABSTOP and WS_GROUP styles.

You can use the bitwise OR (|) operator to combine styles.

If you do not specify a style, the default style is BS_CHECKBOX and WS_TABSTOP.

Comments   The current dialog units are computed from the height and width of the current system font. The **GetDialogBaseUnits** function returns the dialog units in pixels.

Examples   This example creates a check-box control that is labeled "Italic":

```
CHECKBOX "Italic", 3, 10, 10, 40, 10
```

See Also   **GetDialogBaseUnits**

CLASS

CLASS *class*

The **CLASS** statement defines the class of the dialog box. If no statement is given, the Windows standard dialog class will be used as the default.

Parameters   *class*
Specifies an integer or a string, enclosed in double quotation marks, that identifies the class of the dialog box. If the window procedure for the class does not process a message sent to it, it must call the **DefDlgProc** function to ensure that all messages are handled properly for the dialog box. A private class can use **DefDlgProc** as the default window procedure. The class must be registered with the **cbWndExtra** member of the **WNDCLASS** structure set to DLGWINDOWEXTRA.

Comments   The **CLASS** statement should only be used with special cases, since it overrides the normal processing of a dialog box. The **CLASS** statement converts a dialog box to a window of the specified class; depending on the class, this could give undesirable results. Do not use the predefined control-class names with this statement.

Examples   The following example demonstrates the usage of the **CLASS** statement:

```
CLASS "myclass"
```

See Also   **DefDlgProc**

COMBOBOX

COMBOBOX *id*, *x*, *y*, *width*, *height*[, *style*]

The **COMBOBOX** statement creates a combination box control (a combo box). A combo box consists of either a static text box or an edit box combined with a list box. The list box can be displayed at all times or pulled down by the user. If the combo box contains a static text box, the text box always displays the selection (if any) in the list box portion of the combo box. If it uses an edit box, the user can type in the desired selection; the list box highlights the first item (if any) that matches what the user has entered in the edit box. The user can then select the item highlighted in the list box to complete the choice. In addition, the combo box can be owner-drawn and of fixed or variable height.

Parameters   *id*

Specifies the control identifier. This value must be an integer in the range 0 through 65,535 or a simple expression that evaluates to a value in that range.

x

Specifies the x-coordinate of the left side of the control relative to the left side of the dialog box. This value must be an integer in the range 0 through 65,535 or an expression consisting of integers and the addition (+) or subtraction (−) operator. The coordinate is assumed to be in dialog units and is relative to the origin of the dialog box, window, or control containing the specified control.

y

Specifies the y-coordinate of the top side of the control relative to the top of the dialog box. This value must be an integer in the range 0 through 65,535 or an expression consisting of integers and the addition (+) or subtraction (−) operator. The coordinate is assumed to be in dialog units and is relative to the origin of the dialog box, window, or control containing the specified control.

width

Specifies the width of the control. This value must be an integer in the range 1 through 65,535 or an expression consisting of integers and the addition (+) or subtraction (−) operator. The width is in 1/4-character units.

height

Specifies the height of the control. This value must be an integer in the range 1 through 65,535 or an expression consisting of integers and the addition (+) or subtraction (–) operator. The height is in 1/8-character units.

style

Specifies the control styles. This value can be a combination of the COMBOBOX class styles and any of the following styles: WS_TABSTOP, WS_GROUP, WS_VSCROLL, and WS_DISABLED.

You can use the bitwise OR (|) operator to combine styles.

If you do not specify a style, the default style is CBS_SIMPLE and WS_TABSTOP.

Comments

The current dialog units are computed from the height and width of the current system font. The **GetDialogBaseUnits** function returns the dialog units in pixels.

Examples

This example creates a combo-box control with a vertical scroll bar:

```
COMBOBOX 777, 10, 10, 50, 54, CBS_SIMPLE | WS_VSCROLL | WS_TABSTOP
```

CONTROL

CONTROL *text*, *id*, *class*, *style*, *x*, *y*, *width*, *height*

The **CONTROL** statement defines a control as belonging to the specified class. The statement defines the position and dimensions of the control within the parent window as well as the control style. The **CONTROL** statement is most often used in a **DIALOG** statement.

Parameters

text

Specifies displayed text. Its position depends on the control class. This parameter must contain zero or more characters enclosed in double quotation marks. Character values must be in the range 1 through 255. If a double quotation mark is required in the text, you must include the double quotation mark twice. In the appropriate styles, an ampersand (&) character in the text indicates that the following character is used as a mnemonic character for the control. When the control is displayed, the ampersand is not shown, but the mnemonic character is underlined. The user can choose the control by pressing the key corresponding to the character.

id

Specifies the control identifier. This value must be an integer in the range 0 through 65,535 or a simple expression that evaluates to a value in that range.

class

Specifies the control class. This value can be a predefined name, character string, or integer value that defines the class. For a list of predefined classes, see the following Comments section.

style

Specifies the control style. For a list of control styles, see the following Comments section.

You can use the bitwise OR (|) operator to combine styles.

x

Specifies the x-coordinate of the upper-left corner of the control. This value must be an integer in the range 0 through 65,535 or an expression consisting of integers and the addition (+) or subtraction (–) operator. The coordinate is assumed to be in dialog units and is relative to the origin of the parent window.

y

Specifies the y-coordinate of the upper-left corner of the control. This value must be an integer in the range 0 through 65,535 or an expression consisting of integers and the addition (+) or subtraction (–) operator. The coordinate is assumed to be in dialog units and is relative to the origin of the parent window.

width

Specifies the width of the control. This value must be an integer in the range 1 through 65,535 or an expression consisting of integers and the addition (+) or subtraction (–) operator. The value is in 1/4-character units.

height

Specifies the height of the control. This value must be an integer in the range 1 through 65,535 or an expression consisting of integers and the addition (+) or subtraction (–) operator. The value is in 1/8-character units.

Comments

The following list describes the six control classes:

Class	Description
BUTTON	A button control is a small rectangular child window that represents a "button" the user can turn on or off by clicking it with the mouse. Button controls can be used alone or in groups and can either be labeled or appear without text. Button controls typically change appearance when the user clicks them.
COMBOBOX	A combo box control consists of a text box similar to an edit control, plus a list box. The list box may be displayed at all times or may be dropped down when the user selects a "pop box" next to the text box.

Class	Description
	The style of the combo box determines whether the user can edit the contents of the text box. If the list box is visible, typing characters into the text box causes the first list box entry that matches the characters typed to be highlighted. Conversely, selecting an item in the list box displays the selected text in the text box.
EDIT	An edit control is a rectangular child window in which the user can enter text from the keyboard. The user selects the control and gives it the input focus by clicking the mouse inside it or pressing the TAB key. The user can enter text when the control displays a flashing caret. The mouse can be used to move the cursor and select characters to be replaced or to position the cursor for inserting characters. The BACKSPACE key can be used to delete characters.
	Edit controls expand tab characters into as many space characters as are required to move the cursor to the next tab stop. The default for tab stops is eight characters.
LISTBOX	A list box control consists of a list of items. The control is used whenever an application needs to present a list of names, such as filenames, that the user can view and select. The user can select an item by pointing to the name with the mouse and clicking a mouse button. When an item is selected, it is highlighted, and a notification message is passed to the parent window. A scroll bar can be used with a list box control to scroll lists that are too long or too wide for the control window.
SCROLLBAR	A scroll bar control is a rectangle that contains a scroll box and has direction arrows at both ends. The scroll bar sends a notification message to its parent whenever the user clicks the mouse in the control. The parent is responsible for updating the scroll box position, if necessary. Scroll bar controls have the same appearance and function as the scroll bars used in ordinary windows. But unlike scroll bars, scroll bar controls can be positioned anywhere within a window and used whenever needed to provide scrolling input for a window.
	The scroll bar class also includes size box controls. A size box control is a small rectangle that the user can expand to change the size of the window.
STATIC	A static control is a simple text field, box, or rectangle that can be used to label, box, or separate other controls. Static controls take no input and provide no output.

The following lists describe the control styles for each of the control classes:

BUTTON Class

Value	Meaning
BS_3STATE	Creates a button that is the same as a check box, except that the box can be grayed as well as checked. The grayed state typically is used to show that a check box has been disabled.
BS_AUTO3STATE	Creates a button that is the same as a 3-state check box, except that the box changes its state when the user selects it. The state cycles through checked, grayed, and normal.
BS_AUTOCHECKBOX	Creates a button that is the same as a check box, except that an X appears in the check box when the user selects the box; the X disappears (is cleared) the next time the user selects the box.
BS_AUTORADIOBUTTON	Creates a button that is the same as a radio button, except that when the user selects it, the button automatically highlights itself and clears (removes the selection from) any other auto radio buttons in the same group.
BS_CHECKBOX	Creates a small square that has text displayed to its right (unless this style is combined with the BS_LEFTTEXT style).
BS_DEFPUSHBUTTON	Creates a button that has a heavy black border. The user can select this button by pressing the ENTER key. This style is useful for enabling the user to quickly select the most likely option (the default option).
BS_GROUPBOX	Creates a rectangle in which other controls can be grouped. Any text associated with this style is displayed in the rectangle's upper-left corner.
BS_LEFTTEXT	Places text on the left side of the radio button or check box when combined with a radio button or check box style.
BS_OWNERDRAW	Creates an owner-drawn button. The owner window receives a WM_MEASUREITEM message when the button is created and it receives a WM_DRAWITEM message when a visual aspect of the button has changed. The BS_OWNERDRAW style cannot be combined with any other button styles.

Value	Meaning
BS_PUSHBUTTON	Creates a push button that posts a WM_COMMAND message to the owner window when the user selects the button.
BS_RADIOBUTTON	Creates a small circle that has text displayed to its right (unless this style is combined with the BS_LEFTTEXT style). Radio buttons are usually used in groups of related but mutually exclusive choices.

COMBOBOX Class

Style	Description
CBS_AUTOHSCROLL	Automatically scrolls the text in the edit control to the right when the user types a character at the end of the line. If this style is not set, only text that fits within the rectangular boundary is allowed.
CBS_DISABLENOSCROLL	Shows a disabled vertical scroll bar in the list box when the box does not contain enough items to scroll. Without this style, the scroll bar is hidden when the list box does not contain enough items.
CBS_DROPDOWN	Similar to CBS_SIMPLE, except that the list box is not displayed unless the user selects an icon next to the text box.
CBS_DROPDOWNLIST	Similar to CBS_DROPDOWN, except that the edit control is replaced by a static text item that displays the current selection in the list box.
CBS_HASSTRINGS	Specifies that an owner-drawn combo box contains items consisting of strings. The combo box maintains the memory and pointers for the strings so the application can use the CB_GETLBTEXT message to retrieve the text for a particular item.
CBS_NOINTEGRALHEIGHT	Specifies that the size of the combo box is exactly the size specified by the application when it created the combo box. Normally, Windows sizes a combo box so that the combo box does not display partial items.

Style	Description
CBS_OEMCONVERT	Converts text entered in the combo-box edit control from the Windows character set to the OEM character set and then back to the Windows set. This ensures proper character conversion when the application calls the **AnsiToOem** function to convert a Windows string in the combo box to OEM characters. This style is most useful for combo boxes that contain filenames and applies only to combo boxes created with the CBS_SIMPLE or CBS_DROPDOWN styles.
CBS_OWNERDRAWFIXED	Specifies that the owner of the list box is responsible for drawing its contents and that the items in the list box are all the same height. The owner window receives a WM_MEASUREITEM message when the combo box is created and a WM_DRAWITEM message when a visual aspect of the combo box has changed.
CBS_OWNERDRAWVARIABLE	Specifies that the owner of the list box is responsible for drawing its contents and that the items in the list box are variable in height. The owner window receives a WM_MEASUREITEM message for each item in the combo box when the combo box is created and a WM_DRAWITEM message whenever the visual aspect of the combo box changes.
CBS_SIMPLE	Displays the list box at all times. The current selection in the list box is displayed in the edit control.
CBS_SORT	Automatically sorts strings entered into the list box.

EDIT Class

Style	Meaning
ES_AUTOHSCROLL	Automatically scrolls text to the right by 10 characters when the user types a character at the end of the line. When the user presses the ENTER key, the control scrolls all text back to position zero.

Style	Meaning
ES_AUTOVSCROLL	Automatically scrolls text up one page when the user presses ENTER on the last line.
ES_CENTER	Centers text in a multiline edit control.
ES_LEFT	Aligns text to the left.
ES_LOWERCASE	Converts all characters to lowercase as they are typed into the edit control.
ES_MULTILINE	Designates multiline edit control. (The default is single-line edit control.)
	When the multiline edit control is in a dialog box, the default response to pressing the ENTER key is to activate the default button. To use the ENTER key as a carriage return, an application should use the style ES_WANTRETURN.
	When the multiline edit control is not in a dialog box and the ES_AUTOVSCROLL style is specified, the edit control shows as many lines as possible and scrolls vertically when the user presses the ENTER key. If ES_AUTOVSCROLL is not specified, the edit control shows as many lines as possible and beeps if the user presses ENTER when no more lines can be displayed.
	If the ES_AUTOHSCROLL style is specified, the multiline edit control automatically scrolls horizontally when the caret goes past the right edge of the control. To start a new line, the user must press ENTER. If ES_AUTOHSCROLL is not specified, the control automatically wraps words to the beginning of the next line when necessary. A new line is also started if the user presses ENTER. The position of the wordwrap is determined by the window size. If the window size changes, the wordwrap position changes and the text is redisplayed.
	Multiline edit controls can have scroll bars. An edit control with scroll bars processes its own scroll bar messages. Edit controls without scroll bars scroll as described in the previous two paragraphs and process any scroll messages sent by the parent window.
ES_NOHIDESEL	Negates the default behavior for an edit control. The default behavior is to hide the selection when the control loses the input focus and invert the selection when the control receives the input focus.

Style	Meaning
ES_READONLY	Prevents the user from typing or editing text in the edit control.
ES_RIGHT	Aligns text to the right in a multiline edit control.
ES_UPPERCASE	Converts all characters to uppercase as they are typed into the edit control.
ES_WANTRETURN	Specifies that a carriage return be inserted when the user presses the ENTER key while entering text into a multiline edit control in a dialog box. If this style is not specified, pressing the ENTER key has the same effect as pressing the dialog box's default push button. This style has no effect on a single-line edit control.

LISTBOX Class

Style	Meaning
LBS_DISABLENOSCROLL	Shows a disabled vertical scroll bar for the list box when the box does not contain enough items to scroll. If this style is not specified, the scroll bar is hidden when the list box does not contain enough items.
LBS_EXTENDEDSEL	Allows multiple items to be selected by using the SHIFT key and the mouse or special key combinations.
LBS_HASSTRINGS	Specifies that a list box contains items consisting of strings. The list box maintains the memory and pointers for the strings so the application can use the LB_GETTEXT message to retrieve the text for a particular item. By default, all list boxes except owner-drawn list boxes have this style. An application can create an owner-drawn list box either with or without this style.
LBS_MULTICOLUMN	Specifies a multicolumn list box that is scrolled horizontally. The LB_SETCOLUMNWIDTH message sets the width of the columns.
LBS_MULTIPLESEL	Turns string selection on or off each time the user clicks or double-clicks the string. Any number of strings can be selected.

Style	Meaning
LBS_MULTICOLUMN	Specifies a multicolumn list box that is scrolled horizontally. The LB_SETCOLUMNWIDTH message sets the width of the columns.
LBS_MULTIPLESEL	Turns string selection on or off each time the user clicks or double-clicks the string. Any number of strings can be selected.
LBS_NOINTEGRALHEIGHT	Specifies that the size of the list box is exactly the size specified by the application when it created the list box. Normally, Windows sizes a list box so that the list box does not display partial items.
LBS_NOREDRAW	Specifies that the list box's appearance is not updated when changes are made. This style can be changed at any time by sending a WM_SETREDRAW message.
LBS_NOTIFY	Notifies the parent window with an input message whenever the user clicks or double-clicks a string.
LBS_OWNERDRAWFIXED	Specifies that the owner of the list box is responsible for drawing its contents and that the items in the list box are the same height. The owner window receives a WM_MEASUREITEM message when the list box is created and a WM_DRAWITEM message when a visual aspect of the list box has changed.
LBS_OWNERDRAWVARIABLE	Specifies that the owner of the list box is responsible for drawing its contents and that the items in the list box are variable in height. The owner window receives a WM_MEASUREITEM message for each item in the combo box when the combo box is created and a WM_DRAWITEM message whenever the visual aspect of the combo box changes.
LBS_SORT	Sorts strings in the list box alphabetically.
LBS_STANDARD	Sorts strings in the list box alphabetically. The parent window receives an input message whenever the user clicks or double-clicks a string. The list box has borders on all sides.

Style	Meaning
LBS_USETABSTOPS	Allows a list box to recognize and expand tab characters when drawing its strings. The default tab positions are 32 dialog units. (A dialog unit is a horizontal or vertical distance. One horizontal dialog unit is equal to one-fourth of the current dialog base width unit. The dialog base units are computed based on the height and width of the current system font. The **GetDialogBaseUnits** function returns the current dialog base units in pixels.)
LBS_WANTKEYBOARDINPUT	Specifies that the owner of the list box receives WM_VKEYTOITEM or WM_CHARTOITEM messages whenever the user presses a key and the list box has input focus. This allows an application to perform special processing on the keyboard input. If a list box has the LBS_HASSTRINGS style, the list box can receive WM_VKEYTOITEM messages but not WM_CHARTOITEM messages. If a list box does not have the LBS_HASSTRINGS style, the list box can receive WM_CHARTOITEM messages but not WM_VKEYTOITEM messages.

SCROLLBAR Class

Style	Meaning
SBS_BOTTOMALIGN	Aligns the bottom edge of the scroll bar with the bottom edge of the rectangle defined by the following **CreateWindow** parameters: *X, Y, nWidth,* and *nHeight.* The scroll bar has the default height for system scroll bars. Used with the SBS_HORZ style.
SBS_HORZ	Designates a horizontal scroll bar. If neither the SBS_BOTTOMALIGN nor SBS_TOPALIGN style is specified, the scroll bar has the height, width, and position specified by the **CreateWindow** parameters.

Style	Meaning
SBS_LEFTALIGN	Aligns the left edge of the scroll bar with the left edge of the rectangle defined by the **CreateWindow** parameters. The scroll bar has the default width for system scroll bars. Used with the SBS_VERT style.
SBS_RIGHTALIGN	Aligns the right edge of the scroll bar with the right edge of the rectangle defined by the **CreateWindow** parameters. The scroll bar has the default width for system scroll bars. Used with the SBS_VERT style.
SBS_SIZEBOX	Designates a size box. If neither the SBS_SIZEBOXBOTTOMRIGHTALIGN nor SBS_SIZEBOXTOPLEFTALIGN style is specified, the size box has the height, width, and position specified by the **CreateWindow** parameters.
SBS_SIZEBOXBOTTOMRIGHTALIGN	Aligns the lower-right corner of the size box with the lower-right corner of the rectangle specified by the **Create-Window** parameters. The size box has the default size for system size boxes. Used with the SBS_SIZEBOX style.
SBS_SIZEBOXTOPLEFTALIGN	Aligns the upper-left corner of the size box with the upper-left corner of the rectangle specified by the following **CreateWindow** parameters: *X*, *Y*, *nWidth*, and *nHeight*. The size box has the default size for system size boxes. Used with the SBS_SIZEBOX style.
SBS_TOPALIGN	Aligns the top edge of the scroll bar with the top edge of the rectangle defined by the **CreateWindow** parameters. The scroll bar has the default height for system scroll bars. Used with the SBS_HORZ style.
SBS_VERT	Designates a vertical scroll bar. If neither the SBS_RIGHTALIGN nor SBS_LEFTALIGN style is specified, the scroll bar has the height, width, and position specified by the **CreateWindow** parameters.

STATIC Class

A static control can have only one of the following styles:

Style	Meaning
SS_BLACKFRAME	Specifies a box with a frame drawn with the same color as window frames. This color is black in the default Windows color scheme.
SS_BLACKRECT	Specifies a rectangle filled with the color used to draw window frames. This color is black in the default Windows color scheme.
SS_CENTER	Designates a simple rectangle and displays the given text centered in the rectangle. The text is formatted before it is displayed. Words that would extend past the end of a line are automatically wrapped to the beginning of the next centered line.
SS_GRAYFRAME	Specifies a box with a frame drawn with the same color as the screen background (desktop). This color is gray in the default Windows color scheme.
SS_GRAYRECT	Specifies a rectangle filled with the color used to fill the screen background. This color is gray in the default Windows color scheme.
SS_ICON	Designates an icon displayed in the dialog box. The given text is the name of an icon (not a filename) defined elsewhere in the resource file. The *nWidth* and *nHeight* parameters are ignored; the icon automatically sizes itself.
SS_LEFT	Designates a simple rectangle and displays the given text left-aligned in the rectangle. The text is formatted before it is displayed. Words that would extend past the end of a line are automatically wrapped to the beginning of the next left-aligned line.
SS_LEFTNOWORDWRAP	Designates a simple rectangle and displays the given text left-aligned in the rectangle. Tabs are expanded but words are not wrapped. Text that extends past the end of a line is clipped.
SS_NOPREFIX	Prevents interpretation of any & characters in the control's text as accelerator prefix characters (which are displayed with the & removed and the next character in the string underlined). This static-control style may be included with any of the defined static controls.

Style	Meaning
	You can combine SS_NOPREFIX with other styles by using the bitwise OR operator. This is most often used when filenames or other strings that may contain an & need to be displayed in a static control in a dialog box.
SS_RIGHT	Designates a simple rectangle and displays the given text right-aligned in the rectangle. The text is formatted before it is displayed. Words that would extend past the end of a line are automatically wrapped to the beginning of the next right-aligned line.
SS_SIMPLE	Designates a simple rectangle and displays a single line of text left-aligned in the rectangle. The line of text cannot be shortened or altered in any way. (The control's parent window or dialog box must not process the WM_CTLCOLOR message.)
SS_WHITEFRAME	Specifies a box with a frame drawn with the same color as window backgrounds. This color is white in the default Windows color scheme.
SS_WHITERECT	Specifies a rectangle filled with the color used to fill window backgrounds. This color is white in the default Windows color scheme.

CTEXT

CTEXT *text*, *id*, *x*, *y*, *width*, *height*[, *style*]

The **CTEXT** statement creates a centered-text control. The control is a simple rectangle displaying the given text centered in the rectangle. The text is formatted before it is displayed. Words that would extend past the end of a line are automatically wrapped to the beginning of the next line. The **CTEXT** statement, which you can use only in a **DIALOG** statement, defines the text, identifier, dimensions, and attributes of the control.

Parameters

text
Specifies text that is centered in the rectangular area of the control. This parameter must contain zero or more characters enclosed in double quotation marks.

Character values must be in the range 1 through 255. If a double quotation mark is required in the text, you must include the double quotation mark twice.

id

Specifies the control identifier. This value must be an integer in the range 0 through 65,535 or a simple expression that evaluates to a value in that range.

x

Specifies the x-coordinate of the upper-left corner of the control. This value must be an integer in the range 0 through 65,535 or an expression consisting of integers and the addition (+) or subtraction (−) operator. The coordinate is assumed to be in dialog units and is relative to the origin of the dialog box, window, or control containing the specified control.

y

Specifies the y-coordinate of the upper-left corner of the control. This value must be an integer in the range 0 through 65,535 or an expression consisting of integers and the addition (+) or subtraction (−) operator. The coordinate is assumed to be in dialog units and is relative to the origin of the dialog box, window, or control containing the specified control.

width

Specifies the width of the control. This value must be an integer in the range 1 through 65,535 or an expression consisting of integers and the addition (+) or subtraction (−) operator. The width is in 1/4-character units.

height

Specifies the height of the control. This value must be an integer in the range 1 through 65,535 or an expression consisting of integers and the addition (+) or subtraction (−) operator. The height is in 1/8-character units.

style

Specifies the control styles. This value can be any combination of the following styles: SS_CENTER, WS_TABSTOP, and WS_GROUP.

You can use the bitwise OR (|) operator to combine styles.

If you do not specify a style, the default style is SS_CENTER and WS_GROUP.

Examples

This example creates a centered-text control that is labeled "Filename":

```
CTEXT "Filename", 101, 10, 10, 100, 100
```

See Also

CONTROL, DIALOG, LTEXT, RTEXT

CURSOR

nameID **CURSOR** [*load-option*] [*mem-option*] *filename*

The **CURSOR** statement specifies a bitmap that defines the shape of the cursor on the display screen.

Parameters

nameID
Specifies either a unique name or an integer identifying the resource.

load-option
Specifies when the resource is to be loaded. The parameter must be one of the following:

Option	Description
PRELOAD	Resource is loaded immediately.
LOADONCALL	Resource is loaded when called. This is the default option.

mem-option
Specifies whether the resource is fixed or movable and whether it is discardable. The parameter must be one of the following:

Option	Description
FIXED	Resource remains at a fixed memory location.
MOVEABLE	Resource can be moved if necessary in order to compact memory.
DISCARDABLE	Resource can be discarded if no longer needed.

The default is **MOVEABLE** and **DISCARDABLE** for cursor, icon, and font resources. The default for bitmap resources is **MOVEABLE**.

filename
Specifies the name of the file that contains the resource. The name must be a valid MS-DOS filename; it must be a full path if the file is not in the current working directory. The path can either be a quoted or non-quoted string.

Comments

Icon and cursor resources can contain more than one image. If the resource is marked with the **PRELOAD** option, Windows loads all images in the resource when the application executes.

Examples

The following example specifies two cursor resources; one by name (cursor1) and the other by number (2):

```
cursor1 CURSOR bullseye.cur
2       CURSOR "d:\\cursor\\arrow.cur"
```

#define

#define *name value*

The **#define** directive assigns the given value to the specified name. All subsequent occurrences of the name are replaced by the value.

Parameters

name

Specifies the name to be defined. This value is any combination of letters, digits, and punctuation.

value

Specifies any integer, character string, or line of text.

Examples

This example assigns values to the names "NONZERO" and "USERCLASS":

```
#define    NONZERO     1
#define    USERCLASS   "MyControlClass"
```

See Also

#ifdef, **#ifndef**, **#undef**

DEFPUSHBUTTON

DEFPUSHBUTTON *text*, *id*, *x*, *y*, *width*, *height*[, *style*]

The **DEFPUSHBUTTON** statement creates a default push-button control. The control is a small rectangle with a bold outline that represents the default response for the user. The given text is displayed inside the button. The control highlights the button in the usual way when the user clicks the mouse in it and sends a message to its parent window.

Parameters

text

Specifies text that is centered in the rectangular area of the control. This parameter must contain zero or more characters enclosed in double quotation marks. Character values must be in the range 1 through 255. If a double quotation mark is required in the text, you must include the double quotation mark twice. An ampersand (&) character in the text indicates that the following character is used as a mnemonic character for the control. When the control is displayed, the ampersand is not shown but the mnemonic character is underlined. The user can choose the control by pressing the key corresponding to the underlined mnemonic character. To use the ampersand as a character in a string, insert two ampersands (&&).

id

Specifies the control identifier. This value must be an integer in the range 0 through 65,535 or a simple expression that evaluates to a value in that range.

x

Specifies the x-coordinate of the upper-left corner of the control. This value must be an integer in the range 0 through 65,535 or an expression consisting of integers and the addition (+) or subtraction (–) operator. The coordinate is assumed to be in dialog units and is relative to the origin of the dialog box, window, or control containing the specified control.

y

Specifies the y-coordinate of the upper-left corner of the control. This value must be an integer in the range 0 through 65,535 or an expression consisting of integers and the addition (+) or subtraction (–) operator. The coordinate is assumed to be in dialog units and is relative to the origin of the dialog box, window, or control containing the specified control.

width

Specifies the width of the control. This value must be an integer in the range 1 through 65,535 or an expression consisting of integers and the addition (+) or subtraction (–) operator. The width is in 1/4-character units.

height

Specifies the height of the control. This value must be an integer in the range 1 through 65,535 or an expression consisting of integers and the addition (+) or subtraction (–) operator. The height is in 1/8-character units.

style

Specifies the control styles. This value can be a combination of the following styles: BS_DEFPUSHBUTTON, WS_TABSTOP, WS_GROUP, and WS_DISABLED.

You can use the bitwise OR (|) operator to combine styles.

If you do not specify a style, the default style is BS_DEFPUSHBUTTON and WS_TABSTOP.

Examples   This example creates a default push-button control that is labeled "Cancel":

```
DEFPUSHBUTTON "Cancel", 101, 10, 10, 24, 50
```

See Also   **PUSHBUTTON, RADIOBUTTON**

DIALOG

nameID **DIALOG** [*load-option*] [*mem-option*] *x, y, width, height*
BEGIN
  control-statements
  .
  .
  .
END

The **DIALOG** statement defines a window that an application can use to create dialog boxes. The statement defines the position and dimensions of the dialog box on the screen as well as the dialog box style.

Parameters

nameID

Identifies the dialog box. This is either a unique name or a unique integer value in the range 1 to 65,535.

load-option

Specifies when the resource is to be loaded. This parameter is optional. If it is specified, it must be one of the following:

Option	Description
PRELOAD	Resource is loaded immediately.
LOADONCALL	Resource is loaded when called. This is the default option.

mem-option

Specifies whether the resource is fixed or movable and whether it is discardable. This parameter is optional. If it is specified, it must be either **FIXED** or **MOVEABLE**. An additional value, **DISCARDABLE** may also be specified. The following list describes the options in more detail:

Option	Description
FIXED	Resource remains at a fixed memory location.
MOVEABLE	Resource can be moved if necessary in order to compact memory. This is the default option.
DISCARDABLE	Resource can be discarded if no longer needed.

x

Specifies the x-coordinate of the left side of the dialog box. This value must be an integer in the range 0 through 65,535 or an expression consisting of integers and the addition (+) or subtraction (–) operator. The coordinate is assumed to be in dialog units.

y
> Specifies the y-coordinate of the top side of the dialog box. This value must be an integer in the range 0 through 65,535 or an expression consisting of integers and the addition (+) or subtraction (–) operator. The coordinate is assumed to be in dialog units.

width
> Specifies the width of the dialog box. This value must be an integer in the range 1 through 65,535 or an expression consisting of integers and the addition (+) or subtraction (–) operator. The width is in 1/4-character units.

height
> Specifies the height of the dialog box. This value must be an integer in the range 1 through 65,535 or an expression consisting of integers and the addition (+) or subtraction (–) operator. The height is in 1/8-character units.

style
> Specifies the dialog box styles.

Comments

The **GetDialogBaseUnits** function returns the dialog base units in pixels. The exact meaning of the coordinates depends on the style defined by the **STYLE** option statement. For child-style dialog boxes, the coordinates are relative to the origin of the parent window, unless the dialog box has the style DS_ABSALIGN; in that case, the coordinates are relative to the origin of the display screen.

Do not use the WS_CHILD style with a modal dialog box. The **DialogBox** function always disables the parent/owner of the newly created dialog box. When a parent window is disabled, its child windows are implicitly disabled. Since the parent window of the child-style dialog box is disabled, the child-style dialog box is too.

If a dialog box has the DS_ABSALIGN style, the dialog coordinates for its upper-left corner are relative to the screen origin instead of to the upper-left corner of the parent window. You would typically use this style when you wanted the dialog box to start in a specific part of the display no matter where the parent window may be on the screen.

The name **DIALOG** can also be used as the class-name parameter to the **CreateWindow** function to create a window with dialog box attributes.

Examples

The following demonstrates the usage of the **DIALOG** statement:

```
#include <windows.h>

ErrorDialog DIALOG  10, 10, 300, 110
STYLE WS_POPUP|WS_BORDER
CAPTION "Error!"
```

```
BEGIN
    CTEXT "Select One:", 1, 10, 10, 280, 12
    PUSHBUTTON "&Retry", 2, 75, 30, 60, 12
    PUSHBUTTON "&Abort", 3, 75, 50, 60, 12
    PUSHBUTTON "&Ignore", 4, 75, 80, 60, 12
END
```

See Also   **CreateWindow, DialogBox, GetDialogBaseUnits**

EDITTEXT

EDITTEXT *id*, *x*, *y*, *width*, *height*[, *style*]

The **EDITTEXT** statement defines an EDIT control belonging to the EDIT class. It creates a rectangular region in which the user can enter and edit text. The control displays a cursor when the user clicks the mouse in it. The user can then use the keyboard to enter text or edit the existing text. Editing keys include the BACKSPACE and DELETE keys. The user can also use the mouse to select characters to be deleted or to select the place to insert new characters.

Parameters   *id*

Specifies the control identifier. This value must be an integer in the range 0 through 65,535 or a simple expression that evaluates to a value in that range.

x

Specifies the x-coordinate of the left side of the control relative to the left side of the dialog box. This value must be an integer in the range 0 through 65,535 or an expression consisting of integers and the addition (+) or subtraction (–) operator. The coordinate is assumed to be in dialog units and is relative to the origin of the dialog box, window, or control containing the specified control.

y

Specifies the y-coordinate of the top side of the control relative to the top of the dialog box. This value must be an integer in the range 0 through 65,535 or an expression consisting of integers and the addition (+) or subtraction (–) operator. The coordinate is assumed to be in dialog units and is relative to the origin of the dialog box, window, or control containing the specified control.

width

Specifies the width of the control. This value must be an integer in the range 1 through 65,535 or an expression consisting of integers and the addition (+) or subtraction (–) operator. The width is in 1/4-character units.

height
> Specifies the height of the control. This value must be an integer in the range 1 through 65,535 or an expression consisting of integers and the addition (+) or subtraction (–) operator. The height is in 1/8-character units.

style
> Specifies the control styles. This value can be a combination of the edit class styles and the following styles: WS_TABSTOP, WS_GROUP, WS_VSCROLL, WS_HSCROLL, and WS_DISABLED.
>
> You can use the bitwise OR (|) operator to combine styles.
>
> If you do not specify a style, the default style is ES_LEFT, WS_BORDER, and WS_TABSTOP.

Examples   The following example demonstrates the usage of the **EDITTEXT** statement:

```
EDITTEXT  3, 10, 10, 100, 10
```

#elif

#elif *constant-expression*

> The **#elif** directive marks an optional clause of a conditional-compilation block defined by a **#ifdef**, **#ifndef**, or **#if** directive. The directive controls conditional compilation of the resource file by checking the specified constant expression. If the constant expression is nonzero, **#elif** directs the compiler to continue processing statements up to the next **#endif**, **#else**, or **#elif** directive and then skip to the statement after **#endif**. If the constant expression is zero, **#elif** directs the compiler to skip to the next **#endif**, **#else**, or **#elif** directive. You can use any number of **#elif** directives in a conditional block.

Parameters   *constant-expression*
> Specifies the expression to be checked. This value is a defined name, an integer constant, or an expression consisting of names, integers, and arithmetic and relational operators.

Examples   In this example, **#elif** directs the compiler to process the second **BITMAP** statement only if the value assigned to the name "Version" is less than 7. The **#elif** directive itself is processed only if Version is greater than or equal to 3.

```
#if Version < 3
BITMAP 1 errbox.bmp
#elif Version < 7
BITMAP 1 userbox.bmp
#endif
```

See Also   #else, #endif, #if, #ifdef, #ifndef

#else

#else

The **#else** directive marks an optional clause of a conditional-compilation block defined by a **#ifdef**, **#ifndef**, or **#if** directive. The **#else** directive must be the last directive before the **#endif** directive.

This directive has no arguments.

Examples   This example compiles the second **BITMAP** statement only if the name "DEBUG" is not defined:

```
#ifdef DEBUG
    BITMAP 1 errbox.bmp
#else
    BITMAP 1 userbox.bmp
#endif
```

See Also   #elif, #endif, #if, #ifdef, #ifndef

#endif

#endif

The **#endif** directive marks the end of a conditional-compilation block defined by a **#ifdef** directive. One **#endif** is required for each **#if**, **#ifdef**, or **#ifndef** directive.

This directive has no arguments.

See Also   #elif, #else, #if, #ifdef, #ifndef

FONT

FONT pointsize, typeface

The **FONT** statement defines the font with which Windows will draw text in the dialog box. The font must have been previously loaded, either from the WIN.INI file or by calling the **LoadResource** function.

Parameters   *pointsize*
Specifies the size, in points, of the font.

typeface
Specifies the name of the typeface. This name must be identical to the name defined in the [fonts] section of WIN.INI. This parameter must be enclosed in double quotes.

Examples   The following example demonstrates the usage of the **FONT** statement:

```
FONT 12, "MS Sans Serif"
```

See Also   **DIALOG**, **LoadResource**

FONT

nameID **FONT** [*load-option*] [*mem-option*] *filename*

The **FONT** resource-definition statement specifies a file that contains a font.

For a font resource, *nameID* must be a number; it cannot be a name.

Parameters   *nameID*
Specifies either a unique name or an integer value identifying the resource.

load-option
Specifies when the resource is to be loaded. The parameter must be one of the following options:

Option	Description
PRELOAD	Resource is loaded immediately.
LOADONCALL	Resource is loaded when called. This is the default option.

mem-option
Specifies whether the resource is fixed or movable and whether it is discardable. The parameter must be one of the following options:

Option	Description
FIXED	Resource remains at a fixed memory location.
MOVEABLE	Resource can be moved if necessary in order to compact memory.
DISCARDABLE	Resource can be discarded if no longer needed.

The default is **MOVEABLE** and **DISCARDABLE** for cursor, icon, and font resources. The default for bitmap resources is **MOVEABLE**.

filename
Specifies the name of the file that contains the resource. The name must be a valid MS-DOS filename; it must be a full path if the file is not in the current working directory. The path can either be a quoted or non-quoted string.

Examples   The following example specifies a single font resource:

```
5 FONT  CMROMAN.FNT
```

GROUPBOX

GROUPBOX *text*, *id*, *x*, *y*, *width*, *height*[, *style*]

The **GROUPBOX** statement creates a group box control. The control is a rectangle that groups other controls together. The controls are grouped by drawing a border around them and displaying the given text in the upper-left corner. The **GROUPBOX** statement, which you can use only in a **DIALOG** statement, defines the text, identifier, dimensions, and attributes of a control window.

Parameters   *text*
Specifies text that is displayed to the right of the control. This parameter must contain zero or more characters enclosed in double quotation marks. Character values must be in the range 1 through 255. If a double quotation mark is required in the text, you must include the double quotation mark twice. An ampersand (&) character in the text indicates that the following character is used as a mnemonic character for the control. When the control is displayed, the ampersand is not shown but the mnemonic character is underlined. The user can

choose the control by pressing the key corresponding to the underlined mnemonic character. To use the ampersand as a character in a string, insert two ampersands (&&).

id

Specifies the control identifier. This value must be an integer in the range 0 through 65,535 or a simple expression that evaluates to a value in that range.

x

Specifies the x-coordinate of the left side of the control relative to the left side of the dialog box. This value must be an integer in the range 0 through 65,535 or an expression consisting of integers and the addition (+) or subtraction (–) operator. The coordinate is assumed to be in dialog units and is relative to the origin of the dialog box, window, or control containing the specified control.

y

Specifies the y-coordinate of the top side of the control relative to the top of the dialog box. This value must be an integer in the range 0 through 65,535 or an expression consisting of integers and the addition (+) or subtraction (–) operator. The coordinate is assumed to be in dialog units and is relative to the origin of the dialog box, window, or control containing the specified control.

width

Specifies the width of the control. This value must be an integer in the range 1 through 65,535 or an expression consisting of integers and the addition (+) or subtraction (–) operator. The width is in 1/4-character units.

height

Specifies the height of the control. This value must be an integer in the range 1 through 65,535 or an expression consisting of integers and the addition (+) or subtraction (–) operator. The height is in 1/8-character units.

style

Specifies the control styles. This value can be a combination of the button class style BS_GROUPBOX and the WS_TABSTOP and WS_DISABLED styles.

You can use the bitwise OR (|) operator to combine styles.

If you do not specify a style, the default style is BS_GROUPBOX.

Examples   This example creates a group-box control that is labeled "Options":

```
GROUPBOX "Options", 101, 10, 10, 100, 100
```

See Also   **DIALOG**

ICON

ICON *text*, *id*, *x*, *y*, [*width*, *height*, *style*]

The **ICON** statement creates an icon control. This control is an icon displayed in a dialog box. The **ICON** statement, which you can use only in a **DIALOG** statement, defines the icon-resource identifier, icon-control identifier, position, and attributes of a control.

Parameters

text

Specifies the name of an icon (not a filename) defined elsewhere in the resource file.

id

Specifies the control identifier. This value must be an integer in the range 0 through 65,535 or a simple expression that evaluates to a value in that range.

x

Specifies the x-coordinate of the left side of the control relative to the left side of the dialog box. This value must be an integer in the range 0 through 65,535 or an expression consisting of integers and the addition (+) or subtraction (−) operator. The coordinate is assumed to be in dialog units and is relative to the origin of the dialog box, window, or control containing the specified control.

y

Specifies the y-coordinate of the top side of the control relative to the top of the dialog box. This value must be an integer in the range 0 through 65,535 or an expression consisting of integers and the addition (+) or subtraction (−) operator. The coordinate is assumed to be in dialog units and is relative to the origin of the dialog box, window, or control containing the specified control.

width

This value is ignored and should be set to zero.

height

This value is ignored and should be set to zero.

style

Specifies the control style. This parameter is optional. The only value that can be specified is the SS_ICON style. This is the default style whether this parameter is specified or not.

Examples

This example creates an icon control whose icon identifier is 901 and whose name is "myicon":

```
ICON "myicon" 901, 30, 30
```

See Also

DIALOG

ICON

nameID **ICON** [*load-option*] [*mem-option*] *filename*

The **ICON** resource-definition statement specifies a bitmap that defines the shape of the icon to be used for a given application.

Parameters

nameID
Specifies either a unique name or an integer value identifying the resource.

load-option
Specifies when the resource is to be loaded. The parameter must be one of the following options:

Option	Description
PRELOAD	Resource is loaded immediately.
LOADONCALL	Resource is loaded when called. This is the default option.

mem-option
Specifies whether the resource is fixed or movable and whether it is discardable. The parameter must be one of the following options:

Option	Description
FIXED	Resource remains at a fixed memory location.
MOVEABLE	Resource can be moved if necessary in order to compact memory.
DISCARDABLE	Resource can be discarded if no longer needed.

The default is **MOVEABLE** and **DISCARDABLE** for cursor, icon, and font resources. The default for bitmap resources is **MOVEABLE**.

filename
Specifies the name of the file that contains the resource. The name must be a valid MS-DOS filename; it must be a full path if the file is not in the current working directory. The path can either be a quoted or non-quoted string.

Comments

Icon and cursor resources can contain more than one image. If the resource is marked as **PRELOAD**, Windows loads all images in the resource when the application executes.

Examples

The following example specifies two icon resources:

```
desk1    ICON desk.ico
11       ICON DISCARDABLE custom.ico
```

#if

#if constant-expression

The **#if** directive controls conditional compilation of the resource file by checking the specified constant expression. If the constant expression is nonzero, **#if** directs the compiler to continue processing statements up to the next **#endif**, **#else**, or **#elif** directive and then skip to the statement after the **#endif** directive. If the constant expression is zero, **#if** directs the compiler to skip to the next **#endif**, **#else**, or **#elif** directive.

Parameters   *constant-expression*
Specifies the expression to be checked. This value is a defined name, an integer constant, or an expression consisting of names, integers, and arithmetic and relational operators.

Examples   This example compiles the **BITMAP** statement only if the value assigned to the name "Version" is less than 3:

```
#if Version < 3
BITMAP 1 errbox.bmp
#endif
```

See Also   **#elif, #else, #endif, #ifdef, #ifndef**

#ifdef

#ifdef name

The **#ifdef** directive controls conditional compilation of the resource file by checking the specified name. If the name has been defined by using a **#define** directive or by using the **-d** command-line option with the Resource Compiler, **#ifdef** directs the compiler to continue with the statement immediately after the **#ifdef** directive. If the name has not been defined, **#ifdef** directs the compiler to skip all statements up to the next **#endif** directive.

Parameters   *name*
Specifies the name to be checked by the directive.

Examples   This example compiles the **BITMAP** statement only if the name "Debug" is defined:

```
#ifdef Debug
BITMAP 1 errbox.bmp
#endif
```

See Also   **#define, #endif, #if, #ifndef, #undef**

#ifndef

#ifndef *name*

The **#ifndef** directive controls conditional compilation of the resource file by checking the specified name. If the name has not been defined or if its definition has been removed by using the **#undef** directive, **#ifndef** directs the compiler to continue processing statements up to the next **#endif**, **#else**, or **#elif** directive and then skip to the statement after the **#endif** directive. If the name is defined, **#ifndef** directs the compiler to skip to the next **#endif**, **#else**, or **#elif** directive.

Parameters   *name*
    Specifies the name to be checked by the directive.

Examples   This example compiles the **BITMAP** statement only if the name "Optimize" is not defined:

```
#ifndef Optimize
BITMAP 1 errbox.bmp
#endif
```

See Also   **#elif, #else, #endif, #if, #ifdef, #undef**

#include

#include (*filename*)

The **#include** directive causes Resource Compiler to process the file specified in the *filename* parameter. This file should be a header file that defines the constants used in the resource-definition file.

Parameters   *filename*

Specifies the name of the file to be included. This value must be an ASCII string. If the file is in the current directory, the string must be enclosed in double quotation marks; if the file is in the directory specified by the INCLUDE environment variable, the string must be enclosed in less-than and greater-than characters (<>). You must give a full path enclosed in double quotation marks if the file is not in the current directory or in the directory specified by the INCLUDE environment variable.

Examples   This example processes the header files WINDOWS.H and HEADERS\MYDEFS.H while compiling the resource-definition file:

```
#include <windows.h>
#include "headers\mydefs.h"
```

See Also   **#define**

LISTBOX

LISTBOX *id, x, y, width, height*[, *style*]

The **LISTBOX** statement creates commonly used controls for a dialog box or window. The control is a rectangle containing a list of strings (such as filenames) from which the user can select. The **LISTBOX** statement, which can only be used in a **DIALOG** or **WINDOW** statement, defines the identifier, dimensions, and attributes of a control window.

Parameters   *id*

Specifies the control identifier. This value must be an integer in the range 0 through 65,535 or a simple expression that evaluates to a value in that range.

x

Specifies the x-coordinate of the left side of the control relative to the left side of the dialog box. This value must be an integer in the range 0 through 65,535 or an expression consisting of integers and the addition (+) or subtraction (–) operator. The coordinate is assumed to be in dialog units and is relative to the origin of the dialog box, window, or control containing the specified control.

y

Specifies the y-coordinate of the top side of the control relative to the top of the dialog box. This value must be an integer in the range 0 through 65,535 or an expression consisting of integers and the addition (+) or subtraction (−) operator. The coordinate is assumed to be in dialog units and is relative to the origin of the dialog box, window, or control containing the specified control.

width
Specifies the width of the control. This value must be an integer in the range 1 through 65,535 or an expression consisting of integers and the addition (+) or subtraction (−) operator. The width is in 1/4-character units.

height
Specifies the height of the control. This value must be an integer in the range 1 through 65,535 or an expression consisting of integers and the addition (+) or subtraction (−) operator. The height is in 1/8-character units.

style
Specifies the control styles. This value can be a combination of the list-box class styles and any of the following styles: WS_BORDER and WS_VSCROLL.

You can use the bitwise OR (|) operator to combine styles.

If you do not specify a style, the default style is LBS_NOTIFY and WS_BORDER.

Examples   This example creates a list-box control whose identifier is 101:

```
LISTBOX 101, 10, 10, 100, 100
```

See Also   **COMBOBOX**, **DIALOG**

LTEXT

LTEXT *text*, *id*, *x*, *y*, *width*, *height*, [*style*]

The **LTEXT** statement creates a left-aligned text control. The control is a simple rectangle displaying the given text left-aligned in the rectangle. The text is formatted before it is displayed. Words that would extend past the end of a line are automatically wrapped to the beginning of the next line. The **LTEXT** statement, which can be used only in a **DIALOG** statement, defines the text, identifier, dimensions, and attributes of the control.

Parameters   *text*
Specifies text that is left-aligned in the rectangular area of the control. This parameter must contain zero or more characters enclosed in double quotation

marks. Character values must be in the range 1 through 255. If a double quotation mark is required in the text, you must include the double quotation mark twice.

id

Specifies the control identifier. This value must be an integer in the range 0 through 65,535 or a simple expression that evaluates to a value in that range.

x

Specifies the x-coordinate of the upper-left corner of the control. This value must be an integer in the range 0 through 65,535 or an expression consisting of integers and the addition (+) or subtraction (–) operator. The coordinate is assumed to be in dialog units and is relative to the origin of the dialog box, window, or control containing the specified control.

y

Specifies the y-coordinate of the upper-left corner of the control. This value must be an integer in the range 0 through 65,535 or an expression consisting of integers and the addition (+) or subtraction (–) operator. The coordinate is assumed to be in dialog units and is relative to the origin of the dialog box, window, or control containing the specified control.

width

Specifies the width of the control. This value must be an integer in the range 1 through 65,535 or an expression consisting of integers and the addition (+) or subtraction (–) operator. The width is in 1/4-character units.

height

Specifies the height of the control. This value must be an integer in the range 1 through 65,535 or an expression consisting of integers and the addition (+) or subtraction (–) operator. The height is in 1/8-character units.

style

Specifies the control styles. This value can be any combination of the BS_RADIOBUTTON style and the following styles: SS_LEFT, WS_GROUP, and WS_TABSTOP.

You can use the bitwise OR (|) operator to combine styles.

If you do not specify a style, the default style is SS_LEFT and WS_GROUP.

Examples

This example creates a left-aligned text control that is labeled "Filename":

```
LTEXT "Filename", 101, 10, 10, 100, 100
```

See Also

CONTROL, CTEXT, DIALOG, RTEXT

MENU

MENU *menuname*

The **MENU** statement defines the dialog box's menu. If no statement is given, the dialog box has no menu.

Parameters   *menuname*
Specifies the menu to use. This value is either the name of the menu or the integer identifier of the menu.

Examples   The following example demonstrates the usage of the **MENU** dialog statement:

```
MENU errmenu
```

MENU

menuID **MENU** [*load-option*] [*mem-option*]
BEGIN
   item-definitions
   .
   .
   .
END

The **MENU** statement defines the contents of a menu resource. A menu resource is a collection of information that defines the appearance and function of an application menu. A menu is a special input tool that lets a user select commands from a list of command names.

Parameters   *menuID*
Identifies the menu. This value is either a unique string or a unique integer value in the range of 1 to 65,535.

load-option
Specifies when the resource is to be loaded. This parameter is optional. If it is specified, it must be one of the following:

Option	Description
PRELOAD	Resource is loaded immediately.
LOADONCALL	Resource is loaded when called. This is the default option.

mem-option

Specifies whether the resource is fixed or movable and whether it is discardable. This parameter is optional. If it is specified, it must be either **FIXED** or **MOVEABLE**. An additional value, **DISCARDABLE**, may also be specified. A description of the memory options follows:

Option	Description
FIXED	Resource remains at a fixed memory location.
MOVEABLE	Resource can be moved if necessary in order to compact memory. This is the default option.
DISCARDABLE	Resource can be discarded if no longer needed.

The default is **MOVEABLE** and **DISCARDABLE**.

Examples

Following is an example of a complete **MENU** statement:

```
sample MENU
BEGIN
    MENUITEM "&Soup", 100
    MENUITEM "S&alad", 101
    POPUP "&Entree"
    BEGIN
        MENUITEM "&Fish", 200
        MENUITEM "&Chicken", 201, CHECKED
        POPUP "&Beef"
        BEGIN
            MENUITEM "&Steak", 301
            MENUITEM "&Prime Rib", 302
        END
    END
    MENUITEM "&Dessert", 103
END
```

See Also

MENUITEM, POPUP

MENUITEM

MENUITEM *text*, *result*, [*optionlist*]

The **MENUITEM** statement, which is optional, defines a menu item.

Parameters

text

Specifies the name of the menu item. This parameter takes an ASCII string, enclosed in double quotation marks.

The string can contain the escape characters **\t** and **\a.** The **\t** character inserts a tab in the string and is used to align text in columns. Tab characters should be used only in pop-up menus, not in menu bars. (For information on pop-up menus, see the **POPUP** statement.) The **\a** character aligns all text that follows it flush right to the menu bar or pop-up menu.

To insert a double quotation mark in the string, use two double quotation marks.

To add a mnemonic to the text string, place the ampersand (&) ahead of the letter that will be the mnemonic. This will cause the letter to appear underlined in the control and to function as the mnemonic. To use the ampersand as a character in a string, insert two ampersands (&&).

result

Specifies the result generated when the user selects the menu item. This parameter takes an integer value. Menu-item results are always integers; when the user clicks the menu-item name, the result is sent to the window that owns the menu.

optionlist

Specifies the appearance of the menu item. This optional parameter takes one or more predefined menu options, separated by commas or spaces. The menu options are as follows:

Option	Description
CHECKED	Item has a check mark next to it.
GRAYED	Item name is initially inactive and appears on the menu in gray or a lightened shade of the menu-text color.
HELP	Identifies a help item.
INACTIVE	Item name is displayed but it cannot be selected.
MENUBARBREAK	Same as MF_MENUBREAK except that for pop-up menus, it separates the new column from the old column with a vertical line.
MENUBREAK	Places the menu item on a new line for static menu-bar items. For pop-up menus, it places the menu item in a new column with no dividing line between the columns.

The **INACTIVE** and **GRAYED** options cannot be used together.

Examples

The following example demonstrates the usage of the **MENUITEM** statement:

```
MENUITEM  "&Alpha", 1, CHECKED, GRAYED
MENUITEM  "&Beta", 2
```

POPUP

POPUP *text*, [*optionlist*]
BEGIN
   item-definitions
   .
   .
   .
END

The **POPUP** statement marks the beginning of the definition of a pop-up menu. A pop-up menu (which is also known as a drop-down menu) is a special menu item that displays a sublist of menu items when it is selected.

Parameters

text
Specifies the name of the pop-up menu. This string must be enclosed in double quotation marks.

optionlist
Specifies one or more predefined menu options that specify the appearance of the menu item. The menu options follow:

Option	Description
CHECKED	Item has a check mark next to it. This option is not valid for a top-level pop-up menu.
GRAYED	Item name is initially inactive and appears on the menu in gray or a lightened shade of the menu-text color.
INACTIVE	Item name is displayed but it cannot be selected.
MENUBARBREAK	Same as MF_MENUBREAK except that for pop-up menus, it separates the new column from the old column with a vertical line.
MENUBREAK	Places the menu item on a new line for static menu-bar items. For pop-up menus, it places the menu item in a new column with no dividing line between the columns.

The options can be combined using the bitwise OR operator. The **INACTIVE** and **GRAYED** options cannot be used together.

Examples   The following example demonstrates the usage of the **POPUP** statement:

```
chem MENU
BEGIN

    POPUP "&Elements"
    BEGIN
        MENUITEM "&Oxygen", 200
        MENUITEM "&Carbon", 201, CHECKED
        MENUITEM "&Hydrogen", 202
        MENUITEM "&Sulfur", 203
        MENUITEM "Ch&lorine", 204
    END

    POPUP "&Compounds"
    BEGIN
        POPUP "&Sugars"
        BEGIN
            MENUITEM "&Glucose", 301
            MENUITEM "&Sucrose", 302, CHECKED
            MENUITEM "&Lactose", 303, MENUBREAK
            MENUITEM "&Fructose", 304
        END

        POPUP "&Acids"
        BEGIN
            "&Hydrochloric", 401
            "&Sulfuric", 402
        END

    END

END
```

See Also   **MENU, MENUITEM**

PUSHBUTTON

PUSHBUTTON *text*, *id*, *x*, *y*, *width*, *height*, [*style*]

The **PUSHBUTTON** statement creates a push-button control. The control is a round-cornered rectangle containing the given text. The control sends a message to its parent whenever the user chooses the control.

Parameters

text

Specifies text that is centered in the rectangular area of the control. This parameter must contain zero or more characters enclosed in double quotation marks. Character values must be in the range 1 through 255. If a double quotation mark is required in the text, you must include the double quotation mark twice. An ampersand (&) character character in the text indicates that the following character is used as a mnemonic character for the control. When the control is displayed, the ampersand is not shown but the mnemonic character is underlined. The user can choose the control by pressing the key corresponding to the underlined mnemonic character.

id

Specifies the control identifier. This value must be an integer in the range 0 through 65,535 or an expression consisting of integers and the additon (+) operator that evaluates to a value in that range.

x

Specifies the x-coordinate of the upper-left corner of the control. This value must be an integer in the range 0 through 65,535 or an expression consisting of integers and the addition (+) operator that evaluates to a value in that range. The coordinate is assumed to be in dialog units and is relative to the origin of the dialog box containing the pushbutton.

y

Specifies the y-coordinate of the upper-left corner of the control. This value must be an integer in the range 0 through 65,535 or an expression consisting of integers and the addition (+) operator that evaluates to a value in that range. The coordinate is assumed to be in dialog units and is relative to the origin of the dialog box containing the pushbutton.

width

Specifies the width of the control. This value must be an integer in the range 1 through 65,535 or an expression consisting of integers and the addition (+) operator that evaluates to a value in that range. The width units are 1/4 of the dialog base width unit.

height

Specifies the height of the control. This value must be an integer in the range 1 through 65,535 or an expression consisting of integers and the addition (+) operator that evaluates to a value in that range. The height units are 1/8 of the dialog base height unit.

style

This optional parameter specifies styles for the pushbutton, which can be a combination of the BS_PUSHBUTTON style and the following styles: WS_DISABLED, WS_GROUP, and WS_TABSTOP.

Comments   The current dialog base units are computed from the height and width of the current system font. The **GetDialogBaseUnits** function returns the dialog base units in pixels. The coordinates are relative to the origin of the dialog box.

The default style for **PUSHBUTTON** is BS_PUSHBUTTON and WS_TABSTOP.

Examples   The following example demonstrates the usage of the **PUSHBUTTON** statement:

```
PUSHBUTTON "ON", 7, 10, 10, 20, 10
```

See Also   **GetDialogBaseUnits**

RADIOBUTTON

RADIOBUTTON *text*, *id*, *x*, *y*, *width*, *height*, [*style*]

The **RADIOBUTTON** statement creates a radio-button control. The control is a small circle that has the given text displayed next to it, typically to its right. The control highlights the circle and sends a message to its parent window when the user selects the button. The control removes the highlight and sends a message when the button is next selected.

Parameters   *text*

Specifies text that is centered in the rectangular area of the control. This parameter must contain zero or more characters enclosed in double quotation marks. Character values must be in the range 1 through 255. If a double quotation mark is required in the text, you must include the double quotation mark twice. An ampersand (&) character in the text indicates that the following character is used as a mnemonic character for the control. When the control is displayed, the ampersand is not shown, but the mnemonic character is underlined. The user can choose the control by pressing the key corresponding to the underlined mnemonic character.

id

Specifies the control identifier. This value must be an integer in the range 0 through 65,535 or an expression consisting of integers and the additon (+) operator that evaluates to a value in that range.

x

Specifies the x-coordinate of the upper-left corner of the control. This value must be an integer in the range 0 through 65,535 or an expression consisting of integers and the addition (+) operator that evaluates to a value in that range. The coordinate is assumed to be in dialog units and is relative to the origin of the dialog box containing the radio button.

y

Specifies the y-coordinate of the upper-left corner of the control. This value must be an integer in the range 0 through 65,535 or an expression consisting of integers and the addition (+) operator that evaluates to a value in that range. The coordinate is assumed to be in dialog units and is relative to the origin of the dialog box containing the radio button.

width

Specifies the width of the control. This value must be an integer in the range 1 through 65,535 or an expression consisting of integers and the addition (+) operator that evaluates to a value in that range. The width is in dialog units.

height

Specifies the height of the control. This value must be an integer in the range 1 through 65,535 or an expression consisting of integers and the addition (+) operator that evaluates to a value in that range. The height is in dialog units.

style

This optional parameter specifies styles for the radio button, which can be a combination of BUTTON-class styles and the following styles: WS_TABSTOP, WS_DISABLED, and WS_GROUP.

Comments

Horizontal dialog units are 1/4 of the dialog base width unit. Vertical units are 1/8 of the dialog base height unit. The current dialog base units are computed from the height and width of the current system font. The **GetDialogBaseUnits** function returns the dialog base units in pixels. The coordinates are relative to the origin of the dialog box.

The default style for **RADIOBUTTON** is BS_RADIOBUTTON and WS_TABSTOP.

The following example demonstrates the usage of the **RADIOBUTTON** statement:

```
RADIOBUTTON "Italic", 100, 10, 10, 40, 10
```

See Also   **GetDialogBaseUnits**

RCDATA

nameID **RCDATA** [*load-option*] [*mem-option*]
BEGIN
  raw-data
  .
  .
  .
END

The **RCDATA** statement defines a raw data resource for an application. Raw data resources permit the inclusion of binary data directly in the executable file.

Parameters   *nameID*
Specifies either a unique name or an integer value that identifies the resource.

load-option
Specifies when the resource is to be loaded. It takes one of the following keywords:

Option	Description
PRELOAD	Resource is loaded immediately.
LOADONCALL	Resource is loaded when called. This is the default option.

mem-option
Specifies whether the resource is fixed or movable and whether it is discardable. This optional parameter takes one or more of the following keywords:

Option	Description
FIXED	Resource remains at a fixed memory location.
MOVEABLE	Resource can be moved if necessary in order to compact memory.
DISCARDABLE	Resource can be discarded if no longer needed.

The default memory option is **MOVEABLE** and **DISCARDABLE**.

raw-data
> Specifies one or more integers and strings. Integers can be in decimal, octal, or hexadecimal format.

Examples   The following example demonstrates the usage of the **RCDATA** statement:

```
resname RCDATA
BEGIN
   "Here is a data string\0", /* A string. Note: explicitly
                                  null-terminated */
   1024,                      /* int        */
   0x029a,                    /* hex int    */
   0o733,                     /* octal int  */
   "\07"                      /* octal byte */
END
```

RTEXT

RTEXT *text, id, x, y, width, height,* [*style*]

> The **RTEXT** statement creates a right-aligned text control. The control is a simple rectangle displaying the given text right-aligned in the rectangle. The text is formatted before it is displayed. Words that would extend past the end of a line are automatically wrapped to the beginning of the next line.

Parameters   *text*
> Specifies text that is aligned on the right side of the rectangular area of the control. This parameter must contain zero or more characters enclosed in double quotation marks. Character values must be in the range 1 through 255. If a double quotation mark is required in the text, you must include the double quotation mark twice. An ampersand (&) character in the text indicates that the following character is used as a mnemonic character for the control. When the control is displayed, the ampersand is not shown, but the mnemonic character is underlined. The user can choose the control by pressing the key corresponding to the underlined mnemonic character.

id
> Specifies the control identifier. This value must be an integer in the range 0 through 65,535 or an expression consisting of integers and the additon (+) operator that evaluates to a value in that range.

x
> Specifies the x-coordinate of the upper-left corner of the control. This value must be an integer in the range 0 through 65,535 or an expression consisting of integers and the addition (+) operator that evaluates to a value in that range. The coordinate is assumed to be in dialog units and is relative to the origin of the dialog box containing the text control.

y
> Specifies the y-coordinate of the upper-left corner of the control. This value must be an integer in the range 0 through 65,535 or an expression consisting of integers and the addition (+) operator that evaluates to a value in that range. The coordinate is assumed to be in dialog units and is relative to the origin of the dialog box containing the text control.

width
> Specifies the width of the control. This value must be an integer in the range 1 through 65,535 or an expression consisting of integers and the addition (+) operator that evaluates to a value in that range. The width is in dialog units.

height
> Specifies the height of the control. This value must be an integer in the range 1 through 65,535 or an expression consisting of integers and the addition (+) operator that evaluates to a value in that range. The height is in dialog units.

style
> This optional parameter specifies styles for the text control, which can be any combination of the following: WS_TABSTOP and WS_GROUP.

Comments

Horizontal dialog units are 1/4 of the dialog base width unit. Vertical units are 1/8 of the dialog base height unit. The current dialog base units are computed from the height and width of the current system font. The **GetDialogBaseUnits** function returns the dialog base units in pixels. The coordinates are relative to the origin of the dialog box.

The default style for **RTEXT** is SS_RIGHT and WS_GROUP.

Examples

The following example demonstrates the usage of the **RTEXT** statement:

```
RTEXT "Number of Messages", 4, 30, 50, 100, 10
```

SCROLLBAR

SCROLLBAR *id*, *x*, *y*, *width*, *height*, [*style*]

The **SCROLLBAR** statement creates a scroll-bar control. The control is a rectangle that contains a scroll box and has direction arrows at both ends. The scroll-bar control sends a notification message to its parent whenever the user clicks the mouse in the control. The parent is responsible for updating the scroll-box position. Scroll-bar controls can be positioned anywhere in a window and used whenever needed to provide scrolling input.

Parameters

id
Identifies the control. This parameter takes a unique integer value.

x
Specifies the x-coordinate of the upper-left corner of the control in dialog units relative to the origin of the dialog box. The horizontal units are 1/4 of the dialog base width unit.

y
Specifies the y-coordinate of the upper-left corner of the control in dialog units relative to the origin of the dialog box. The vertical units are 1/8 of the dialog base height unit.

width
Specifies the width of the control. The width units are 1/4 of the dialog base width unit.

height
Specifies the height of the control. The height units are 1/8 of the dialog base height unit.

style
Specifies a combination (or none) of the following styles: WS_TABSTOP, WS_GROUP, and WS_DISABLED.

In addition to these styles, the *style* parameter may contain a combination (or none) of the SCROLLBAR-class styles. Styles can be combined by using the bitwise OR operator.

Comments   The *x, y, width,* and *height* parameters can use the addition operator (+) for relative positioning. For example, "15 + 6" can be used for the *x* parameter.

The default style for **SCROLLBAR** is SBS_HORZ.

The current dialog base units are computed from the height and width of the current system font. The **GetDialogBaseUnits** function returns the dialog base units in pixels.

Examples   The following example demonstrates the usage of the **SCROLLBAR** statement:

```
SCROLLBAR 999, 25, 30, 10, 100
```

SEPARATOR

MENUITEM SEPARATOR

The **MENUITEM SEPARATOR** form of the **MENUITEM** statement creates an inactive menu item that serves as a dividing bar between two active menu items in a pop-up menu.

Examples   The following example demonstrates the usage of the **MENUITEM SEPARATOR** statement:

```
MENUITEM "&Roman", 206
MENUITEM SEPARATOR
MENUITEM "&20 Point", 301
```

STRINGTABLE

STRINGTABLE [*load-option*] [*mem-option*]
BEGIN
   stringID string
   .
   .
   .
END

The **STRINGTABLE** statement defines one or more string resources for an application. String resources are simply null-terminated ASCII strings that can be loaded when needed from the executable file, using the **LoadString** function.

Parameters

load-option
Specifies when the resource is to be loaded. This optional parameter must be one of the following keywords:

Option	Description
PRELOAD	Resource is loaded immediately.
LOADONCALL	Resource is loaded when called. This is the default option.

mem-option
Specifies whether the resource is fixed or movable and whether or not it is discardable. This optional parameter can be one of the following keywords:

Option	Description
FIXED	Resource remains at a fixed memory location.
MOVEABLE	Resource can be moved if necessary in order to compact memory.
DISCARDABLE	Resource can be discarded if no longer needed.

The default is **MOVEABLE** and **DISCARDABLE**.

stringID
Specifies an integer value that identifies the resource.

string
Specifies one or more ASCII strings, enclosed in double quotation marks. The string must be no longer than 255 characters and must occupy a single line in the source file. To add a carriage return to the string, use this character sequence: \012. For example, "Line one\012Line two" would define a string that would be displayed as follows:

```
Line one
Line two
```

Comments

Grouping strings in separate segments allows all related strings to be read in at one time and discarded together. When possible, an application should make the table movable and discardable. The Resource Compiler allocates 16 strings per segment and uses the identifier value to determine which segment is to contain the string. Strings with the same upper-12 bits in their identifiers are placed in the same segment.

Examples   The following example demonstrates the usage of the **STRINGTABLE** statement:

```
#define IDS_HELLO    1
#define IDS_GOODBYE  2

STRINGTABLE
BEGIN
    IDS_HELLO,   "Hello"
    IDS_GOODBYE, "Goodbye"
END
```

STYLE

STYLE *style*

The **STYLE** statement defines the window style of the dialog box. The window style specifies whether the box is a pop-up or a child window. The default style has the following attributes: WS_POPUP, WS_BORDER, and WS_SYSMENU.

Parameters   *style*
Specifies the window style. This parameter takes an integer value or predefined name. The following lists the predefined styles:

Style	Meaning
DS_LOCALEDIT	Specifies that edit controls in the dialog box will use memory in the application's data segment. By default, all edit controls in dialog boxes use memory outside the application's data segment. This feature can be suppressed by adding the DS_LOCALEDIT flag to the STYLE command for the dialog box. If this flag is not used, EM_GET-HANDLE and EM_SETHANDLE messages must not be used since the storage for the control is not in the application's data segment. This feature does not affect edit controls created outside of dialog boxes.
DS_MODALFRAME	Creates a dialog box with a modal dialog box frame that can be combined with a title bar and System menu by specifying the WS_CAPTION and WS_SYSMENU styles.

Style	Meaning
DS_NOIDLEMSG	Suppresses WM_ENTERIDLE messages that Windows would otherwise send to the owner of the dialog box while the dialog box is displayed.
DS_SYSMODAL	Creates a system-modal dialog box.
WS_BORDER	Creates a window that has a border.
WS_CAPTION	Creates a window that has a title bar (implies the WS_BORDER style).
WS_CHILD	Creates a child window. It cannot be used with the WS_POPUP style.
WS_CHILDWINDOW	Creates a child window that has the WS_CHILD style.
WS_CLIPCHILDREN	Excludes the area occupied by child windows when drawing within the parent window. Used when creating the parent window.
WS_CLIPSIBLINGS	Clips child windows relative to each other; that is, when a particular child window receives a WM_PAINT message, this style clips all other top-level child windows out of the region of the child window to be updated. (If the WS_CLIPSIBLINGS style is not given and child windows overlap, it is possible, when drawing in the client area of a child window, to draw in the client area of a neighboring child window.) For use with the WS_CHILD style only.
WS_DISABLED	Creates a window that is initially disabled.
WS_DLGFRAME	Creates a window with a modal dialog box frame but no title.
WS_GROUP	Specifies the first control of a group of controls in which the user can move from one control to the next by using the arrow keys. All controls defined with the WS_GROUP style after the first control belong to the same group. The next control with the WS_GROUP style ends the style group and starts the next group (that is, one group ends where the next begins). This style is valid only for controls.

Style	Meaning
WS_HSCROLL	Creates a window that has a horizontal scroll bar.
WS_ICONIC	Creates a window that is initially iconic. For use with the WS_OVERLAPPED style only.
WS_MAXIMIZE	Creates a window of maximum size.
WS_MAXIMIZEBOX	Creates a window that has a Maximize box.
WS_MINIMIZE	Creates a window of minimum size.
WS_MINIMIZEBOX	Creates a window that has a Minimize box.
WS_OVERLAPPED	Creates an overlapped window. An overlapped window has a caption and a border.
WS_OVERLAPPEDWINDOW	Creates an overlapped window having the WS_OVERLAPPED, WS_CAPTION, WS_SYSMENU, WS_THICKFRAME, WS_MINIMIZEBOX, and WS_MAXIMIZEBOX styles.
WS_POPUP	Creates a pop-up window. It cannot be used with the WS_CHILD style.
WS_POPUPWINDOW	Creates a pop-up window that has the WS_POPUP, WS_BORDER, and WS_SYSMENU styles. The WS_CAPTION style must be combined with the WS_POPUPWINDOW style to make the System menu visible.
WS_SIZEBOX	Creates a window that has a size box. Used only for windows with a title bar or with vertical and horizontal scroll bars.
WS_SYSMENU	Creates a window that has a System-menu box in its title bar. Used only for windows with title bars. If used with a child window, this style creates a Close box instead of a System-menu box.
WS_TABSTOP	Specifies one of any number of controls through which the user can move by using the TAB key. The TAB key moves the user to the next control specified by the WS_TABSTOP style. This style is valid only for controls.

Style	Meaning
WS_THICKFRAME	Creates a window with a thick frame that can be used to size the window.
WS_VISIBLE	Creates a window that is initially visible. This applies to overlapping and pop-up windows. For overlapping windows, the *y* parameter is used as a parameter for the **ShowWindow** function.
WS_VSCROLL	Creates a window that has a vertical scroll bar.

Comments

If the predefined names are used, the **#include** directive must be used so that the WINDOWS.H file will be included in the resource script.

#undef

#undef *name*

The **#undef** directive removes the current definition of the specified name. All subsequent occurrences of the name are processed without replacement.

Parameters

name
Specifies the name to be removed. This value is any combination of letters, digits, and punctuation.

Examples

This example removes the definitions for the names "nonzero" and "USER-CLASS":

```
#undef    nonzero
#undef    USERCLASS
```

See Also

#define

User-Defined

nameID typeID [*load-option*] [*mem-option*] *filename*

nameID typeID [*load-option*] [*mem-option*]
BEGIN
   raw-data
   .
   .
   .
END

A user-defined resource statement specifies a resource that contains application-specific data. The data can have any format and can be defined either as the content of a given file (if the *filename* parameter is given) or as a series of numbers or strings (if the *raw-data* parameter is given).

Parameters

nameID
Specifies either a unique name or an integer that identifies the resource.

typeID
Specifies either a unique name or an integer that identifies the resource type. If a number is given, it must be greater than 255. The numbers 1 through 255 are reserved for existing and future predefined resource types.

load-option
Specifies when the resource is to be loaded. The parameter must be one of the following options:

Option	Description
PRELOAD	Resource is loaded immediately.
LOADONCALL	Resource is loaded when called. This is the default option.

mem-option
Specifies whether the resource is fixed or movable and whether it is discardable. The parameter must be one of the following options:

Option	Description
FIXED	Resource remains at a fixed memory location.
MOVEABLE	Resource can be moved if necessary in order to compact memory.
DISCARDABLE	Resource can be discarded if no longer needed.

The default is **MOVEABLE** and **DISCARDABLE** for cursor, icon, and font resources. The default for bitmap resources is **MOVEABLE**.

filename
Specifies the name of the file that contains the resource data. The parameter must be a valid MS-DOS filename; it must be a full path if the file is not in the current working directory.

raw-data
Specifies one or more integers and strings. Integers can be in decimal, octal, or hexadecimal format.

Examples

The following example shows several user-defined statements:

```
array   MYRES   data.res
14      300     custom.res
18 MYRES2
BEGIN
  "Here is a data string\0", /* A string. Note: explicitly
                                 null-terminated */
  1024,                      /* int        */
  0x029a,                    /* hex int    */
  0o733,                     /* octal int  */
  "\07"                      /* octal byte */
END
```

VERSIONINFO

versionID **VERSIONINFO** *fixed-info*
BEGIN
   block-statement
   .
   .
   .
END

The **VERSIONINFO** statement creates a version-information resource. The resource contains such information about the file as its version number, its intended operating system, and its original filename. The resource is intended to be used with the File Installation library functions.

Parameters

versionID
Specifies the version-information resource identifier. This value must be 1.

fixed-info

Specifies the version information, such as the file version and the intended operating system. This parameter consists of the following statements:

Statement	Description
FILEVERSION *version*	Specifies the binary version number for the file. The *version* consists of two 32-bit integers, defined by four 16-bit integers. For example, "FILEVERSION 3,10,0,61" is translated into two doublewords: 0x0003000a and 0x0000003d, in that order. If *version* is defined by the doublewords dw1 and dw2, they need to appear in the **FILEVERSION** statement as follows: **HIWORD**(dw1), **LOWORD**(dw1), **HIWORD**(dw2), **LOWORD**(dw2).
PRODUCTVERSION *version*	Specifies the binary version number for the product with which the file is distributed. The *version* parameter is two 32-bit integers, defined by four 16-bit integers. For more information about *version*, see the **FILEVERSION** description.
FILEFLAGSMASK *fileflagsmask*	Specifies which bits in the **FILEFLAGS** statement are valid. If a bit is set, the corresponding bit in **FILEFLAGS** is valid.
FILEFLAGS *fileflags*	Specifies the Boolean attributes of the file. The *fileflags* parameter must be the combination of all the file flags that are valid at compile time. For Windows 3.1, this value is 0x3f.
FILEOS *fileos*	Specifies the operating system for which this file was designed. The *fileos* parameter can be one of the operating system values given in the Comments section.
FILETYPE *filetype*	Specifies the general type of file. The *filetype* parameter can be one of the file type values listed in the Comments section.
FILESUBTYPE *subtype*	Specifies the function of the file. The *subtype* parameter is zero unless the *type* parameter in the **FILETYPE** statement is VFT_DRV, VFT_FONT, or VFT_VXD. For a list of file subtype values, see the Comments section.

block-statement

Specifies one or more version-information blocks. A block can contain string information or variable information.

Comments

To use the constants specified with the **VERSIONINFO** statement, the VER.H file must be included in the resource-definition file.

The following list describes the parameters used in the **VERSIONINFO** statement:

Parameter	Description
fileflags	Specifies a combination of the following values:

Value	Meaning
VS_FF_DEBUG	File contains debugging information or is compiled with debugging features enabled.
VS_FF_INFOINFERRED	File contains a dynamically created version-information resource. Some of the blocks for the resource may be empty or incorrect. This value is not intended to be used in version-information resources created by using the **VERSIONINFO** statement.
VS_FF_PATCHED	File has been modified and is not identical to the original shipping file of the same version number.
VS_FF_PRERELEASE	File is a development version, not a commercially released product.
VS_FF_PRIVATEBUILD	File was not built using standard release procedures. If this value is given, the **String-FileInfo** block must contain a **PrivateBuild** string.
VS_FF_SPECIALBUILD	File was built by the original company using standard release procedures but is a variation of the standard file of the same version number. If this value is given, the **String-FileInfo** block must contain a **SpecialBuild** string.

Parameter	Description
fileos	Specifies one of the following values:

Value	Meaning
VOS_UNKNOWN	Operating system for which the file was designed is unknown to Windows.
VOS_DOS	File was designed for MS-DOS.

Parameter	Description

Value	Meaning
VOS_NT	File was designed for Windows NT.
VOS_WINDOWS16	File was designed for Windows 3.0 or later.
VOS_WINDOWS32	File was designed for 32-bit Windows.
VOS_DOS_WINDOWS16	File was designed for Windows 3.0 or later running with MS-DOS.
VOS_DOS_WINDOWS32	File was designed for 32-bit Windows running with MS-DOS.
VOS_NT_WINDOWS32	File was designed for 32-bit Windows running with Windows NT.

The values 0x00002L, 0x00003L, 0x20000L and 0x30000L are reserved.

filetype   Specifies one of the following values:

Value	Meaning
VFT_UNKNOWN	File type is unknown to Windows.
VFT_APP	File contains an application.
VFT_DLL	File contains a dynamic-link library (DLL).
VFT_DRV	File contains a device driver. If the **dwFileType** member is VFT_DRV, the **dwFileSubtype** member contains a more specific description of the driver.
VFT_FONT	File contains a font. If the **dwFileType** member is VFT_FONT, the **dwFileSubtype** member contains a more specific description of the font file.
VFT_VXD	File contains a virtual device.
VFT_STATIC_LIB	File contains a static-link library.
	All other values are reserved for use by Microsoft.

Parameter	Description
subtype	Specifies additional information about the file type.

If the **FILETYPE** statement specifies VFT_DRV, this parameter can be one of the following values:

Value	Meaning
VFT2_UNKNOWN	Driver type is unknown to Windows.
VFT2_DRV_COMM	File contains a communications driver.
VFT2_DRV_PRINTER	File contains a printer driver.
VFT2_DRV_KEYBOARD	File contains a keyboard driver.
VFT2_DRV_LANGUAGE	File contains a language driver.
VFT2_DRV_DISPLAY	File contains a display driver.
VFT2_DRV_MOUSE	File contains a mouse driver.
VFT2_DRV_NETWORK	File contains a network driver.
VFT2_DRV_SYSTEM	File contains a system driver.
VFT2_DRV_INSTALLABLE	File contains an installable driver.
VFT2_DRV_SOUND	File contains a sound driver.

If the **FILETYPE** statement specifies VFT_FONT, this parameter can be one of the following values:

Value	Meaning
VFT2_UNKNOWN	Font type is unknown to Windows.
VFT2_FONT_RASTER	File contains a raster font.
VFT2_FONT_VECTOR	File contains a vector font.
VFT2_FONT_TRUETYPE	File contains a TrueType font.

If the **FILETYPE** statement specifies VFT_VXD, this parameter must be the virtual-device identifier included in the virtual-device control block.

Parameter	Description
	All *subtype* values not listed here are reserved for use by Microsoft.
langID	Specifies one of the following language identifiers:

Value	Language
0x0401	Arabic
0x0402	Bulgarian
0x0403	Catalan
0x0404	Traditional Chinese
0x0405	Czech
0x0406	Danish
0x0407	German
0x0408	Greek
0x0409	U.S. English
0x040A	Castilian Spanish
0x040B	Finnish
0x040C	French
0x040D	Hebrew
0x040E	Hungarian
0x040F	Icelandic
0x0410	Italian
0x0411	Japanese
0x0412	Korean
0x0413	Dutch
0x0414	Norwegian – Bokmål
0x0415	Polish
0x0416	Brazilian Portuguese
0x0417	Rhaeto-Romanic
0x0418	Romanian
0x0419	Russian
0x041A	Croato-Serbian (Latin)
0x041B	Slovak
0x041C	Albanian
0x041D	Swedish
0x041E	Thai

Parameter	Description

Value	Language
0x041F	Turkish
0x0420	Urdu
0x0421	Bahasa
0x0804	Simplified Chinese
0x0807	Swiss German
0x0809	U.K. English
0x080A	Mexican Spanish
0x080C	Belgian French
0x0810	Swiss Italian
0x0813	Belgian Dutch
0x0814	Norwegian – Nynorsk
0x0816	Portuguese
0x081A	Serbo-Croatian (Cyrillic)
0x0C0C	Canadian French
0x100C	Swiss French

charsetID   Specifies one of the following character-set identifiers:

Value	Character set
0	7-bit ASCII
932	Windows, Japan (Shift – JIS X-0208)
949	Windows, Korea (Shift – KSC 5601)
950	Windows, Taiwan (GB5)
1200	Unicode
1250	Windows, Latin-2 (Eastern European)
1251	Windows, Cyrillic
1252	Windows, Multilingual
1253	Windows, Greek
1254	Windows, Turkish
1255	Windows, Hebrew
1256	Windows, Arabic

Parameter	Description
string-name	Specifies one of the following predefined names:

Name	Value
Comments	Specifies additional information that should be displayed for diagnostic purposes.
CompanyName	Specifies the company that produced the file—for example, "Microsoft Corporation" or "Standard Microsystems Corporation, Inc.". This string is required.
FileDescription	Specifies a file description to be presented to users. This string may be displayed in a list box when the user is choosing files to install—for example, "Keyboard Driver for AT-Style Keyboards" or "Microsoft Word for Windows". This string is required.
FileVersion	Specifies the version number of the file—for example, "3.10" or "5.00.RC2". This string is required.
InternalName	Specifies the internal name of the file, if one exists—for example, a module name if the file is a dynamic-link library. If the file has no internal name, this string should be the original filename, without extension. This string is required.
LegalCopyright	Specifies all copyright notices that apply to the file. This should include the full text of all notices, legal symbols, copyright dates, and so on—for example, "Copyright Microsoft Corp. 1990,1991". This string is optional.
LegalTrademarks	Specifies all trademarks and registered trademarks that apply to the file. This should include the full text of all notices, legal symbols, trademark numbers, and so on—for example, "Windows(TM) is a trademark of Microsoft Corporation". This string is optional.

Parameter	Description	
	Name	**Value**
	OriginalFilename	Specifies the original name of the file, not including a path. This information enables an application to determine whether a file has been renamed by a user. The format of the name depends on the file system for which the file was created. This string is required.
	PrivateBuild	Specifies information about a private version of the file—for example, "Built by TESTER1 on \TESTBED". This string should be present only if the VS_FF_PRIVATEBUILD flag is set in the **dwFileFlags** member of the **VS_FIXEDFILEINFO** structure of the root block.
	ProductName	Specifies the name of the product with which the file is distributed—for example, "Microsoft Windows". This string is required.
	ProductVersion	Specifies the version of the product with which the file is distributed—for example, "3.10" or "5.00.RC2". This string is required.
	SpecialBuild	Specifies how this version of the file differs from the standard version—for example, "Private build for TESTER1 solving mouse problems on M250 and M250E computers". This string should be present only if the VS_FF_SPECIALBUILD flag is set in the **dwFileFlags** member of the **VS_FIXEDFILEINFO** structure in the root block.

A string information block has the following form:

BLOCK "**StringFileInfo**"
BEGIN
  BLOCK "*lang-charset*"
  BEGIN
    VALUE "*string-name*", "*value*"

    .
    .
    .

  END
END

Following are the parameters in the **StringFileInfo** block:

lang-charset
    Specifies a language and character-set identifier pair. It is a hexadecimal string consisting of the concatenation of the language and character-set identifiers listed earlier in this section.

string-name
    Specifies the name of a value in the block and can be one of the predefined names listed earlier in this section.

value
    Specifies, as a character string, the value of the corresponding string name. More than one **VALUE** statement can be given.

A variable information block has the following form:

BLOCK "**VarFileInfo**"
BEGIN
  VALUE "**Translation**",
    langID, *charsetID*

    .
    .
    .

END

Following are the parameters in the variable information block:

langID
    Specifies one of the language identifiers listed earlier in this section.

charsetID
    Specifies one of the character-set identifiers listed earlier in this section.

    More than one identifier pair can be given, but each pair must be separated from the preceding pair with a comma.

Assembly-Language Macros

Assembly-language Microsoft Windows applications are highly structured assembly-language programs that use high-level–language calling conventions as well as Windows functions, data types, and programming conventions. Although you create assembly-language Windows programs by using a macro assembler, the goal is to generate object files that are similar to the object files generated by a C compiler. This chapter gives some guidelines that can help you meet this goal when creating assembly-language Windows applications.

The Microsoft Windows 3.1 Software Development Kit (SDK) includes the CMACROS.INC file. This file contains high-level–language macros, called Cmacros, that define segments, programming models, function interfaces, and data types needed to create Windows applications. The Cmacros provide assembly-time options that define the memory model and the calling conventions that an application will use. The options must be selected in the assembly-language source file before the **INCLUDE** directive is used.

This chapter provides an overview of the Cmacros and supplies the information necessary to create an assembly-language Windows application.

14.1 Creating Assembly-Language Windows Applications

When creating an assembly-language Windows application using the Cmacros, you should do the following in your application's assembly-language source file:

1. Specify the memory model by setting one of the following options to 1: **memS**, **memM**, **memC**, or **memL**.
2. Specify the Pascal calling convention by setting the **?PLM** option to 1.

   This specification is required for functions that will be called by Windows.
3. Enable Windows prolog and epilog code by setting the **?WIN** option to 1.

   This specification is required for callback functions or for exported functions in Windows libraries.
4. Include the CMACROS.INC file in the application source file.

   The statement that includes the CMACROS.INC file must come after the statements described in the preceding steps.
5. Create the application entry point, **WinMain**, and make sure that it is declared a public function.
6. Declare callback functions as described in Section 14.1.6, "Declaring Callback Functions."

After assembling the application source files, link your application's assembled object files with the appropriate C-language library for Windows and C run-time libraries.

The rest of this section describes these steps in greater detail.

14.1.1 Specifying a Memory Model

The Cmacro memory-model options specify the memory model that the application will use. The memory model defines how many code and data segments are in the application. Following is a list of the possible memory models:

Model	Description
Small	One code segment and one data segment
Medium	Multiple code segments and one data segment
Compact	One code segment and multiple data segments
Large	Multiple code and data segments
Huge	Multiple code segments and multiple data segments, with one or more data items larger than 64K

Select a memory model by defining the option name at the beginning of the assembly-language source file. These option names are available:

Option name	Memory model	Code size	Data size
memS	Small	Small	Small
memM	Medium	Large	Small
memC	Compact	Small	Large
memL	Large	Large	Large
memH	Huge	Large	Large

You can define a name by using the **EQU** directive. The definition has the following form:

```
memM     EQU     1
```

If no option is selected, the default model is small.

When you select a memory-model option, two symbols are defined: **SizeC** and **SizeD**. These two symbols can be used for code that is dependent on the memory model. They can have the following values:

Symbol	Value	Meaning
SizeC	0	Small code
	1	Large code
SizeD	0	Small data
	1	Large data
	2	Huge data

14.1.2 Selecting a Calling Convention

The Cmacro calling-convention option specifies the high-level–language calling convention that the application will use. You can select the calling convention by defining the value of the **?PLM** option. The values for the calling conventions are described as follows:

Value	Convention	Description
0	Standard C	The caller pushes the rightmost argument onto the stack first, the leftmost last. The caller pops the arguments off the stack after control is returned.
1	Pascal	The caller pushes the leftmost argument onto the stack first, the rightmost last. The called function pops the arguments off the stack.

You can set the **?PLM** value by using the = directive. The statement has the following form:

```
?PLM = 1
```

The default is the Pascal calling convention. That convention is required for functions called by Windows.

14.1.3 Enabling the Windows Prolog/Epilog Option

The Windows prolog/epilog option is required for Windows applications. It specifies whether to use special prolog and epilog code with each function; this code defines the current data segment for the given function.

You set this option by defining the value of the **?WIN** option.

Value	Meaning
0	Disable the special prolog/epilog code.
1	Enable the special prolog/epilog code.

You can set the **?WIN** value by using the = directive. The statement has the following form:

```
?WIN = 1
```

By default, prolog and epilog code are enabled.

14.1.4 Including the CMACROS.INC File

The CMACROS.INC file contains the assembly-language definitions for all Cmacros. You must include this file at the beginning of the assembly-language source file by using the **INCLUDE** directive. The line has the following form:

```
INCLUDE CMACROS.INC
```

You must give the full path if the macro file is not in the current directory or in a directory specified on the command line.

For a complete description of each of the Cmacros, see Section 14.4, "Alphabetic Reference."

14.1.5 Creating the Application Entry Point

Create the application entry point, **WinMain**, and make sure that it is declared a public function. The function should have the following form:

```
cProc WinMain, <PUBLIC>, <si,di>
    parmW hInstance
    parmW hPrevInstance
    parmD lpCmdLine
    parmW nCmdShow
cBegin WinMain
    .
    .
    .
cEnd WinMain

sEnd
```

The **WinMain** function should be defined within the standard code segment, **CODE**.

14.1.6 Declaring Callback Functions

Callback functions must be declared as follows:

```
cProc TestWndProc, <FAR,PUBLIC>, <si,di>
     parmW hWnd
     parmW message
     parmW wParam
     parmD lParam
cBegin TestWndProc
     .
     .
     .
cEnd TestWndProc
```

Callback functions must be defined within a code segment.

14.1.7 Linking with Libraries

After assembling your application's source files, you should link the assembled object files with the appropriate C-language libraries.

If the entire application is written in assembly language, you may need to add an external definition for the absolute symbol **__acrtused** in your application source file in order to link properly.

14.1.8 Enabling Stack Checking

You can enable stack checking by defining the **?CHKSTK** option. When stack checking is enabled, the prolog code calls the externally defined routine **CHKSTK** to allocate local variables.

You can define the **?CHKSTK** option by using the = directive. The statement has the following form:

```
?CHKSTK = 1
```

Once **?CHKSTK** is defined, stack checking is enabled for the entire file.

The default (when **?CHKSTK** is not defined) is no stack checking.

14.2 Cmacro Groups

This chapter lists and describes the Cmacros, a set of assembly-language macros that can be used with the Microsoft Macro Assembler (ML) to create assembly-language Windows applications. The Cmacros provide a simplified interface to the function and segment conventions of high-level languages such as C.

The Cmacros are divided into the following groups:

- Segment macros
- Storage-allocation macros
- Function macros
- Call macros
- Special-definition macros
- Error macros

The rest of this section briefly describes each group of macros.

14.2.1 Segment Macros

Segment macros give access to the code and data segments that an application will use. These segments have the names, attributes, classes, and groups required by Windows:

Macro name	Description
createSeg	Creates a new segment that has the specified name and segment attributes.
sBegin	Opens up a segment. This macro is similar to the **SEGMENT** assembler directive.
sEnd	Closes a segment. This macro is similar to the **ENDS** assembler directive.
assumes	Makes all references to data and code in the *segName* segment relative to the segment register given by *segReg*. This macro is similar to the **ASSUME** assembler directive.
dataOFFSET	Generates an offset relative to the start of the group to which the **DATA** segment belongs. This macro is similar to the **OFFSET** assembler operator but automatically provides the group name.
codeOFFSET	Generates an offset relative to the start of the group to which the **CODE** segment belongs. This macro is similar to the **OFFSET** assembler operator but automatically provides the group name.

Macro name	Description
*segName*OFFSET	Generates an offset relative to the start of the group to which the user-defined *segName* segment belongs. This macro is similar to the **OFFSET** assembler operator, but automatically provides the group name.

The Cmacros have two predefined segments, **CODE** and **DATA**, that any application can use without special definition.

14.2.2 Storage-Allocation Macros

Storage-allocation macros allocate static memory (either private or public), declare externally defined memory and procedures, and allow the definition of public labels:

Macro name	Description
static*X*	Allocates private static-memory storage.
global*X*	Allocates public static-memory storage.
extern*X*	Defines one or more names that will be the labels of external variables or functions.
label*X*	Defines one or more names that will be the labels of public (global) variables or functions.

14.2.3 Function Macros

Function macros define the names, attributes, parameters, and local variables of functions:

Macro name	Description
cProc	Defines the name and attributes of a function.
parm*X*	Defines one or more function parameters. The parameters provide access to the arguments passed to the function.
local*X*	Defines one or more frame variables for the specified function.
cBegin	Defines the actual entry point for the specified function.
cEnd	Defines the exit point for the specified function.

14.2.4 Call Macros

Call macros can be used to call **cProc** functions and high-level–language functions. These macros pass arguments according to the calling convention defined by the **?PLM** option:

Macro name	Description
cCall	Pushes the specified arguments onto the stack, saves registers (if any), and calls the specified function.
Save	Directs the next **cCall** macro to save the specified registers on the stack before calling a function and to restore the registers after the function returns.
Arg	Defines the arguments to be passed to a function by the next **cCall** macro.

14.2.5 Special-Definition Macros

Special-definition macros inform the Cmacros about user-defined variables, function-register use, and register pointers:

Macro name	Description
Def	Registers the name of a user-defined variable with the Cmacros.
FarPtr	Defines a 32-bit pointer value that can be passed as a single argument in a **cCall** macro.

14.2.6 Error Macros

Error macros generate an error message to the console and an error message in the listing. Both the text that caused the error and the result of its evaluation are displayed in the generated error message:

Macro name	Description
errnz	Evaluates a given expression. If the result is not zero, an error is displayed.
errn$	Subtracts the offset of the *label* parameter from the offset of the location counter and then adds the *bias* parameter to the result. If this result is not zero, an error message is displayed.

Error macros let you code assertions into an assembly-language source program. This enables you to code optimum instruction sequences for some operations based on the variable allocation or bit position of a flag in a word and assert that the assumptions made are true.

14.3 Using the Cmacros

This section explains the assembly-language statements generated by some of the Cmacros and illustrates their use with an example of a Cmacros function, **BITBLT**.

14.3.1 Overriding Types

Parameters and local variables created by using the **parm**X and **local**X macros actually correspond to expressions of the following form:

```
localB x        ==>        x equ byte ptr [bp+nn]
parmB y         ==>        y equ byte ptr [bp+nn]
```

In this example, the *nn* parameter specifies an offset from the current BP register value.

These expressions let you use the names without having to explicitly type in operators. This means that *x* can be referred to as follows:

```
mov     al,x
```

and that *y* can be referred to as follows:

```
mov     ax,y
```

A problem arises if the type must be overridden. The assembler creates an error message if it encounters the following line:

```
mov     ax,word ptr x
```

This can be solved by enclosing the name in parentheses:

```
mov     ax,word ptr (x)
```

One exception to this pattern is the **localV** macro. The expression generated by this macro does not have a type associated with it. It can, therefore, be overridden without the parentheses:

```
localV  horse,10   = = >        horse equ [bp+nn]
```

14.3.2 Symbol Redefinition

Any symbol defined by a **parm**X macro in one function can be redefined as a parameter in any other function. This allows different functions to refer to the same parameter by the same name, regardless of its location on the stack.

14.3.3 Sample Cmacros Function

The following example defines the **BITBLT** assembly function, which is a **FAR** and **PUBLIC** type function. When **BITBLT** is invoked, the SI and DI registers are automatically saved, and they are automatically restored upon exit. The BP register is always saved.

The **BITBLT** function is passed seven doubleword pointers on the stack. Space will be allocated on the stack for eight frame variables (one structure, five bytes, and two words).

The **cBegin** macro defines the start of the actual code. The *pExt* parameter is loaded, and some values are loaded into registers. The AX and BX registers are saved on execution of the subsequent **cCall** macro.

A C function, There, is called by the **cCall** macro. Four arguments are passed to There: *pDestBitmap*, the 32-bit pointer in the DS:SI registers, the value in the AX register, and the value in the BX register. The **cCall** macro places the arguments on the stack in the correct order.

When There returns, the arguments placed on the stack are automatically removed and the AX and BX registers are restored.

When the **cEnd** macro is reached, the frame variables are removed, any autosave registers are restored, and a return of the correct type (near or far) is performed.

The following example shows how the **BITBLT** function is defined:

```
cProc BITBLT,<FAR,PUBLIC>,<si,di>

    parmD   pDestBitmap     ; --> to dest bitmap descriptor
    parmD   pDestOrg        ; --> to dest origin (a point)
    parmD   pSrcBitmap      ; --> to source bitmap descriptor
    parmD   pSrcOrg         ; --> to source origin
    parmD   pExt            ; --> to rectangle extent
    parmD   pRop            ; --> to rasterop descriptor
    parmD   pBrush          ; --> to a physical brush

    localV  nOps,4          ; # of each operand used

    localB  phaseH          ; horizontal phase (rotate count)
    localB  PatRow          ; current row for patterns [0..7]
    localB  direction       ; increment/decrement flag

    localW  startMask       ; mask for first dest byte
    localW  lastMask        ; mask for last dest byte

    localB  firstFetch      ; number of first fetches needed
    localB  stepDirection   ; direction of move (left, right)
```

```
        cBegin

        lds     si,pExt
        mov     ax,extentX[si]
        mov     bx,extentY[si]

        RegPtr  dest,ds,si
        Save    <ax,bx>

        cCall   THERE,<pDestBitmap,dest,ax,bx>

        mov     extentX[si],cx
        mov     extentY[si],dx
                .
                .
                .

        cEnd
```

14.4 Alphabetic Reference

This section describes the Cmacros, a set of assembly-language macros that can be used with the Microsoft Macro Assembler (ML) to create assembly-language Windows applications. It lists the Cmacros in alphabetic order and describes each macro in detail.

Arg

Arg *namelist*

The **Arg** macro defines the arguments to be passed to a function by the next **cCall** macro. The arguments are pushed onto the stack in the order given. This order must correspond to the order of the function parameters.

More than one **Arg** macro can be given before each **cCall** macro. Multiple **Arg** macros have the same effect as a single macro.

Parameters

namelist

Specifies a list of argument names to be passed to the function. All names must be previously defined.

Comments	Byte-type parameters are passed as words. There is no sign extension or zeroing of the high-order byte.
	Immediate arguments arc not supported.
Examples	The following examples demonstrate the usage of the **Arg** macro:

```
Arg     var1
Arg     var2
Arg     var3
Arg     <var1,var2,var3>
```

Assumes

Assumes *segReg*, *segName*

The **assumes** macro makes all references to data and code in the predefined segment given by the *segName* parameter relative to the segment register given by the *segReg* parameter. This macro is similar to the **ASSUME** assembler directive.

Parameters	*segReg*
	Specifies the name of a segment register.
	segName
	Specifies the name of a predefined segment, **CODE** or **DATA**, or of a user-defined segment.
Examples	The following examples demonstrate the usage of the **assumes** macro:

```
assumes CS, CODE
assumes DS, CODE
```

cBegin

cBegin [*procName*]

The **cBegin** macro defines the actual entry point for the function given by the *procName* parameter. The macro creates code that sets up the frame and saves registers.

Parameters   *procName*
                      Specifies a function name. This parameter is optional; if the parameter is given, it must be the same as the name given in the **cProc** macro immediately preceding the **cBegin** macro.

cCall

cCall procName, [<*argList*>], [<*underscores*>]

The **cCall** macro pushes the arguments in the *argList* parameter onto the stack, saves registers (if any), and calls the function given by the *procName* parameter.

Parameters   *procName*
                      Specifies the name of the function to be called.

                      argList
                      Specifies a list of the names of arguments to be passed to the function. This parameter is optional; it is not required if the **Arg** macro is used before the **cCall** macro.

                      underscores
                      Specifies whether an underscore should be added to the beginning of the *procName* parameter. This parameter is optional; if this argument is blank and the calling convention is the C calling convention, an underscore is added.

Comments   The arguments of an **Arg** macro are pushed onto the stack before any arguments in the *argList* parameter of a **cCall** macro.

                      Byte-type parameters are passed as words. There is no sign extension or zeroing of the high-order byte.

                      Immediate arguments are not supported.

Examples   The following examples demonstrate the usage of the **cCall** macro:

```
cCall    there,<pExt,ax,bx,pResult>

Arg      pExt
Arg      ax
cCall    there,<bx,pResult>
```

cEnd

cEnd [*procName*]

The **cEnd** macro defines the exit point for the function given by the *procName* parameter. The macro creates code that discards the frame, restores registers, and returns to the caller.

Parameters

procName

Specifies a function name. This parameter is optional; if the parameter is given, it must be the same as the name given in the **cBegin** macro immediately preceding the **cEnd** macro.

Comments

Once a function has been defined using the **cProc** macro, any formal parameters should be declared with the **parmX** macro and any local variables with the **localX** macro. The **cBegin** and **cEnd** macros must be used to delineate the code for the function.

Examples

The following example demonstrates the usage of the **cEnd** macro:

```
cProc   strcpy,<PUBLIC>,<si,di>
    parmW   dst
    parmW   src
    localW  cnt

cBegin
    cld
    mov     si,src
    mov     di,dest
    push    ds
    pop     es
    xor     cx,cx
    mov     cnt,cx
loop:
    lodsb
    stosb
    inc     cnt
    cmp     al,0
    jnz     loop
    mov     ax,cnt
cEnd
```

codeOFFSET

codeOFFSET *arg*

The **codeOFFSET** macro generates an offset relative to the start of the group to which the **CODE** segment belongs. It is similar to the **OFFSET** assembler operator but automatically provides the group name. For this reason, it should be used instead of **OFFSET**.

Parameters

arg
Specifies a label name or offset value.

Examples

The following example demonstrates the usage of the **codeOFFSET** macro:

```
mov ax,codeOFFSET label
```

---

cProc

cProc *procName*, *<attributes>*, *<autoSave>*

The **cProc** macro defines the name and attributes of a function.

Parameters

procName
Specifies the name of the function.

attributes
Specifies the function type. This parameter can be a combination of the following types:

Type	Description
NEAR	Near function. It can be called only from the segment in which it is defined.
FAR	Far function. It can be called from any segment.
PUBLIC	Public function. It can be externally declared in other source files.

The default attribute is **NEAR** and private (that is, the function cannot be declared externally in other source files). The **NEAR** and **FAR** attributes cannot be used together. If more than one attribute is selected, angle brackets are required.

autoSave
Specifies a list of registers to be saved when the function is invoked and restored when exited. Any 8086 register can be specified.

Comments   If this function is called by a function written in C, it must save and restore the SI and DI registers.

The BP register is always saved, regardless of whether it is present in the list given by the *autoSave* parameter.

Examples   The following examples demonstrate the usage of the **cProc** macro:

```
cProc proc1, <FAR, ds,es>
cProc proc2, <NEAR,PUBLIC>
cProc proc3,,ds
```

createSeg

createSeg *segName*, *logName*, *align*, *combine*, *class*

The **createSeg** macro creates a new segment that has the specified name and segment attributes. The macro automatically creates an **assumes** macro and an **OFFSET** macro for the new segment. This macro is intended to be used in medium-model Windows applications to define nonresident segments.

Parameters   *segName*
Specifies the actual name of the segment. This name is passed to the linker.

logName
Specifies the logical name of the segment. This name is used in all subsequent **sBegin**, **sEnd**, and **assumes** macros that refer to the segment.

align
Specifies the alignment type. This parameter can be one of the following types: **BYTE**, **WORD**, **PARA**, and **PAGE**.

combine
Specifies the combine type for the segment. This parameter can be one of the following types: **COMMON**, **MEMORY**, **PUBLIC**, and **STACK**.

If no combine type is given, a private segment is assumed.

class
Specifies the class name of the segment. The class name defines the segments that must be loaded in consecutive memory.

Comments   The Cmacros have two predefined segments, **CODE** and **DATA**, that any application can use without special definition. Medium-, large-, and huge-model applications can define additional segments by using the **createSeg** macro.

Examples   The following example demonstrates the usage of the **createSeg** macro:

```
createSeg    _INIT,INITCODE,BYTE,PUBLIC,CODE

sBegin  INITCODE
assumes CS:INITCODE

        mov ax,initcodeOFFSET  sample

sEnd    INITCODE
```

dataOFFSET

dataOFFSET *arg*

The **dataOFFSET** macro generates an offset relative to the start of the group to which the **DATA** segment belongs. It is similar to the **OFFSET** assembler operator but automatically provides the group name. For this reason, it should be used instead of **OFFSET**.

Parameters   *arg*
    Specifies a label name or offset value.

Examples   The following example demonstrates the usage of the **dataOFFSET** macro:

```
mv ax,dataOFFSET label
```

Def*X*

Def*X* <*namelist*>

The **Def***X* macro registers the name of a user-defined variable with the Cmacros. Variables that are not defined using the **static***X*, **global***X*, **extern***X*, **parm***X*, or **local***X* macros cannot be referred to in other macros, unless the name is registered or the variable was defined with the **DW** assembler directive.

Parameters   *X*
Specifies the storage size of the variable. This parameter can be one of the following types:

Type	Description
B	Byte
W	Word
D	Doubleword
Q	Quadruple word
T	10-byte word
CP	Code pointer (one word for small and compact models)
DP	Data pointer (one word for small and medium models)

namelist
Specifies a list of variable names to be defined.

Examples   The following example demonstrates the usage of the **Def*X*** macro:

```
maxSize db      132
        DefB    maxSize
dest equ  wordptr es:[di]
    DefW <dest>
```

errn$

errn$ *label*, [*bias*]

The **errn$** macro subtracts the offset of the *label* parameter from the offset of the location counter and then adds the *bias* parameter to the result. If this result is not zero, an error message is displayed.

Parameters   *label*
Specifies a label corresponding to a memory location.

bias
Specifies a signed bias value. A plus or minus sign is required. This parameter is optional.

Examples   The following example demonstrates the usage of the **errn$** macro:

```
;   end of previous code
    errn$   function1
function1:
```

If a function that was originally located immediately after another piece of code is ever moved, the **errn$** macro displays an error message.

errnz

errnz <*expression*>

The **errnz** macro evaluates a given expression. If the result is not zero, an error is displayed.

Parameters

expression
Specifies the expression to be evaluated. Angle brackets are required if there are any spaces in the expression.

Examples

The following examples demonstrate the usage of the **errnz** macro:

```
x       db      ?
y       db      ?

mov     ax, word ptr x
errnz   <(OFFSET y) - (OFFSET x) -1>
```

If during assembly, *x* and *y* receive anything but sequential storage locations, the **errnz** macro displays an error message.

```
table1   struc
    .
    .
    .
table1len equ  $-table1
table1   ends

table2   struc
    .
    .
    .
table2len equ  $-table2
table2   ends

errnz   table1Len-table2Len
```

If during assembly the length of two tables is not the same, the **errnz** macro displays an error message.

extern*X*

extern*X* *<namelist>*

The **extern*X*** macro defines one or more names that will be the labels of external variables or functions.

Parameters

X

Specifies the storage size or function type. This parameter can be one of the following types:

Type	Description
A	Constant value declared with the **EQU** and = directives in a separate file
B	Byte
W	Word
D	Doubleword
Q	Quadruple word
T	10 bytes
CP	Code pointer (one word for small and compact models)
DP	Data pointer (one word for small and medium models)
NP	Near-function pointer
FP	Far-function pointer
P	Near for small and compact models; far for other models

namelist

Specifies the list of the names of the variables or functions.

Examples

The following examples demonstrate the usage of the **extern*X*** macro:

```
externB <DataBase>
externFP <SampleRead>
```

FarPtr

FarPtr *name,* *segment,* *offset*

>The **FarPtr** macro defines a 32-bit pointer value that can be passed as a single argument in a **cCall** macro. In the **FarPtr** macro, the *segment* and *offset* values do not have to be in registers.

Parameters

>*name*
>>Specifies the name of the pointer to be created.
>
>*segment*
>>Specifies the text that defines the segment portion of the pointer.
>
>*offset*
>>Specifies the text that defines the offset portion of the pointer.

Examples

>The following example demonstrates the usage of the **FarPtr** macro:

```
FarPtr  destPtr,es,<wordptr 3[si]>
cCall   proc,<destPtr,ax>
```

---

globalX

global *X name,* [*initialValue*] [*replication*]

>The **globalX** macro allocates public static-memory storage.

Parameters

>*X*
>>Specifies the size of the storage to be allocated. This parameter can be one of the following types:

Type	Description
B	Byte
W	Word
D	Doubleword
Q	Quadruple word
T	10 bytes
CP	Code pointer (one word for small and compact models)
DP	Data pointer (one word for small and medium models)

name
Specifies the reference name of the allocated memory.

initialValue
Specifies an initial value for the storage. This parameter is optional; the default is zero if no value is specified.

replication
Specifies a count of the number of times the allocation is to be duplicated. This parameter, which is optional, generates the **DUP** assembler operator.

Examples   The following example demonstrates the usage of the **global*X*** macro:

```
globalW  flag,1
globalB  string,0, 30
```

label*X*

label*X* <*namelist*>

The **label*X*** macro defines one or more names that will be the labels of public (global) variables or functions.

Parameters   *X*
Specifies the storage size or function type. This parameter can be one of the following types:

Type	Description
B	Byte
W	Word
D	Doubleword
Q	Quadruple word
T	10 bytes
CP	Code pointer (one word for small and compact models)
DP	Data pointer (one word for small and medium models)
NP	Near-function pointer
FP	Far-function pointer
P	Near for small and compact models; far for other models

namelist
Specifies the list of the names of the external variables or functions.

Examples

The following examples demonstrate the usage of the **label***X* macro:

```
labelB <DataBase>
labelFP <SampleRead>
```

local*X*

local*X* *<namelist>*, *size*

The **local***X* macro defines one or more frame variables for the function. To keep the words in the stack aligned, the macro ensures that the total space allocated is an even number of bytes.

Parameters

X

Specifies the storage size. This parameter can be one of the following types:

Type	Description
B	Byte (allocates a single byte of storage on the stack)
W	Word (allocated on a word boundary)
D	Doubleword (allocated on a word boundary)
V	Variable size (allocated on a word boundary)
Q	Quadruple word (aligned on a word boundary)
T	10-byte word (aligned on a word boundary)
CP	Code pointer (one word for small and compact models)
DP	Data pointer (one word for small and medium models)

namelist

Specifies the list of the names of the frame variables for the function.

size

Specifies the size of the variable. It is used with the **local V** macro only.

Comments

B-type variables are not necessarily aligned on word boundaries.

The **localD** macro creates two additional symbols, **OFF_***name* and **SEG_***name*. **OFF_***name* is the offset portion of the parameter and **SEG_***name* is the segment portion.

Only the name is required when referencing a variable. Write your code in the following manner:

```
mov     al,var1
```

It should not be written like this:

```
mov     al,byte ptr var1[bp]
```

Examples

The following examples demonstrate the usage of the **local*X*** macro:

```
localB <L1,L2,L3>
localW L4
localD <L5>
localV L6,%(size struc)
```

parm*X*

parm*X* <*namelist*>

The **parm*X*** macro defines one or more function parameters. The parameters provide access to the arguments passed to the function and must appear in the same order as the arguments in the function call.

Parameters

X
Specifies the storage size. This parameter can be one of the following types:

Type	Description
B	Byte (allocated on a word boundary on the stack)
W	Word (allocated on a word boundary)
D	Doubleword (allocated on a word boundary)
Q	Quadruple word (aligned on a word boundary)
T	10-byte word (aligned on a word boundary)
CP	Code pointer (one word for small and compact models)
DP	Data pointer (one word for small and medium models)

namelist
Specifies the list of the parameter names.

Comments   The **parmD** macro creates two additional symbols, **OFF**_*name* and **SEG**_*name*. **OFF**_*name* is the offset portion of the parameter and **SEG**_*name* is the segment portion.

Only the parameter name is required when referring to the corresponding argument. Write your code in the following manner:

```
mov     al,var1
```

It should not be written like this:

```
mov     al,byte ptr var1[bp]
```

Examples   The following examples demonstrate the usage of the **parm***X* macro:

```
parmW var1
parmB <var2,var3,var4>
parmD <var5>
```

Save

Save <*regList*>

The **Save** macro directs the next **cCall** macro to save the specified registers on the stack before calling a function and to restore the registers after the function returns. The macro can be used to save registers that are destroyed by the called function.

The **Save** macro applies to only one **cCall** macro; each new **cCall** must have a corresponding **Save**. If two **Save** macros appear before a **cCall** macro, only the second macro is recognized.

Parameters   *regList*
     Specifies a list of registers to be saved.

Examples   The following examples demonstrate the usage of the **Save** macro:

```
Save    <cl,bh,si>
Save    <ax>
```

sBegin

sBegin *segName*

> The **sBegin** macro opens up a segment. This macro is similar to the **SEGMENT** assembler directive.

Parameters
> *segName*
> Specifies the name of the segment to be opened. It can be one of the predefined segments, **CODE** or **DATA**, or the name of a user-defined segment.

Examples
> The following examples demonstrate the usage of the **sBegin** macro:

```
sBegin Data
sBegin Code
```

---

*segName*OFFSET

*segName***OFFSET** *arg*

> The *segName***OFFSET** macro generates an offset relative to the start of the group to which the user-defined segment *segName* belongs. It is similar to the **OFFSET** assembler operator but automatically provides the group name. For this reason, it should be used instead of **OFFSET**.

Parameters
> *arg*
> Specifies a label name or offset value.

Examples
> The following example demonstrates the usage of the *segName***OFFSET** macro:

```
mv ax,initcodeOFFSET label
```

sEnd

sEnd [*segName*]

The **sEnd** macro closes a segment. This macro is similar to the **ENDS** assembler directive.

Parameters   *segName*
Specifies a name used for readability. This parameter is optional; if it is given, it must be the same as the name given in the matching **sBegin** macro.

Examples   The following examples demonstrate the usage of the **sEnd** macro:

```
sEnd
sEnd data
```

staticX

staticX *name*, [*initialValue*], [*replication*]

The **staticX** macro allocates private static-memory storage.

Parameters   *X*
Specifies the size of storage to be allocated. This parameter can be one of the following types:

Type	Description
B	Byte
W	Word
D	Doubleword
Q	Quadruple word
T	10 bytes
CP	Code pointer (one word for small and compact models)
DP	Data pointer (one word for small and medium models)

name
Specifies the reference name of the allocated memory.

initialValue
> Specifies an initial value for the storage. This parameter is optional; if no value is specified, the default is zero.

replication
> Specifies a count of the number of times the allocation is to be duplicated. This parameter, which is optional, generates the **DUP** assembler operator.

Examples   The following examples demonstrate the usage of the **static*X*** macro:

```
staticW  flag,1
staticB  string, , 30
```

Windows Help Statements and Macros

This chapter describes the syntax and purpose of statements and macros used in topic and project files for the Microsoft Windows Help application. The Windows Help statements define the format and placement of text and graphics in the Help file. The Windows Help macros define actions to take while the Help file is being viewed, such as creating custom buttons and carrying out menu commands. For more information about using statements and macros to create Help files, see *Microsoft Windows Programming Tools*.

15.1 Help Statement Syntax

Windows Help statements are an extended subset of tokens defined by the rich-text-format (RTF) standard. The statements specify character and paragraph properties, such as font, color, spacing and alignment, for text in the Help file.

The Help statements are presented to the Microsoft Help Compiler in topic files, which are specified in the [FILES] section of a project file. A topic file consists of statements, groups, and unformatted text. Each statement consists of a backslash (\) followed by a statement name. For example, the following line demonstrates usage of the **\tab** statement:

```
left column\tab right column
```

Statements must be separated from subsequent text or statement parameters by a delimiter. A delimiter can be one of the following:

- A space.
- A digit or minus sign, which indicates that a numeric parameter follows. The subsequent digit sequence is then delimited by a space or character other than a letter or digit.
- Any character other than a letter or digit.

When a space is used as a delimiter, the Microsoft Help Compiler discards it. If any other character is used, the compiler processes it as text or the start of another statement. For example, if a backslash is used as a delimiter, the compiler interprets it as the beginning of the next statement.

A group consists of Help statements and text enclosed in braces ({ }). Formatting specified within a group affects only the text within that group. Text within a group inherits any formatting of the text preceding the group.

Unformatted text consists of any combination of 7-bit ASCII characters. Although characters whose values are greater than 127 are not permitted in topic files, the \' statement can be used to insert them in the final Help file. The Microsoft Help Compiler treats spaces as part of the text, but it discards carriage return and linefeed characters.

Although the Microsoft Help Compiler supports many RTF tokens, it does not support them all. The compiler ignores any RTF statement that is not explicitly defined in this chapter. Furthermore, the compiler may interpret an RTF token differently than it is specified by the standard. For example, the standard specifies that the **\uldb** statement indicates a double underline, but the Microsoft Help Compiler uses this statement to indicate a hot spot.

15.2 Help Macro Syntax

Windows Help macros specify actions that Windows Help takes when it loads Help or displays a topic. (Help macros can also be executed when the user selects a hot spot or clicks on a designated segmented graphic.) A Help macro consists of a macro name and parameters enclosed in parentheses.

Macro names specify the action to take, such as creating buttons or inserting menu items. The names are not sensitive to case, so any combination of uppercase and lowercase letters may be used.

Macro parameters specify the files, buttons, menus, or topics on which to carry out the action. The parameters must be enclosed in parentheses and separated by spaces. Parameters in many macros must also be enclosed in quotation marks. This is especially true if the parameter contains space characters. The valid quotation characters are the matching double quotation marks (" ") and the opening and closing single quotation marks (' '). If a quotation character is needed as part of a parameter, the parameter should be enclosed in single quotation marks. When using single quotation marks in this manner, you can omit the backslash escape character for the double quotation marks, as shown in the following example:

```
`command "string as parameter"'
```

Macros can be used as parameters in other macros. In most cases, embedded macros must be enclosed in quotation marks. If the embedded macro also has quoted parameters, the quotation character that is used must be different than the quotation characters enclosing the macro. The following example shows the correct way to use nested quotation marks:

```
CreateButton("time_btn", "&Time", "ExecProgram(`clock', 0)")
```

A Help macro and all of its parameters must not exceed 512 characters.

Help macros can be combined into macro strings by separating the macros with semicolons (;). The Microsoft Help Compiler processes the macro string as a unit and executes the individual macros sequentially.

15.3 Help Statement Reference

This section lists the Windows Help statements in alphabetic order.

\ansi

\ansi

The **\ansi** statement sets the American National Standards Institute (ANSI) character set. The Windows character set is essentially equivalent to the ANSI character set.

See Also   **\windows**

\b

\b

The **\b** statement starts bold text. The statement applies to all subsequent text up to the next **\plain** or **\b0** statement.

Comments   No **\plain** or **\b0** statement is required if the **\b** statement and subsequent text are enclosed in braces. Braces limit the scope of a character property statement to just the enclosed text.

The **\b0** statement was first supported in the Microsoft Help Compiler version 3.1.

Examples   The following example sets "Note" to bold:

```
{\b Note}  Setting the Auto option frees novice users from
determining their system configurations.
```

See Also   **\i, \plain, \scaps**

\bin

\bin*n*

The **\bin** statement indicates the start of binary picture data. The Help compiler interprets subsequent bytes in the file as binary data. This statement is used in conjunction with the **\pict** statement.

Parameters   *n*

Specifies the number of bytes of binary data following the statement.

Comments   A single space character must separate the **\bin** statement from subsequent bytes. The Microsoft Help Compiler assumes that all subsequent bytes, including linefeed and carriage return characters, are binary data. These bytes can have any value in the range 0 through 255. For this reason, the **\bin** statement is typically used in program-generated files only.

If the **\bin** statement is not given with a **\pict** statement, the default picture data format is hexadecimal.

See Also   **\pict**

---

bmc

\{bmc *filename***\}**

The **bmc** statement displays a specified bitmap or metafile in the current line of text. The statement positions the bitmap or metafile as if it were the next character in the line, aligning it on the base line and applying the current paragraph properties.

Parameters   *filename*

Specifies the name of a file containing either a Windows bitmap, a placeable Windows metafile, a multiresolution bitmap, or a segmented-graphics bitmap.

Comments   Since the **bmc** statement is not a standard RTF statement, the Microsoft Help Compiler relies on the opening and closing braces, including the backslashes (\), to distinguish the statement from regular text.

If a file containing a metafile is specified, the file must contain a placeable Windows metafile; the Microsoft Help Compiler will not accept standard Windows metafiles. Furthermore, Windows Help sets the MM_ANISOTROPIC mode prior to displaying the metafile, so the placeable Windows metafile must either set the window origin and extents or set some other mapping mode.

Examples

The following example inserts a bitmap representing a keyboard key in a paragraph:

```
\par
Press the \{bmc escape.bmp\} key to return to the main window.
\par
```

See Also

bmr, bml, \wbitmap

bml

\{**bml** *filename*\}

The **bml** statement displays a specified bitmap or metafile at the left margin of the Help window. The first line of subsequent text aligns with the upper-right corner of the image and subsequent lines wrap along the right edge of the image.

Parameters

filename
    Specifies the name of a file containing either a Windows bitmap, a placeable Windows metafile, a multiresolution bitmap, or a segmented-graphics bitmap.

Comments

Since the **bml** statement is not a standard RTF statement, the Microsoft Help Compiler relies on the opening and closing braces, including the backslashes (\), to distinguish the statement from regular text.

If a file containing a metafile is specified, the file must contain a placeable Windows metafile; the Microsoft Help Compiler will not accept standard Windows metafiles. Furthermore, Windows Help sets the MM_ANISOTROPIC mode prior to displaying the metafile, so the placeable Windows metafile must either set the window origin and extents or set some other mapping mode.

Examples

The following example places a bitmap at the left margin. The subsequent paragraph wraps around the bitmap:

```
\par
\{bml roadmap.bmp\}
The map at the left shows the easiest route to the school.
Although many people use Highway 125, there are fewer stops
and less traffic if you use Ames Road.
```

See Also   bmc, bmr, \wbitmap

---

bmr

\{**bmr** *filename*\}

The **bmr** statement displays a specified bitmap or metafile at the right margin of the Help window. The first line of subsequent text aligns with the upper-left corner of the image and subsequent lines wrap along the left edge of the image.

Parameters   *filename*
   Specifies the name of a file containing either a Windows bitmap, a placeable Windows metafile, a multiresolution bitmap, or a segmented-graphics bitmap.

Comments   Since the **bmr** statement is not a standard RTF statement, the Microsoft Help Compiler relies on the opening and closing braces, including the backslashes (\), to distinguish the statement from regular text.

If a file containing a metafile is specified, the file must contain a placeable Windows metafile; the Help compiler will not accept standard Windows metafiles. Furthermore, Windows Help sets the MM_ANISOTROPIC mode prior to displaying the metafile, so the placeable Windows metafile must either set the window origin and extents or set some other mapping mode.

Examples   The following example places a bitmap at the right margin. The subsequent paragraph wraps around the bitmap:

```
\par
\{bmr roadmap.bmp\}
The map at the right shows the easiest route to the school.
Although many people use Highway 125, there are fewer stops
and less traffic if you use Ames Road.
```

See Also   bmc, bml, \wbitmap

\box

\box

The **\box** statement draws a box around the current paragraph or picture. The statement applies to all subsequent paragraphs or pictures up to the next **\pard** statement.

Comments

For paragraphs, Windows Help uses the height of the paragraph, excluding space before or after the paragraph, as the height of the box. For pictures (as defined by **\pict** statements), Windows Help uses the specified height of the picture as the height of the box. For both paragraphs and pictures, the width of the box is equal to the space between the left and right indents.

Windows Help draws the box using the current border style.

Examples

The following example draws a box around the paragraph:

```
\par \box
{\b Note}  Setting the Auto option frees novice users from
determining their system configurations.
\par \pard
```

See Also

\brdrb, \brdrl, \brdrr, \brdrt, \pard

\brdrb

\brdrb

The **\brdrb** statement draws a border below the current paragraph or picture. The statement applies to all subsequent paragraphs or pictures up to the next **\pard** statement.

Comments

Windows Help draws the border using the current border style.

See Also

\box, \brdrbar, \brdrl, \brdrr, \brdrt, \pard

\brdrbar

\brdrbar

The **\brdrbar** statement draws a vertical bar to the left of the current paragraph or picture. The statement applies to all subsequent paragraphs or pictures up to the next **\pard** statement.

Comments

Windows Help draws the border using the current border style.

In a print-based document, the **\brdrbar** statement draws the bar on the right side of paragraphs on odd-numbered pages, but on the left side of paragraphs on even-numbered pages.

See Also

\box, \brdrl, \brdrb, \brdrr, \brdrt, \pard

\brdrdb

\brdrdb

The **\brdrdb** statement selects a double line for drawing borders. The selection applies to all subsequent paragraphs or pictures up to the next **\pard** statement.

See Also

\brdrdot, \brdrs, \brdrsh, \brdrth, \pard

\brdrdot

\brdrdot

The **\brdrdot** statement selects a dotted line for drawing borders. The selection applies to all subsequent paragraphs or pictures up to the next **\pard** statement.

See Also

\brdrs, \brdrth, \brdrsh, \brdrdb, \pard

\brdrl

\brdrl

The **\brdrl** statement draws a border to the left of the current paragraph or picture. The statement applies to all subsequent paragraphs or pictures up to the next **\pard** statement.

Comments   Windows Help draws the border using the current border style.

See Also   **\box, \brdrb, \brdrbar, \brdrr, \brdrt, \pard**

\brdrr

\brdrr

The **\brdrr** statement draws a border to the right of the current paragraph or picture. The statement applies to all subsequent paragraphs or pictures up to the next **\pard** statement.

Comments   Windows Help draws the border using the current border style.

See Also   **\box, \brdrb, \brdrbar, \brdrl, \brdrt, \pard**

\brdrs

\brdrs

The **\brdrs** statement selects a standard-width line for drawing borders. The selection applies to all subsequent paragraphs or pictures up to the next **\pard** statement.

See Also   **\brdrdb, \brdrdot, \brdrsh, \brdrth, \pard**

\brdrsh

\brdrsh

The **\brdrsh** statement selects a shadow outline for drawing borders. The selection applies to all subsequent paragraphs or pictures up to the next **\pard** statement.

See Also   \bdrddb, \brdrdot, \brdrs, \brdrth, \pard

\brdrt

\brdrt

The **\brdrt** statement draws a border above the current paragraph or picture. The statement applies to all subsequent paragraphs or pictures up to the next **\pard** statement.

Comments   Windows Help draws the border using the current border style.

See Also   \box, \brdrb, \brdrbar, \brdrl, \brdrr, \pard

\brdrth

\brdrth

The **\brdrth** statement selects a thick line for drawing borders. The selection applies to all subsequent paragraphs or pictures up to the next **\pard** statement.

See Also   \brdrdb, \brdrdot, \brdrs, \brdrsh, \pard

\cell

\cell

The **\cell** statement marks the end of a cell in a table. A cell consists of all paragraphs from a preceding **\intbl** or **\cell** statement to the ending **\cell** statement. Windows Help formats and displays these paragraphs using the left and right margins of the cell and any current paragraph properties.

Comments

This statement was first supported in the Microsoft Help Compiler version 3.1.

Examples

The following example creates a two-column table. The second column contains three separate paragraphs, each having different paragraph properties:

```
\cellx2880\cellx5760
\intbl
Alignment\cell
\ql
Left-aligned
\par
\qc
Centered
\par
\qr
Right-aligned\cell
\row \pard
```

See Also

\cellx, \intbl, \row, \trgaph, \trleft, \trowd

\cellx

\cellx*n*

The **\cellx** statement sets the absolute position of the right edge of a table cell. One **\cellx** statement must be given for each cell in the table. The first **\cellx** statement applies to the left-most cell, the last to the right-most cell. For each **\cellx** statement, the specified position applies to the corresponding cell in each subsequent row of the table up to the next **\trowd** statement.

Parameters

n

Specifies the position of the cell's right edge, in twips. The position is relative to the left edge of the Help window. It is not affected by the current indents.

Comments   A table consists of a grid of cells in columns and rows. Each cell has an explicitly defined right edge; the position of a cell's left edge is the same as the position of the right edge of the adjacent cell. For the left-most cell in a row, the left edge position is equal to the Help window's left margin position. Each cell has a left and right margin between which Windows Help aligns and wraps text. By default, the margin positions are equal to the left and right edges. The **\trgaph** and **\trleft** statements can be used to set different margins for all cells in a row.

This statement was first supported in the Microsoft Help Compiler version 3.1.

Examples   The following example creates a three-column table having two rows. The positions of the right edges of the three cells are 2, 4, and 6 inches, respectively:

```
\cellx2880\cellx5760\cellx8640
\intbl
Row 1 Cell 1\cell
Row 1 Cell 2\cell
Row 1 Cell 3\cell
\row
\intbl
Row 2 Cell 1\cell
Row 2 Cell 2\cell
Row 2 Cell 3\cell
\row \pard
```

See Also   **\cell, \intbl, \row, \trgaph, \trleft, \trowd**

\cf

\cf*n*

The **\cf** statement sets the foreground color. The new color applies to all subsequent text up to the next **\plain** or **\cf** statement.

Parameters   *n*
Specifies the color number to set as foreground. The number must be an integer number in the range 1 to the maximum number of colors specified in the color table for the Help file. If an invalid color number is specified, Windows Help uses the default foreground color.

Comments   No **\plain** or **\cf** statement is required if the **\cf** statement and subsequent text are enclosed in braces. Braces limit the scope of a character property statement to the enclosed text only.

If the **\cf** statement is not given, the default foreground color is the text color set by Control Panel.

Examples   The following example displays green text:

```
{\colortbl;\red0\green255\blue0;}
{\cf1 This text is green.}
```

See Also   **\cb, \colortbl**

\chftn

\chftn*n*

The **chftn** statement sets the footnote reference character for subsequent **\footnote** statements.

The Microsoft Help Compiler ignores this statement.

Parameters   *n*
  Specifies the footnote reference character.

See Also   **\footnote**

\clmgf

\clmgf

The **\clmgf** statement specifies the first cell in a range of cells to be merged.

The Microsoft Help Compiler ignores this statement.

Comments   All cells between the **\clmgf** statement and a subsequent **\clmrg** statement are combined into a single cell. The left edge of the new cell is the same as that of the leftmost cell to be merged; the right-edge is the same as that of the rightmost cell.

This statement was first supported in the Microsoft Help Compiler version 3.1.

See Also   **\clmrg**

\clmrg

\clmrg

The **\clmrg** statement merges the current cell with the preceding cell.

The Microsoft Help Compiler ignores this statement.

Comments   All cells between the **\clmgf** statement and a subsequent **\clmrg** statement are combined into a single cell. The left edge of the new cell is the same as that of the leftmost cell to be merged; the right-edge is the same as that of the rightmost cell.

This statement was first supported in the Microsoft Help Compiler version 3.1.

See Also   **\clmgf**

\colortbl

{\colortbl
\red$r$\green$g$\blue$b$;

  .

  .

  .

}

The **\colortbl** statement creates a color table for the Help file. The color table consists of one or more color definitions. Each color definition consists of one **\red**, **\green**, and **\blue** statement specifying the amount of primary color to use to generate the final color. Each color definition must end with a semicolon (;).

Parameters r

Specifies the intensity of red in the color. It must be an integer in the range 0 through 255.

g

Specifies the intensity of green in the color. It must be an integer in the range 0 through 255.

b

Specifies the intensity of blue in the color. It must be an integer in the range 0 through 255.

Comments   Color definitions are implicitly numbered starting at zero. A color definition's implicit number can be used in the **\cf** statement to set the foreground color.

The default colors are the window-text and window-background colors set by Control Panel. To override the default colors, both a **\colortbl** statement and a **\cf** statement must be given.

Examples   The following example creates a color table containing two color definitions. The first color definition is empty (only the semicolon is given), so color number 0 always represents the default color. The second definition specifies green; color number 1 can be used to display green text:

```
{\colortbl;\red0\green255\blue0;}
```

See Also   **\cf**

\deff

\deffn

The **\deff** statement sets the default font number. Windows Help uses the number to set the default font whenever a **\plain** statement is given or an invalid font number is given in a **\f** statement.

Parameters   n
Specifies the number of the font to be used as the default font. This parameter must be a valid font number as specified by the **\fonttbl** statement for the Help file.

Comments   If the **\deff** statement is not given, the default font number is zero.

See Also   **\f**, **\fonttbl**, **\plain**

\f

\fn

The **\f** statement sets the font. The new font applies to all subsequent text up to the next **\plain** or **\f** statement.

Parameters   *n*

Specifies the font number. This parameter must be one of the integer font numbers defined in the font table for the Help file.

Comments   The **\f** statement does not set the point size of the font; use the **\fs** statement instead.

No **\plain** or **\f** statement is required if the **\f** statement and subsequent text are enclosed in braces. Braces limit the scope of a character property statement to just the enclosed text.

If the **\f** statement is not given, the default font is defined by the **\deff** statement (or is zero if no **\deff** statement is given).

Examples   The following example uses the Arial font to display text:

```
{\fonttbl {\f0\fswiss Arial;}}
\par
{\f0
This text illustrates the Arial font.}
\par
```

See Also   **\deff, \fonttbl, \fs, \plain**

\fi

\fin

The **\fi** statement sets the first-line indent for the paragraph. The new indent applies to the first line of each subsequent paragraph up to the next **\pard** statement or **\fi** statement. The first-line indent is always relative to the current left indent.

Parameters   *n*

Specifies the indent, in twips. This parameter can be either a positive or negative number.

Comments	If the **\fi** statement is not given, the first-line indent is zero by default.
Examples	The following example uses the first-line indent and a tab stop to make a numbered list:

```
\tx360\li360\fi-360
1
\tab
Insert the disk in drive A.
\par
2
\tab
Type a:setup and press the ENTER key.
\par
3
\tab
Follow the instructions on the screen.
\par \pard
```

See Also	**\li, \pard**

\field

\field

The **\field** statement defines a field.

Comments	The Microsoft Help Compiler ignores this statement and all related field statements except the **\fldrslt** statement.
See Also	**\fldrslt**

\fldrslt

\fldrslt

The **\fldrslt** statement specifies the most recently calculated result of a field. The Microsoft Help Compiler interprets the result as text and formats it using the current character and paragraph properties.

Comments	The Help compiler ignores all field statements except the **\fldrslt** statement. Any text associated with other field statements is ignored.
See Also	**\field**

\fonttbl

\fonttbl {
\f_n_****_family font-name_**;**

   .
   .
   .

}

The **\fonttbl** statement creates a font table for the Help file. The font table consists of one or more font definitions. Each definition consists of a font number, a font family, and a font name.

Parameters

_n_

Specifies the font number. This parameter must be an integer. This number can be used in subsequent **\f** statements to set the current font to the specified font. In the font table, font numbers should start at zero and increase by one for each new font definition.

family

Specifies the font family. This parameter must be one of the following:

Value	Meaning
fnil	Unknown or default fonts (default)
froman	Roman, proportionally spaced serif fonts (for example, MS Serif and Palatino®)
fswiss	Swiss, proportionally spaced sans serif fonts (for example, Swiss)
fmodern	Fixed-pitch serif and sans serif fonts (for example, Courier, Elite, and Pica)
fscript	Script fonts (for example, Cursive)
fdecor	Decorative fonts (for example, Old English and ITC Zapf Chancery®)
ftech	Technical, symbol, and mathematical fonts (for example, Symbol®)

font-name
> Specifies the name of the font. This parameter should specify an available Windows font.

Comments   If a font with the specified name is not available, Windows Help chooses a font from the specified family. If no font from the given family exists, Windows Help chooses a font having the same character set as specified for the Help file.

The **\deff** statement sets the default font number for the Help file. The default font is set whenever the **\pard** statement is given.

See Also   **\deff, \f, \fs, \pard**

\footnote

n{**\footnote** *text*}

The **\footnote** statement defines topic-specific information, such as the topic's build tags, context string, title, browse number, keywords, and execution macros. Every topic must, at least, have a context string to give the user access to the topic through links.

Parameters   *n*
> Specifies the footnote character. It can be one of the following:

Value	Meaning
*	Specifies a build tag. The Microsoft Help Compiler uses build tags to determine whether it should include the topic in the Help file. The *text* parameter can be any combination of characters but must not contain spaces. Uppercase and lowercase characters are treated as equivalent characters (case-insensitive). If a topic has build-tag statements, they must be the first statements in the topic. The Microsoft Help Compiler checks a topic for build tags if the project file specifies a build expression using the **BUILD** option.
#	Specifies a context string. The *text* parameter can be any combination of letters and digits but must not contain spaces. Uppercase and lowercase characters are treated as equivalent characters (case-insensitive). The context string can be used with the **\v** statement in other topics to create links to this topic.

Value	Meaning
$	Specifies a topic title. Windows Help uses the topic title to identify the topic in the Search and History dialog boxes. The *text* parameter can be any combination of characters including spaces.
+	Specifies the browse-sequence identifier. Windows Help adds topics having an identifier to the browse sequence and allows users to view the topics by using the browse buttons. The *text* parameter can be a combination of letters and digits. Windows Help determines the order of topics in the browse sequence by sorting the identifier alphabetically. If two topics have the same identifier, Windows Help assumes that the topic that was compiled first is to be displayed first. Windows Help uses the browse sequence identifier only if the browse buttons have been enabled by using the **BrowseButtons** macro.
K	Specifies a keyword. Windows Help displays all keywords in the Help file in the Search dialog box and allows a user to choose a topic to view by choosing a keyword. The *text* parameter can be any combination of characters including spaces. If the first character is the letter *K*, it must be preceded with an extra space or a semicolon. More than one keyword can be given by separating the keywords with semicolons (;). A topic cannot contain keywords unless it also has a topic title.
!	Specifies a Help macro. Windows Help executes the macro when the topic is displayed. The *text* parameter can be any Help macro.

If *n* is any letter (other than *K*), the footnote specifies an alternative keyword. Windows applications can search for topics having alternative keywords by using the HELP_MULTIKEY command with the **WinHelp** function.

text
Specifies the build tag, context string, topic title, browse-sequence number, keyword, or macro associated with the footnote. This parameter depends on the footnote type as specified by the *n* parameter.

Comments
A topic can have more than one build-tag, context-string, keyword, and help-macro statement, but must not have more than one topic-title or browse-sequence-number statement.

In print-based documents, the **\footnote** statement creates a footnote and the footnote is anchored to the character immediately preceding the **\footnote** statement.

Examples   The following example defines a topic titled "Short Topic". The context string "topic1" can be used to create links to this topic. The keywords "example topic" and "short topic" appear in the Search dialog box and can be used to choose the topic for viewing:

```
${\footnote Short Topic}
#{\footnote topic1}
K{\footnote example topic;short topic}
This topic has a title, context string, and two keywords.
\par
\page
```

See Also   \chftn, \v

\fs

\fs*n*

The \fs statement sets the size of the font. The new font size applies to all subsequent text up to the next \plain or \fs statement.

Parameters   *n*
              Specifies the size of the font, in half points.

Comments   The \fs statement does not set the font face; use the \f statement instead.

No \plain or \fs statement is required if the \fs statement and subsequent text are enclosed in braces. Braces limit the scope of a character property statement to just the enclosed text.

If the \fs statement is not given, the default font size is 24.

Examples   The following example sets the size of the font to 10 points:

```
{\fs20 This line is in 10 point type.}
\par
```

See Also   \plain, \f

\'

\'hh

The \' statement converts the specified hexadecimal number into a character value and inserts the value into the Help file. The appearance of the character when displayed depends on the character set specified for the Help file.

Parameters

hh
  Specifies a two-digit hexadecimal value.

Comments

Since the Microsoft Help Compiler does not accept character values greater than 127, the \' statement is the only method to insert such character values into the Help file.

Examples

The following example inserts a trademark in a Help file that uses the **\windows** statement to set the character set:

```
ABC\'99 is a trademark of the ABC Product Corporation.
```

See Also

\ansi, \pc, \pca, \windows

\i

\i

The **\i** statement starts italic text. The statement applies to all subsequent text up to the next **\plain** or **\i0** statement.

Comments

No **\plain** or **\i0** statement is required if the **\i** statement and subsequent text are enclosed in braces. Braces limit the scope of a character property statement to just the enclosed text.

Examples

The following example sets "not" to italic:

```
You must {\i not} save the file without first setting the
Auto option.
```

See Also

\b, \plain, \scaps

\intbl

\intbl

The **\intbl** statement marks subsequent paragraphs as part of a table. The statement applies to all subsequent paragraphs up to the next **\row** statement.

Comments   This statement was first supported in Microsoft Help Compiler version 3.1.

Examples   The following example creates a three-column table having two rows:

```
\cellx1440\cellx2880\cellx4320
\intbl
Row 1 Column 1\cell
Row 1 Column 2\cell
Row 1 Column 3\cell \row
\intbl
Row 2 Column 1\cell
Row 2 Column 2\cell
Row 2 Column 3\cell \row \pard
```

See Also   **\cell, \cellx, \row, \trgaph, \trleft, \trowd**

\keep

\keep

The **\keep** statement prevents Windows Help from wrapping text to fit the Help window. The statement applies to all subsequent paragraphs up to the next **\pard** statement.

Comments   If the text in a paragraph exceeds the width of the Help window, Help displays a horizontal scroll bar.

In print-based documents, the **\keep** statement keeps paragraphs intact.

See Also   **\line**

\keepn

\keepn

The **\keepn** statement creates a non-scrolling region at the top of the Help window for the given topic. The **\keepn** statement applies to all subsequent paragraphs up to the next **\pard** statement. All paragraphs with this paragraph property are placed in the non-scrolling region.

Comments

If a **\keepn** statement is used in a topic, it must be applied to the first paragraph in the topic (and subsequent paragraphs as needed). The Help compiler displays an error message and does not create a non-scrolling region if paragraphs are given before the **\keepn** statement. Only one non-scrolling region per topic is allowed.

Windows Help formats, aligns, and wraps text in the non-scrolling region just as it does in the rest of the topic. It separates the non-scrolling region from the rest of the Help window with a horizontal bar. Windows Help sets the height of the non-scrolling region so that all all paragraphs in the region can be viewed if the help window is large enough. If the window is smaller than the non-scrolling region, the user will be unable to view the rest of the topic. For this reason, the non-scrolling region is typically reserved for a single line of text specifying the name or title of the topic.

In print-based documents, the **\keepn** statement keeps the subsequent paragraph with the paragraph that follows it.

See Also

\page

\li

\li_n_

The **\li** statement sets the left indent for the paragraph. The indent applies to all subsequent paragraphs up to the next **\pard** or **\li** statement.

Parameters

_n_
    Specifies the indent, in twips. The value can be either positive or negative.

Comments

If the **\li** statement is not given, the left indent is zero by default. Windows Help automatically provides a small left margin so that if no indent is specified the text does not start immediately at the left edge of the Help window.

Specifying a negative left indent moves the starting point for a line of text to the left of the default left margin. If the negative indent is large enough, the start of the text may be clipped by the left edge of the help window.

Examples
The following example uses the left indent and a tab stop to make a bulleted list. In this example, font number 0 is assumed to be the Symbol font:

```
Use the Auto command to:
\par
\tx360\li360\fi-360
{\f0\'B7}
\tab
Save files automatically
\par
{\f0\'B7}
\tab
Prevent overwriting existing files
\par
{\f0\'B7}
\tab
Create automatic backup files
\par \pard
```

See Also
\fi, \pard, \ri

\line

\line

The **\line** statement breaks the current line without ending the paragraph. Subsequent text starts on the next line and is aligned and indented according to the current paragraph properties.

See Also
\par

\mac

\mac

The **\mac** statement sets the Apple Macintosh character set.

See Also   **\windows**

\page

\page

The **\page** statement marks the end of a topic.

Comments   In a print-based document, the **\page** statement creates a page break.

Examples   The following example shows a complete topic:

```
${\footnote Short Topic}
#{\footnote short_topic}
Most topics in a topic file consist of topic-title and
context-string statements followed by the topic text. Every
topic ends with a {\b \\page} statement.
\par
\page
```

See Also   **\par**

\par

\par

The **\par** statement marks the end of a paragraph. The statement ends the current line of text and moves the current position to the left margin and down by the current line-spacing and space-after-paragraph values.

Comments   The first line of text after a **\par**, **\page**, or **\sect** statement marks the start of a paragraph. When a paragraph starts, the current position is moved down by the current space-before-paragraph value. Subsequent text is formatted using the current text alignment, line spacing, and left, right, and first-line indents.

Examples

The following example has three paragraphs:

```
\ql
This paragraph is left-aligned.
\par \pard
\qc
This paragraph is centered.
\par \pard
\qr
This paragraph is right-aligned.
\par
```

See Also

\line, \pard, \sect

\pard

\pard

The **\pard** statement restores all paragraph properties to default values.

Comments

If the **\pard** statement appears anywhere before the end of a paragraph (that is, before the **\par** statement), the default properties apply to the entire paragraph.

The default paragraph properties are as follows:

Property	Default
Alignment	Left-aligned
First-line indent	0
Left indent	0
Right indent	0
Space before	0
Space after	0
Line spacing	Tallest character
Tab stops	None
Borders	None
Border style	Single-width

See Also

\par

\pc

\pc

The **\pc** statement sets the OEM character set (also known as code page 437).

See Also   **\windows**

\pca

\pca

The **\pca** statement sets the International English character set (also known as code page 850).

See Also   **\windows**

\pich

\pich$n$

The **\pich** statement specifies the height of the picture. This statement must be used in conjunction with a **\pict** statement.

Parameters n

Specifies the height of the picture, in twips or pixels, depending on the picture type. If the picture is a metafile, the width is in twips; otherwise the width is, in pixels.

See Also   **\pict**, **\picw**

\pichgoal

\pichgoal_n_

> The **\pichgoal** statement specifies the desired height of a picture. If necessary, Windows Help stretches or compresses the picture to match the requested height. This statement must be used in conjunction with a **\pict** statement.

Parameters   _n_
> Specifies the desired height, in twips.

See Also   **\pict**, **\picwgoal**

\picscalex

\picscalex_n_

> The **\picscalex** statement specifies the horizontal scaling value. This statement must be used in conjunction with a **\pict** statement.

Parameters   _n_
> Specifies the scaling value as a percentage. If this value is greater than 100, the bitmap or metafile is enlarged.

Comments   If the **\picscalex** statement is not given, the default scaling value is 100.

See Also   **\picscaley**, **\pict**

\picscaley

\picscaley_n_

> The **\picscaley** statement specifies the vertical scaling value. This statement must be used in conjunction with a **\pict** statement.

Parameters   *n*

Specifies the scaling value as a percentage. If this value is greater than 100, the bitmap or metafile is enlarged.

Comments   If the **\picscaley** statement is not given, the default scaling value is 100.

See Also   **\picscalex, \pict**

\pict

\pict*picture-statementspicture-data*

The **\pict** statement creates a picture. A picture consists of hexadecimal or binary data representing a bitmap or metafile.

Parameters   *picture-statements*

Specifies one or more statements defining the type of picture, the dimensions of the picture, and the format of the picture data. It can be a combination of the following statements:

Statement	Descripton
\wbitmap	Specifies a Windows bitmap.
\wmetafile	Specifies a Windows metafile.
\picw	Specifies the picture width.
\pich	Specifies the picture height.
\picwgoal	Specifies the desired picture width.
\pichgoal	Specifies the desired picture height.
\picscalex	Specifies the horizontal scaling value.
\picscaley	Specifies the vertical scaling value.
\wbmbitspixel	Specifies the number of bits per pixel.
\wbmplanes	Specifies the number of planes.
\wbmwidthbytes	Specifies the bitmap width, in bytes.
\bin	Specifies binary picture data.

picture-data

Specifies hexadecimal or binary data representing the picture. The picture data follows the last picture statement.

Comments   If a data format is not specified, the default format is hexadecimal.

See Also   **\wbitmap, \wmetafile, \picw, \pich, \picwgoal, \pichgoal, \picscalex, \picscaley, \wbmbitspixel, \wbmplanes, \wbmwidthbytes, \bin**

\picw

\picw_n_

The **\picw** statement specifies the width of the picture. This statement must be used in conjunction with a **\pict** statement.

Parameters   _n_

Specifies the width of the picture, in twips or pixels, depending on the picture type. If the picture is a metafile, the width is in twips; otherwise, the width is in pixels.

See Also   **\pict, \pich**

\picwgoal

\picwgoal_n_

The **\picwgoal** statement specifies the desired width of the picture, in twips. If necessary, Windows Help stretches or compresses the picture to match the requested height. This statement must be used in conjunction with a **\pict** statement.

Parameters   _n_

Specifies the desired width, in twips.

See Also   **\pict, \pichgoal**

\plain

\plain

The **\plain** statement restores the character properties to default values.

Comments   The default character properties are as follows:

Property	Default
Bold	Off
Italic	Off
Small caps	Off
Font	0
Font size	24

See Also   \b, \i, \scaps, \f, \fs

\qc

\qc

The **\qc** statement centers text between the current left and right indents. The statement applies to subsequent paragraphs up to the next **\pard** statement or text-alignment statement.

Comments   If a **\ql**, **\qr**, **\qc**, or **\qj** statement is not given, the text is left-aligned by default.

See Also   \qj, \ql, \qr, \pard

\qj

\qj

The **\qj** statement justifies text between the current left and right indents. The statement applies to subsequent paragraphs up to the next **\pard** statement or text-alignment statement.

The Microsoft Help Compiler ignores this statement.

Comments   If a **\ql**, **\qr**, **\qc**, or **\qj** statement is not given, the text is left-aligned by default.

See Also   \qc, \ql, \qr, \pard

\ql

\ql

The **\ql** statement aligns text along the left indent. The statement applies to subsequent paragraphs up to the next **\pard** statement or text-alignment statement.

Comments   If a **\ql**, **\qr**, **\qc**, or **\qj** statement is not given, the text is left-aligned by default.

See Also   \qc, \qj, \qr, \pard

\qr

\qr

The **\qr** statement aligns text along the right indent. The statement applies to subsequent paragraphs up to the next **\pard** statement or text-alignment statement.

Comments   If a **\ql**, **\qr**, **\qc**, or **\qj** statement is not given, the text is left-aligned by default.

See Also   \qc, \qj, \ql, \pard

\ri

\rin

The **\ri** statement sets the right indent for the paragraph. The indent applies to all subsequent paragraphs up to the next **\pard** or **\ri** statement.

Parameters

n

Specifies the right indent, in twips. It can be a positive or negative value.

Comments

If the **\ri** statement is not given, the right indent is zero by default. Windows Help automatically provides a small right margin so that when no right indent is specified, the text does not end abruptly at the right edge of the Help window.

Windows Help never displays less than one word for each line in a paragraph even if the right indent is greater than the width of the window.

Examples

In the following example, the right and left indents are set to one inch and the subsequent text is centered between the indents:

```
\li1440\ri1440\qc
Microsoft Windows Help\line
Sample File\line
```

See Also

\li, **\pard**

\row

\row

The **\row** statement marks the end of a table row. The statement ends the current row and begins a new row by moving down pass the end of the longest cell in the row. The next **\cell** statement specifies the text of the leftmost cell in the next row.

Comments

This statement was first supported in the Microsoft Help Compiler version 3.1.

Examples   The following example creates a table having four rows and two columns:

```
\cellx2880\cellx5760
\intbl
Row 1, Column 1\cell
Row 1, Column 2\cell \row
\intbl
Row 2, Column 1\cell
Row 2, Column 2\cell \row
\intbl
Row 3, Column 1\cell
Row 3, Column 2\cell \row
\intbl
Row 4, Column 1\cell
Row 4, Column 2\cell \row
\par \pard
```

See Also   **\cell, \cellx, \intbl**

\rtf

\rtf*n*

The **\rtf** statement identifies the file as a rich-text format (RTF) file and specifies the version of the RTF standard used.

Parameters   *n*
Specifies the version of the RTF standard used. For the Microsoft Help Compiler version 3.1, this parameter must be 1.

Comments   The **\rtf** statement must follow the first open brace in the Help file. A statement specifying the character set for the file must also follow the **\rtf** statement.

See Also   **\windows**

\sa

\sa*n*

The \sa statement sets the amount of vertical spacing after a paragraph. The vertical space applies to all subsequent paragraphs up to the next \pard or \sa statement.

Parameters

n
Specifies the amount of vertical spacing, in twips.

Comments

If the \sa statement is not given, the vertical spacing after a paragraph is zero by default.

See Also

\sb, \pard

\sb

\sb*n*

The \sb statement sets the amount of vertical spacing before the paragraph. The vertical space applies to all subsequent paragraphs up to the next \pard statement or \sb statement.

Parameters

n
Specifies the amount of vertical spacing, in twips.

Comments

If the \sb statement is not given, the vertical spacing before the paragraph is zero by default.

See Also

\sa, \pard

\scaps

\scaps

The **\scaps** statement starts small-capital text. The statement converts all subsequent lowercase letters to uppercase before displaying the text. This statement applies to all subsequent text up to the next **\plain** or **\scaps0** statement.

Comments

No **\plain** or **\scaps0** statement is required if the **\scaps** statement and subsequent text are enclosed in braces. Braces limit the scope of a character property statement to just the enclosed text.

The **\scaps** statement does not reduce the point size of the text. To reduce point size, the **\fs** statement must be used.

Examples

The following example displays the key name ENTER in small capitals:

```
Press the {\scaps enter} key to complete the action.
```

See Also

\plain

\sect

\sect

The **\sect** statement marks the end of a section and paragraph.

See Also

\par

\sl

\sl*n*

The **\sl** statement sets the amount of vertical space between lines in a paragraph. The vertical space applies to all subsequent paragraphs up to the next **\pard** or **\sl** statement.

Parameters	*n*
	Specifies the amount of vertical spacing, in twips. If this parameter is a positive value, Windows Help uses this value if it is greater than the tallest character. Otherwise, Windows Help uses the height of the tallest character as the line spacing. If this parameter is a negative value, Windows Help uses the absolute value of the number even if the tallest character is taller.
Comments	If the **\sl** statement is not given, Windows Help automatically sets the line spacing by using the tallest character in the line.
See Also	**\pard**

\strike

\strike

The **\strike** statement creates a hot spot. The statement is used in conjunction with a **\v** statement to create a link to another topic. When the user chooses a hot spot, Windows Help displays the associated topic in the Help window.

The **\strike** statement applies to all subsequent text up to the next **\plain** or **\strike0** statement.

Comments   No **\plain** or **\strike0** statement is required if the **\strike** statement and subsequent text are enclosed in braces. Braces limit the scope of a character property statement to just the enclosed text.

In print-based documents, or whenever it is not followed by **\v**, the **\strike** statement creates strikeout text.

Examples   The following example creates a hot spot for a topic. When displayed, the hot-spot text, "Hot Spot," is green and has a solid line under it:

```
{\strike Hot Spot}{\v Topic}
```

See Also   **\ul, \uldb, \v**

\tab

\tab

The **\tab** statement inserts a tab character (ASCII character code 9).

Comments   The tab character (ASCII character 9) has the same effect as the **\tab** statement.

See Also   \tb, \tqc, \tqr, \tx

\tb

\tb

The **\tb** statement advances to the next tab stop. The Microsoft Windows Help Compiler ignores this statement.

See Also   \tab, \tqc, \tqr, \tx

\tqc

\tqc

The **\tqc** statement advances to the next tab stop and centers text.

See Also   \tab, \tb, \tqr, \tx

\tqr

\tqr

The **\tqr** statement advances to the next tab stop and aligns text to the right.

See Also   \tab, \tb, \tqc, \tx

\trgaph

\trgaph*n*

The **\trgaph** statement specifies the amount of space between text in adjacent cells in a table. For each cell in the table, Windows Help uses the space to calculate the cell's left and right margins. It then uses the margins to align and wrap the text in the cell. Windows Help applies the same margin widths to each cell ensuring that paragraphs in adjacent cells have the specified space between them.

The **\trgaph** statement applies to cells in all subsequent rows of a table up to the next **\trowd** statement.

Parameters

n

Specifies the space, in twips, between text in adjacent cells. If this parameter exceeds the actual width of the cell, the left and right margins are assumed to be at the same position in the cell.

Comments

The width of the left margin in the first cell is always equal to the space specified by this statement. The **\trleft** statement is typically used to move the left margin to a position similar to the left margins in all other cells.

This statement was first supported in the Microsoft Help Compiler version 3.1.

Examples

The following example creates a three-column table with one-quarter inch space between the text in the columns:

```
\trgaph360 \cellx1440\cellx2880\cellx4320
\intbl
Row 1 Column 1\cell
Row 1 Column 2\cell
Row 1 Column 3\cell \row
\intbl
Row 2 Column 1\cell
Row 2 Column 2\cell
Row 2 Column 3\cell \row \pard
```

See Also

\cell, \cellx, \intbl, \row, \trleft, \trowd

\trleft

\trleftn

The **\trleft** statement sets the position of the left margin for the first (leftmost) cell in a row of a table. This statement applies to the first cell in all subsequent rows of the table up to the next **\trowd** statement.

Parameters

n

Specifies the relative position, in twips, of the left margin. This parameter can be a positive or negative number. The final position of the left margin is the sum of the current position and this value.

Comments

This statement was first supported in the Microsoft Help Compiler version 3.1.

Examples

The following example creates a three-column table with one-quarter inch space between the text in the columns. The left margin in the first cell is flush with the left margin of the Help window:

```
\trgaph360\trleft-360 \cellx1440\cellx2880\cellx4320
\intbl
Row 1 Column 1\cell
Row 1 Column 2\cell
Row 1 Column 3\cell \row
\intbl
Row 2 Column 1\cell
Row 2 Column 2\cell
Row 2 Column 3\cell \row \pard
```

See Also

\cell, \cellx, \intbl, \row, \trgaph, \trowd

\trowd

\trowd

The **\trowd** statement sets default margins and cell positions for subsequent rows in a table.

Comments

This statement was first supported in the Microsoft Help Compiler version 3.1.

See Also

\cell, \cellx, \intbl, \row, \trgaph, \trleft

\trqc

\trqc

The **\trqc** statement directs Windows Help to dynamically adjust the width of table columns to fit in the current window.

Comments

In a print-based document, the **\trqc** statement centers a table row with respect to its containing column.

This statement was first supported in the Microsoft Help Compiler version 3.1.

See Also

\trowd, \trql

\trql

\trql

The **\trql** statement aligns the text in each cell of a table row to the left.

Comments

This statement was first supported in the Microsoft Help Compiler version 3.1.

See Also

\trowd, \trqc

\tx

\tx$n$

The **\tx** statement sets the position of a tab stop. The position is relative to the left margin of the Help window. A tab stop applies to all subsequent paragraphs up the next **\pard** statement.

Parameters

n
Specifies the tab stop position, in twips.

Comments	If the **\tx** statement is not given, tab stops are set at every one-half inch by default.
See Also	**\tab, \tb, \tqc, \tqr**

\ul

\ul

The **\ul** statement creates a link to a pop-up topic. The statement is used in conjunction with a **\v** statement to create a link to another topic. When the user chooses the link, Windows Help displays the associated topic in a pop-up window.

The **\ul** statement applies to all subsequent text up to the next **\plain** or **\ul0** statement.

Comments	No **\plain** or **\ul0** statement is required if the **\ul** statement and subsequent text are enclosed in braces. Braces limit the scope of a character property statement to just the enclosed text. In print-based documents, or whenever it is not followed by **\v**, the **\ul** statement creates a continuous underline.
Examples	The following example creates a pop-up link for a topic. When displayed, the link text, "Popup Link," is green and has a dotted line under it: `{\ul Popup Link}{\v PopupTopic}`
See Also	**\strike, \uldb, \v**

\uldb

\uldb

The **\uldb** statement creates a hot spot. This statement is used in conjunction with a **\v** statement to create a link to another topic. When the user chooses a hot spot, Windows Help displays the associated topic in the Help window.

The **\uldb** statement applies to all subsequent text up to the next **\plain** or **\uldb0** statement.

Comments   No **\plain** or **\uldb0** statement is required if the **\uldb** statement and subsequent text are enclosed in braces. Braces limit the scope of a character property statement to just the enclosed text.

Examples   The following example creates a hot spot for a topic. When displayed, the hot-spot text, "Hot Spot," is green and has a solid line under it:

```
{\uldb Hot Spot}{\v Topic}
```

See Also   **\strike, \ul, \v**

\v

{**\v** *context-string*}

The **\v** statement creates a link to the topic having the specified context string. The **\v** statement is used in conjunction with the **\strike, \ul,** and **\uldb** statements to create hot spots and links to topics.

Parameters   *context-string*
Specifies the context string of a topic in the Help file. The string can be any combination of characters, except spaces, and must also be specified in a context-string **\footnote** statement in some topic in the Help file.

Comments   If the context string is preceded by a percent sign (%), Windows Help displays the associated hot spot or link without applying the standard underline and color. If the context string is preceded by an asterisk (*), Windows Help displays the associated hot spot or link with an underline but without applying the standard color.

In print-based documents, the **\v** statement creates hidden text.

For links or hot spots, the syntax of the **\v** statement is as follows:

[*%|*****] *context* [*>secondary-window*] [*@filename*]

In this syntax, *secondary-window* is the name of the secondary window to jump to. When the secondary window is not specified, the jump is to the same window as the current help topic is using. To jump to the main window, specify "main" for this parameter. This parameter may not be used with pop-up windows.

The *filename* parameter specifies a jump to a topic in a different help file.

For a macro hotspot, the syntax of the **\v** statement is as follows:

[%|*] ! *macro* [;*macro*][;...]

Examples

The following example creates a hot spot for the topic having the context string "Topic". Windows Help applies an underline and the color green the text "Hot Spot" when it displays the topic:

```
{\uldb Hot Spot}{\v Topic}
```

See Also

\footnote, \strike, \ul, \uldb

\wbitmap

\wbitmap*n*

The **\wbitmap** statement sets the picture type to Windows bitmap. This statement must be used in conjunction with a **\pict** statement.

Parameters

n
    Specifies the bitmap type. This parameter is zero for a logical bitmap.

Comments

The **\wbitmap** statement is optional; if a **\wmetafile** statement is not specified, the picture is assumed to be a Windows bitmap.

Examples

The following example creates a 32-by-8 pixel monochrome bitmap:

```
{
\pict \wbitmap0\wbmbitspixel1\wbmplanes1\wbmwidthbytes4\picw32\pich8
3FFFFFFC
F3FFFFCF
FF3FFCFF
FFF3CFFF
FFFC3FFF
FFCFF3FF
FCFFFF3F
CFFFFFF3
}
```

See Also

bmc, bml, bmr, \pict, \wmetafile

\wbmbitspixel

\wbmbitspixel*n*

> The **\wbmbitspixel** statement specifies the number of consecutive bits in the bitmap data that represent a single pixel. This statement must be used in conjunction with the **\pict** statement.

Parameters   *n*
> Specifies the number of bits per pixel.

Comments   If the **\wbmbitspixel** statement is not given, the default bits per pixel value is 1.

See Also   **\pict, \wbitmap, \wbmplanes**

\wbmplanes

\wbmplanes*n*

> The **\wbmplanes** statement specifies the number of color planes in the bitmap data. This statement must be used in conjunction with a **\pict** statement.

Parameters   *n*
> Specifies the number of bitmap planes.

Comments   If the **\wbmplanes** statement is not given, the default number of planes is 1.

See Also   **\pict, \wbitmap, \wbmbitspixel**

\wbmwidthbytes

\wbmwidthbytes*n*

> The **\wbmwidthbytes** statement specifies the number of bytes in each scan line of the bitmap data. This statement must be used in conjunction with the **\pict** statement.

Parameters   *n*
                        Specifies the width of the bitmap, in bytes.

See Also   **\pict**, **\wbitmap**

\windows

\windows

                        The **\windows** statement sets the Windows character set.

Comments   If no **\windows**, **\pc**, or **\pca** statement is given in the Help file, the Windows
                        character set is used by default.

See Also   **\ansi**, **\pc**, **\pca**

\wmetafile

\wmetafile*n*

                        The **\wmetafile** statement sets the picture type to a Windows metafile. This state-
                        ment must be used in conjunction with the **\pict** statement.

Parameters   *n*
                        Specifies the metafile type. This parameter must be 8.

Comments   Windows Help expects the hexadecimal data associated with the picture to
                        represent a valid Windows metafile. By default, Windows Help sets the
                        MM_ANISOTROPIC mapping mode prior to displaying the metafile. To ensure
                        that the picture is displayed correctly, the metafile data must either set the window
                        origin and extents by using the **SetWindowOrg** and **SetWindowExt** records or
                        set another mapping mode by using the **SetMapMode** record.

Examples   The following example creates a picture using a metafile:

```
{{\pict\wmetafile8\picw2880\pich2880
0100090000034f0000000200090000000000
050000000b0200000000050000000c026400
6400090000001d066200ff00640064000000
000008000000fa0200000200000000000000
040000002d010000050000001402000000000
050000001302640064000500000014020000
640005000000130264000000008000000fa02
00000000000000000000040000002d010100
04000000f0010000030000000004e0dff00
8700200000050000020000000000000000000}
\par }
```

See Also   **bmc, bml, bmr, \pict, \wbitmap**

15.4 Help Macro Reference

This section lists the Microsoft Windows Help macros in alphabetic order.

About

About( )

The **About** macro displays Windows Help's About dialog box.

Parameters   This macro does not take any parameters.

Comments   Use of this macro in secondary windows is not recommended.

AddAccelerator

AddAccelerator(*key*, *shift-state*, "*macro*")

The **AddAccelerator** macro assigns a Help macro to an accelerator key (or key combination) so that the macro is carried out when the user presses the accelerator key(s).

Parameters

key

Specifies the Windows virtual-key value. For a list of Virtual-Key Codes, see the *Microsoft Windows Programmer's Reference*, *Volume 3*.

shift-state

Specifies the combination of ALT, SHIFT, and CTRL keys to be used with the accelerator. This parameter may be one of the following values:

Value	Meaning
0	None
1	SHIFT
2	CTRL
3	SHIFT+CTRL
4	ALT
5	ALT+SHIFT
6	ALT+CTRL
7	SHIFT+ALT+CTRL

macro

Specifies the Help macro or macro string executed when the user presses the accelerator key(s). The macro must appear in quotation marks. Multiple macros in a string must be separated by semicolons.

Comments

The **AddAccelerator** macro can be abbreviated as **AA**.

Examples

The following macro executes the Windows Clock program when the user presses ALT+SHIFT+CONTROL+F4:

```
AddAccelerator(0x73, 7, "ExecProgram(`clock.exe', 1)")
```

Annotate

Annotate( )

The **Annotate** macro displays the Annotation dialog box from the Edit menu.

Parameters

This macro does not take any parameters.

Comments

Use of this macro in secondary windows is not recommended.

AppendItem

AppendItem("*menu-id*", "*item-id*", "*item-name*", "*macro*")

The **AppendItem** macro appends a menu item to the end of a menu created with the **InsertMenu** macro.

Parameters

menu-id
Specifies the name used in the **InsertMenu** macro used to create the menu. This name must appear in quotation marks. The new item is appended to this menu.

item-id
Specifies the name that Windows Help uses internally to identify the menu item. This name must appear in quotation marks. This name is used by the **DisableItem** or **DeleteItem** macros.

item-name
Specifies the name that Windows Help displays on the menu for the item. This name must appear in quotation marks. Within the quotation marks, place an ampersand (&) before the character used for the macro's accelerator key.

macro
Specifies one or more macros that are to be executed when the user chooses the menu item. The macro must appear in quotation marks. Multiple macros in a string must be separated by semicolons (;).

Comments

Windows Help ignores this macro if it is executed in a secondary window.

If the keyboard accelerator conflicts with other menu access keys, Windows Help displays the error message "Unable to add item" and ignores the macro.

Examples

The following macro appends a menu item labeled "Tools" to a pop-up menu that has an identifier "IDM_TLS". Choosing the menu item causes a jump to a topic with the context string "tpc1" in the TLS.HLP file:

```
AppendItem("IDM_BKS", "IDM_TLS", "&Tools", "JI(`tls.hlp', `tpc1')")
```

Back

Back( )

The **Back** macro displays the previous topic in the history list. The history list is a list of the last 40 topics the user has displayed since starting Windows Help.

Parameters	This macro does not take any parameters.
Comments	Windows Help ignores this macro if it is executed in a secondary window.
	If the **Back** macro is executed when the Back list is empty, Windows Help takes no action.

BookmarkDefine

BookmarkDefine( )

The **BookmarkDefine** macro displays the Define dialog from the Bookmark menu.

Parameters	This macro does not take any parameters.
Comments	Use of this macro in secondary windows is not recommended.
	If the **BookmarkDefine** macro is executed from a pop-up window, the bookmark is attached to the topic that invoked the pop-up window.

BookmarkMore

BookmarkMore( )

The **BookmarkMore** macro displays the More dialog from the Bookmark menu. The More command appears on the Bookmark menu if the menu lists more than nine bookmarks.

Parameters	This macro does not take any parameters.
Comments	Use of the macro in secondary windows is not recommended.

BrowseButtons

BrowseButtons( )

> The **BrowseButtons** macro adds browse buttons to the button bar.

Parameters   This macro does not take any parameters.

Comments   Windows Help ignores this macro if it is executed from a secondary window.

If the **BrowseButtons** macro is used with one or more **CreateButton** macros in the [CONFIG] section of the project file, the order of the browse buttons on the Windows Help button bar is determined by the order of the **BrowseButtons** macro in relation to the other macros listed in the [CONFIG] section.

Examples   The following macros in the project file cause the Clock button to appear immediately before the two browse buttons on the button bar:

```
[CONFIG]
CreateButton("&Clock", "ExecProgram(`clock', 0)")
BrowseButtons()
```

See Also   **CreateButton**

ChangeButtonBinding

ChangeButtonBinding("*button-id*", "*button-macro*")

> The **ChangeButtonBinding** macro assigns a Help macro to a Help button.

Parameters   *button-id*
Specifies the identifier assigned to the button by the **CreateButton** macro or, for a standard Help button, one of the following predefined button identifiers:

ID	Description
BTN_CONTENTS	Contents
BTN_SEARCH	Index
BTN_BACK	Back
BTN_HISTORY	History

ID	Description
BTN_PREVIOUS	Browse previous
BTN_NEXT	Browse next

The button identifier must be enclosed in quotation marks.

button-macro
Specifies the Help macro executed when the user selects the button. The macro must be enclosed in quotation marks.

Comments

Windows Help ignores this macro if it is executed in a secondary window.

The **ChangeButtonBinding** macro can be abbreviated as **CBB**.

Examples

In the following macro, "conts" is the context string for the table of contents in the DICT.HLP file:

```
ChangeButtonBinding("btn_contents", "JumpId(`dict.hlp', `conts')")
```

ChangeItemBinding

ChangeItemBinding("*item-id***", "***item-macro***")**

The **ChangeItemBinding** macro assigns a Help macro to an item previously added to a Windows Help menu using the **AppendItem** macro.

Parameters

item-id
Identifies the menu item appended by the **AppendItem** macro. The item identifier must be enclosed in quotation marks.

item-macro
Specifies the Help macro to execute when the user selects the item. The macro must be enclosed in quotation marks.

Comments

Windows Help ignores this macro if it is executed in a secondary window.

The **ChangeItemBinding** macro can be abbreviated as **CIB**.

Examples

The following macro changes the menu item identified by "time_item" so that it displays the Windows clock:

```
ChangeItemBinding("time_item", "ExecProgram(`clock', 0)")
```

CheckItem

CheckItem("*item-id***")**

The **CheckItem** macro places a check-mark beside a menu item.

Parameters   *item-id*
Identifies the menu item to check. The item identifier must be enclosed in quotation marks.

Comments   The **CheckItem** macro can be abbreviated as **CI**.

See Also   **UncheckItem**

CloseWindow

CloseWindow("*window-name***")**

The **CloseWindow** macro closes either a secondary window or the main Help window.

Parameters   *window-name*
Specifies the name of the window to close. The name "main" is reserved for the main Help window. For secondary windows, the window name is defined in the [WINDOWS] section of the project file. This name must be enclosed in quotation marks.

Examples   The following macro closes the secondary window named "keys":

```
CloseWindow("keys")
```

Contents

Contents()

The **Contents** macro displays the Contents topic in the current Help file. The Contents topic is defined by the **CONTENTS** option in the [OPTIONS] section of the project file. If the project file does not have a **CONTENTS** option, the Contents topic is the first topic of the first topic file specified in the project file.

CopyDialog

CopyDialog( )

The **CopyDialog** macro displays the Copy dialog from the Edit menu.

Comments   Use of this macro in secondary windows is not recommended.

CopyTopic

CopyTopic( )

The **CopyTopic** macro copies all the text in the currently displayed topic to the Clipboard.

Comments   Use of the macro in secondary windows is not recommended.

CreateButton

CreateButton("*button-id*", "*name*", "*macro*")

The **CreateButton** macro adds a new button to the button bar.

Parameters   *button-id*
Specifies the name that WinHelp uses internally to identify the button. This name must appear in quotation marks. Use this name in the **DisableButton** or **DestroyButton** macro if you want to remove or disable the button or in the **ChangeButtonBinding** if you want to change the Help macro that the button executes in certain topics.

name
> Specifies the text that appears on the button. To make a letter in this text the mnemonic for the button, place an ampersand (&) before that letter. The button name is case-sensitive and can have up to 29 characters in it — any additional characters are ignored.

macro
> Specifies the Help macro or macro string executed when the user clicks on the button. Multiple macros in a macro string must be separated by semicolons.

Comments   Windows Help allows a maximum of 16 custom buttons. It allows a total of 22 buttons, including the standard Browse buttons, on the button bar.

If the **BrowseButtons** macro is used with one or more **CreateButton** macros in the project file, the buttons appear in the same order on the button bar as the macros appear in the project file.

Windows Help ignores this macro if it is executed in a secondary window.

The **CreateButton** macro can be abbreviated as **CB**.

Examples   The following macro creates a new button labeled "Ideas" that jumps to the topic with the context string "dir" in the IDEAS.HLP file when clicked:

```
CreateButton("btn_ideas", "&Ideas", "JumpId(`ideas.hlp', `dir')")
```

DeleteItem

DeleteItem("*item-id*")

The **DeleteItem** macro removes a menu item that was added by using the **AppendItem** macro.

Parameters   *item-id*
> Specifies the item identifier used in the **AppendItem** macro. The item identifier must be enclosed in quotation marks.

Comments   Windows Help ignores this macro if it is executed in a secondary window.

Examples   The following macro removes the menu item "Tools" appended in the example for the **AppendItem** macro:

```
DeleteItem("IDM_TOOLS")
```

DeleteMark

DeleteMark("*marker-text***")**

The **DeleteMark** macro removes a text marker added with the **SaveMark** macro.

Parameters
marker-text
Specifies the text marker previously added by the **SaveMark** macro. The marker text must be enclosed in quotation marks.

Comments
If the marker does not exist when the **DeleteMark** macro is executed, Windows Help displays a "Topic not found" error message.

Examples
The following macro removes the marker "Managing Memory" from a Help file:

```
DeleteMark("Managing Memory")
```

DestroyButton

DestroyButton("*button-id***")**

The **DestroyButton** macro removes a button added with the **CreateButton** macro.

Parameters
button-id
Identifies a button previously created by the **CreateButton** macro. The button identifier must be enclosed in quotation marks.

Comments
The button identifier cannot be an identifier for one of the standard Help buttons. For a list of those identifiers, see the **ChangeButtonBinding** macro.

Windows Help ignores this macro if it is executed in a secondary window.

DisableButton

DisableButton("*button-id***")**

The **DisableButton** macro grays out a button added with the **CreateButton** macro. This button cannot be used in the topic until an **EnableButton** macro is executed.

Parameters   *button-id*
Specifies the identifier assigned to the button by the **CreateButton** macro. The button identifier must be enclosed in quotation marks.

Comments   Windows Help ignores this macro if it is executed in a secondary window.

The **DisableButton** macro can be abbreviated as **DB**.

DisableItem

DisableItem("*item-id***")**

The **DisableItem** macro grays out a menu item added with the **AppendItem** macro. The menu item cannot be used in the topic until an **EnableItem** macro is executed.

Parameters   *item-id*
Identifies a menu item previously appended with the **AppendItem** macro. The item identifier must be enclosed in quotation marks.

Comments   Windows Help ignores this macro if it is executed in a secondary window.

The **DisableItem** macro can be abbreviated as **DI**.

EnableButton

EnableButton("*button-id***")**

The **EnableButton** macro re-enables a button disabled with the **DisableButton** macro.

Parameters   *button-id*
Specifies the identifier assigned to the button by the **CreateButton** macro. The button identifier must be enclosed in quotation marks.

Comments   Windows Help ignores this macro if it is executed in a secondary window.

The **EnableButton** macro can be abbreviated as **EB**.

EnableItem

EnableItem("*item-id*"**)**

The **EnableItem** macro re-enables a menu item disabled with the **DisableItem** macro.

Parameters   *item-id*
Specifies the identifier assigned to the menu item by the **CreateItem** macro. The item identifier must be enclosed in quotation marks.

Comments   Windows Help ignores this macro if it is executed in a secondary window.

The **EnableItem** macro can be abbreviated as **EI**.

ExecProgram

ExecProgram("*command-line*"**,** *display-state***)**

The **ExecProgram** macro executes a Windows application.

Parameters   *command-line*
Specifies the command line for the application to be executed. The command line must be enclosed in quotation marks. Windows Help searches for this application in the current directory, followed by the Windows directory, the user's path, and the directory of the currently viewed Help file.

display-state
Specifies a value indicating how the application is shown when executed. It may be one of the following values:

Value	Meaning
0	Normal
1	Minimized
2	Maximized

Comments

The **ExecProgram** macro can be abbreviated as **EP**.

Do not use the backslash character to escape double quotation-mark characters in macros. Instead, you can enclose the command line in single opening and closing quotation marks and omit the backslash for the double quotation marks, as shown in the following example:

```
`command "string as parameter"'
```

Examples

The following example executes the Clock application. The application is minimized when it starts:

```
ExecProgram(`clock.exe', 1)
```

Exit

Exit( )

The **Exit** macro exits the Windows Help application. It has the same effect as selecting Exit from the File menu.

Parameters

This macro does not take any parameters.

FileOpen

FileOpen( )

The **FileOpen** macro displays the Open dialog box from the File menu.

Parameters This macro does not take any parameters.

Comments Use of the macro in secondary windows is not recommended.

FocusWindow

FocusWindow("*window-name***")**

The **FocusWindow** macro changes the focus to the specified window, either the main Help window or a secondary window.

Parameters *window-name*
Specifies the name of the window to receive the focus. The name "main" is reserved for the main Help window. For secondary windows, the window name is defined in the [WINDOWS] section of the project file. This name must be enclosed in quotation marks.

Comments This macro is ignored if the specified window does not exist.

Examples The following macro changes the focus to the secondary window "keys":

```
FocusWindow("keys")
```

GoToMark

GoToMark("*marker-text***")**

The **GoToMark** macro jumps to a marker set with the **SaveMark** macro.

Parameters *marker-text*
Specifies a text marker previously defined by using the **SaveMark** macro.

Examples The following macros jumps to the marker "Managing Memory".

```
GoToMark("Managing Memory")
```

HelpOn

HelpOn( )

The **HelpOn** macro displays the Help file for the Windows Help application. The macro carries out the same action as choosing the the How to Use Help command on the Help menu.

Parameters   This macro does not take any parameters.

HelpOnTop

HelpOnTop( )

The **HelpOnTop** macro toggles the on-top state of Windows Help. It is equivalent to checking or unchecking the Always On Top command in the Help menu.

Parameters   This macro does not take any parameters.

Comments   Windows Help does not provide a macro to check the current state of the Always On Top command. It is up to the user to determine whether the macro should be used to change the state of the command.

History

History( )

The **History** macro displays the history list, which shows the last 40 topics the user has viewed since opening a Help file in Windows Help. It has the same effect as choosing the History button.

Parameters   This macro does not take any parameters.

Comments   Windows Help ignores this macro if it is executed in a secondary window.

IfThen

IfThen(IsMark("*marker-text***"), "***macro***")**

The **IfThen** macro executes a Help macro if a given marker exists. It uses the **IsMark** macro to make the test.

Parameters
marker-text
Specifies a text marker previously created by using the **SaveMark** macro. The marker must be enclosed in quotation marks.

macro
Specifies a Help macro or macro string to be executed if the marker exists. Multiple macros in a macro string must be separated by semicolons.

Examples
The following macro jumps to the topic with context string "man_mem" if a marker named "Managing Memory" has been set by the **SaveMark** macro:

```
IfThen(IsMark("Managing Memory"), "JI(`trb.hlp', `man_mem')")
```

IfThenElse

IfThenElse(IsMark("*marker-text***"), "***macro1***", "***macro2***")**

The **IfThenElse** macro executes one of two Help macros depending on whether or not a marker exists. It uses the **IsMark** macro to make the test.

Parameters
marker-text
Specifies a text marker previously created by using the **IsMark** macro. The marker must be enclosed in quotation marks.

macro1
Specifies a Help macro or macro string to be executed if the marker exits. Multiple macros in either macro string must be separated by semicolons.

macro2
Specifies a Help macro or macro string to be executed if the marker does not exit. Multiple macros in either macro string must be separated by semicolons.

Examples

The following macro jumps to the topic with context string "mem" if a marker named "Memory" has been set by the **SaveMark** macro. If the marker does not exist, it jumps to the next topic in the browse sequence.

```
IfThenElse(IsMark("Memory"), "JI(`trb.hlp', `mem')", "Next()")
```

InsertItem

InsertItem("*menu-id*", "*item-id*", "*item-name*", "*macro*", *position*)

The **InsertItem** macro inserts a menu item at a given position on an existing menu. The menu can be either one you create with the **InsertMenu** macro or one of the standard Windows Help menus.

Parameters

menu-id

Identifies either a standard Windows Help menu or a menu previously created by using the **InsertMenu** macro. For a standard menu, this parameter can be one of the following:

Name	Menu
MNU_FILE	File
MNU_EDIT	Edit
MNU_BOOKMARK	Bookmark menu
MNU_HELPON	Help

For other menus, this parameter must be the name used with the **InsertMenu** macro. In all cases, the menu identifier must be enclosed in quotation marks. The new item is inserted into this menu.

item-id

Specifies the name that Windows Help uses internally to identify the menu item. The item identifier must be enclosed in quotation marks.

item-name

Specifies the name Windows Help displays in the menu for the item. This name is case-sensitive and must be enclosed in quotation marks. An ampersand (&) before a character in the name identifies it as the item's keyboard access key.

macro

Specifies a Help macro or macro string to be executed when the user chooses the menu item. The macro must be enclosed in quotation marks. Multiple macros in a string must be separated by semicolons (;).

position
>Specifies the position of the menu item in the menu. It must be an integer value. Position 0 is the first or topmost position in the menu.

Comments

The *item-id* parameter can be used in a subsequent **DisableItem** or **DeleteItem** macro to remove or disable the item or to change the operations that the item performs in certain topics.

Windows Help ignores this macro if it is executed in a secondary window.

The specified keyboard access keys must be unique. If a key conflicts with other menu access keys, Windows Help displays the error message "Unable to add item" and ignores the macro.

Examples

The following macro inserts a menu item labeled "Tools" as the third item on a menu that has an identifier "MNU_BKS". Selecting the menu item causes a jump to a topic with the context string "tls1" in the TLS.HLP file:

```
InsertItem("mnu_bks", "m_tls", "&Tools", "JI(`tls.hlp', `tls1')", 3)
```

InsertMenu

InsertMenu("*menu-id***", "***menu-name***", *menu-position*)**

>The **InsertMenu** inserts a new menu in the Windows Help menu bar.

Parameters

menu-id
>Specifies the name that Windows Help uses internally to identify the menu. The menu identifier must be enclosed in quotation marks. This identifier can be used in the **AppendItem** macro to add macros to the menu.

menu-name
>Specifies the name that Windows Help displays on the menu bar. This name must be enclosed in quotation marks. An ampersand (&) before a character in the name identifies it as the menu's keyboard access key.

menu-position
>Specifies the position on the menu bar of the new menu name. This parameter must be an integer number. Positions are numbered from left to right, with position 0 the left-most menu.

Comments

Windows Help ignores this macro if it is executed in a secondary window.

Examples   The following macro adds a menu named "Utilities" to the Windows Help application. The label "Utilities" appears as the fourth item on the Windows Help menu bar. The user presses U with the ALT key to open the menu.

```
InsertMenu("IDM_UTIL", "&Utilities", 3)
```

IsMark

IsMark("*marker-text***")**

The **IsMark** macro tests whether or not a marker set by the **SaveMark** macro exists. It is used as a parameter to the conditional macros **IfThen** and **IfThenElse**. The **IsMark** macro returns nonzero if the mark exists or zero if it does not.

Parameters   *marker-text*
Specifies a text marker previous created using the **SaveMark** macro.

Comments   The **Not** macro can be used to reverse the results of the **IsMark** macro.

Examples   The following macro jumps to the topic with the context string "man_mem" if a marker named "Managing Memory" has been set by the **SaveMark** macro:

```
IfThen(IsMark("Managing Memory"), "JI(`trb.hlp', `man_mem')")
```

JumpContents

JumpContents("*filename***")**

The **JumpContents** macro jumps to the Contents topic of a specified file in the Help file. The Contents topic is indicated by the CONTENTS option entry in the [OPTIONS] section of project file. If the CONTENTS option is not specified, Windows Help jumps to the first topic in the Help file.

Parameters   *filename*
Specifies the name of the destination file for the jump. The filename must be enclosed in quotation marks. If Windows Help cannot find this file, it displays an error message and does not perform the jump.

Comments   Windows Help ignores this macro if it is executed in a secondary window.

Examples   The following macro jumps to the Contents topic of the PROGMAN.HLP file:

```
JumpContents("PROGMAN.HLP")
```

JumpContext

JumpContext("*filename***",** *context-number***)**

Parameters   *filename*
Specifies the name of the destination file for the jump. The filename must be enclosed in quotation marks. If Windows Help cannot find this file, it displays an error message and does not perform the jump.

context-number
Specifies the context number of the topic in the destination file. The context number must be defined in the [MAP] section of the project file. If the context number is not valid, Windows Help jumps to the Contents topic or to the first topic in the file instead and displays an error message.

Comments   The **JumpContext** macro can be abbreviated as **JC**.

Examples   The following macro jumps to the topic mapped to the context number 801 in the PROGMAN.HLP file:

```
JumpContext("PROGMAN.HLP", 801)
```

JumpHelpOn

JumpHelpOn( )

The **JumpHelpOn** macro jumps to the Contents topic of the How to Use Help file. The How To Use Help file is either the default WINHELP.HLP file shipped with Windows 3.1 or the Help file designated by the **SetHelpOnFile** macro in the [CONFIG] section of the project file.

Parameters   This macro does not take any parameters.

Comments   If Windows Help cannot find the specified Help file, it displays an error message
                     and does not perform the jump.

Examples   The following macro jumps to the Contents topic of the designated How to Use
                     Help file:

                     JumpHelpOn()

JumpId

JumpId("*filename***", "***context-string***")**

The **JumpId** macro jumps to the topic with the specified context string in the Help
file.

Parameters   *filename*
                     Specifies the name of the Help file containing the context string. The filename
                     must be enclosed in quotation marks. If Windows Help does not find this file, it
                     displays an error message and does not perform the jump.

                     context-string
                     Context string of the topic in the destination file. The context string must be en-
                     closed in quotation marks. If the context string does not exist, Windows Help
                     jumps to the Contents topic for that file instead.

Comments   The **JumpId** macro may be abbreviated as **JI**.

Examples   The following macro jumps to a topic with "second_topic" as its context string in
                     the SECOND.HLP file:

                     JI("second.hlp", "second_topic")

JumpKeyword

JumpKeyword("*filename***", "***keyword***")**

The **JumpKeyword** macro loads the indicated Help file, searches through the K
keyword table, and displays the first topic containing the index keyword specified
in the macro.

Parameters	*filename*
	Specifies the name of the Help file containing the desired keyword table. The filename must be enclosed in quotation marks. If this file does not exist, Windows Help displays an error message and does not perform the jump.
	keyword
	Specifies the keyword that the macro searches for. The keyword must be enclosed in quotation marks. If Windows Help finds more than one match, it displays the first matched topic. If it does not find any matches, it displays a "Not a keyword" message and displays the Contents topic of the destination file instead.
Comments	The **JumpKeyword** macro can be abbreviated as **JK**.
Examples	The following macro displays the first topic that has "hands" as an index keyword in the CLOCK.HLP file:

```
JumpKeyword("clock.hlp", "hands")
```

Next

Next( )

The **Next** macro displays the next topic in the browse sequence for the Help file.

Parameters   This macro does not take any parameters.

Comments   If the currently displayed topic is the last topic of a browse sequence, this macro does nothing.

Windows Help ignores this macro if it is executed in a secondary window.

Not

Not(IsMark("*marker-text***"))**

The **Not** macro reverses the result (nonzero or zero) returned by the **IsMark** macro. It is used along with the **IsMark** macro as a parameter to the conditional macros **IfThen** and **IfThenElse**.

Parameters

marker-text
Specifies a text marker previously created by using the **SaveMark** macro. The marker text must be enclosed in quotation marks.

Examples

The following macro jumps to the topic with the context string "mem1" if a marker named "Memory" has not been set by the **SaveMark** macro:

```
IfThen(Not(IsMark("Memory")), "JI(`trb.hlp', `mem1')")
```

PopupContext

PopupContext("*filename***",** *context-number***)**

The **PopupContext** macro displays in a pop-up window the topic identified by a specific context number.

Parameters

filename
Specifies the name of the file that contains the topic to be displayed. The filename must be enclosed in quotation marks. If Windows Help cannot find this file, it displays an error message.

context number
Specifies the context number of the topic to be displayed. The context number must be specified in the [MAP] section of the project file. If the context number is not valid, Windows Help displays the Contents topic or the first topic in the file instead.

Comments

The **PopupContext** macro can be abbreviated as **PC**.

Examples

The following macro displays in a pop-up window the topic mapped to the context number 801 in the PROGMAN.HLP file:

```
PopupContext("progman.hlp", 801)
```

PopupId

PopupId("*filename*", "*context-string*")

The **PopupId** macro displays a topic from a specified file in a pop-up window.

Parameters

filename
Specifies the name of the file containing the pop-up window topic. The filename must be enclosed in quotation marks. If this file does not exist, Windows Help displays a warning.

context-string
Specifies the context string of the topic in the destination file. If the requested context string does not exist, Windows Help displays the Contents topic or the first topic in the file.

Comments

The **PopupId** macro can be abbreviated as **PI**.

Examples

The following macro displays a pop-up window with context string "second_topic" from the SECOND.HLP file:

```
PopupId("second.hlp", "second_topic")
```

PositionWindow

PositionWindow(*x*, *y*, *width*, *height*, *state*, "*name*")

The **PositionWindow** macro sets the size and position of a window.

Parameters

x
Specifies the x-coordinate, in help units, of the upper-left corner of the window. Windows Help always assumes the screen (regardless of resolution) is 1024 help units wide. For example, if the x-coordinate is 512, the left edge of the Help window is in the middle of the screen.

y
Specifies the y-coordinate, in help units, of the upper-left corner of the window. Windows Help always assumes the screen (regardless of resolution) is 1024 help units high. For example, if the y-coordinate is 512, the top edge of the Help window is in the middle of the screen.

width
Specifies the default width, in help units, of the window.

height
Specifies the default height, in help units, of the window.

state
Specifies how the window is sized. This parameter can be one of the following values:

Value	Meaning
0	Normal size
1	Maximized

If the parameter is 1, Windows Help ignores the *x*, *y*, *width*, and *height* parameters.

name
Specifies the name of the window to position. The name "main" is reserved for the main Help window. For secondary windows, the window name must be defined in the [WINDOWS] section of the project file. This name must be enclosed in quotation marks.

Comments   If the window to be positioned does not exist, Windows Help ignores the macro.

The **PositionWindow** macro can be abbreviated as **PW**.

Examples   The following macro positions the secondary window "Samples" in the upper-left corner (100, 100) with a width and height of 500 (in help units):

```
PositionWindow(100, 100, 500, 500, 0, "Samples")
```

Prev

Prev( )

The **Prev** macro displays the previous topic in the browse sequence for the Help file. If the currently displayed topic is the first topic of a browse sequence, this macro does nothing.

Parameters   This macro does not take any parameters.

Comments   Windows Help ignores this macro if it is executed in a secondary window.

Print

Print( )

The **Print** macro sends the currently displayed topic to the printer. It should be used only to print topics in windows other than the main Help window (for example, topics in a secondary window).

Parameters This macro does not take any parameters.

PrinterSetup

PrinterSetup( )

The **PrinterSetup** macro displays the Printer Setup dialog box from the File menu.

Parameters This macro does not take any parameters.

Comments Use of the macro in secondary windows is not recommended.

RegisterRoutine

RegisterRoutine("*DLL-name***", "***function-name***", "***format-spec***")**

The **RegisterRoutine** macro registers a function within a dynamic-link library (DLL). Registered functions can be used in macro footnotes in topic files or in the [CONFIG] section of the project file, the same as standard Help macros.

Parameters *DLL-name*
Specifies the filename of the DLL. The filename must be enclosed in quotation marks. If Windows Help cannot find the library, it displays an error message.

function-name
Specifies the name of the function to execute in the designated DLL.

format-spec
Specifies a string indicating the formats of parameters passed to the function. The format string must be enclosed in quotation marks. Characters in the string represent C parameter types:

Character	Description
u	**unsigned short** (WORD)
U	**unsigned long** (DWORD)
i	**short int**
I	**int**
s	**near char *** (PSTR)
S	**far char *** (LPSTR)
v	**void**

If the function is used as a Help macro, Windows Help makes sure the macro parameters match the parameter types given in this macro.

Comments
The **RegisterRoutine** macro can be abbreviated as **RR**.

Examples
The following call registers a routine named PlayAudio in a DLL, MMLIB.DLL. PlayAudio takes arguments of the **far char ***, **int**, and **unsigned long** types:

```
RegisterRoutine("MMLIB", "PlayAudio", "SIU")
```

SaveMark

SaveMark("*marker-text***")**

The **SaveMark** macro saves the location of the currently displayed topic and file and associates a text marker with that location. The **GotoMark** macro can then be used to jump to this location.

Parameters
marker-text
Specifies the text marker to be used to identify the topic location. This text must be enclosed in quotation marks, and it must be unique. If the same text is used for more than one marker, the most recently entered marker is used.

Comments
A text marker can be used with the **GotoMark**, **DeleteMark**, **IfThen**, and **IfThenElse** macros.

If the user exits Windows Help, all text markers are deleted.

Examples   The following macro saves the marker "Managing Memory" in the current topic:

```
SaveMark("Managing Memory")
```

Search

Search( )

The **Search** macro displays the dialog for the Search button, which allows users to search for topics using keywords defined by the K footnote character.

Parameters   This macro does not take any parameters.

Comments   Windows Help ignores this macro if it is executed in a secondary window.

SetContents

SetContents("*filename*", *context-number*)

The **SetContents** macro designates a specific topic as the Contents topic in the specified Help file.

Parameters   *filename*
Specifies the name of the Help file that contains the Contents topic. The filename must be enclosed in quotation marks. If Windows Help cannot find this file, it displays an error message and does not perform the jump.

context number
Specifies the context number of the topic in the specified file. The context number must be defined in the [MAP] section of the project file. If the context number is not valid, Windows Help displays an error message.

Examples   The following example sets the topic mapped to the context number 801 in the PROGMAN.HLP file as the Contents topic. After executing this macro, clicking the Contents button will cause a jump to the topic specified by the *context-number* parameter:

```
SetContents("PROGMAN.HLP", 801)
```

SetHelpOnFile

SetHelpOnFile("*filename*")

Parameters   *filename*
                      Specifies the name of the replacement How to Use Help file. The filename must
                      be enclosed in quotation marks. If Windows Help cannot find this file, it dis-
                      plays an error message.

Comments   If this macro appears in a topic in the Help file, the replacement file is set after ex-
                      ecution of the macro. If this macro appears in the [CONFIG] section of the project
                      file, the replacement file is set when the help file is opened.

Examples   The following macro sets the Using Help file to MYHELP.HLP:

                      ```
                      SetHelpOnFile("myhelp.hlp")
                      ```

UncheckItem

UncheckItem("*item-id*")

                      The **UncheckItem** macro removes the check mark from a menu item.

Parameters   *item-id*
                      Identifies the menu item to uncheck. The item identifier must be enclosed in
                      quotation marks.

Comments   The **UncheckItem** macro can be abbreviated **UI**.

See Also   **CheckItem**

Index

ENHANCE THE VISUAL I.Q. OF YOUR APPLICATIONS WITH WINDOWS CONTROLS

Windows controls elevate a graphical user interface to a higher plane. Nothing can make your application bolder, brighter, and more visual—faster—than knowing how to use the full array of Windows controls to your advantage. Now, there's a video course to help you fast forward through programming techniques using the controls in the Microsoft₀ Windows™ operating system. The Microsoft University *Exploring Controls* video course examines various Windows controls, including buttons, combo boxes, static controls, scroll bars, edit controls, list boxes, and custom controls. Concepts are visually illustrated through 3-D animation and supported with hands-on lab exercises and a student guide.

Learn how to modify and customize controls

▲ Apply techniques for creating, managing, and using common control components of the Windows environment.
▲ Explore how to modify controls through advanced techniques for use when a standard Windows control doesn't meet an application's requirements.
▲ Learn about subclassing, owner draw controls, and what it takes to create your own custom controls.

Get up to speed quickly

Software developers are on a critical path where bringing a product to market a few days late can mean missing the mark completely. Video training from Microsoft University offers the flexibility to meet your needs. Each module includes:
▲ Reference information about the control, such as styles, messages, and notifications.
▲ Procedural techniques for actually implementing the control.
▲ Lab exercises with sample code that you can incorporate into your applications *immediately*.

Exceptional training at a price that's under control

This video course will save you countless development man hours while helping you improve the appearance and usability of your applications. So bring the Microsoft University classroom in-house, and take advantage of this intelligent training solution. The complete *Exploring Controls* video course is just $495* and includes one student guide. To leverage your training investment across a development team, you can purchase additional student guides for just $99 each.

Expertise at the touch of a button

If you want to understand Windows controls from the inside out, pop in the videotape, hit play, and turn up the volume. You'll learn from the training experts at Microsoft, developer of the most popular applications for Windows. Now, put the power of Windows controls to work in YOUR applications—order your copy of the *Exploring Controls* video course today.

TO ORDER:
CALL (206) 828-1507
Once your representative answers, please mention department 605.

Microsoft University offers technical training for developers and support professionals. Please call for more information on other video courses, classroom courses at nine convenient locations in the U.S., on-site training, licensing programs, custom courses, Management Education seminars, or the Microsoft University Training Alliance member nearest you.

Microsoft University

*Plus shipping and applicable state sales taxes.